MOUNTAIN BIKE!
The Southern Appalachian and Smoky Mountains

MOUNTAIN BIKE!
The Southern Appalachian and Smoky Mountains

A GUIDE TO THE CLASSIC TRAILS

STEVE JONES

Menasha
Ridge
Press

Library of Congress Cataloging-in-Publication Data:
Jones, Steve, 1954–
Mountain Bike! Southern Appalachian and Smoky Mountains:
a guide to the classic trails/
Steve Jones.— 1st ed.
p. cm.—(America by mountain bike series)
Includes index.
ISBN 0-89732-270-3
1. All terrain cycling—Appalachian Region, Southern—Guidebooks.
2. All terrain cycling—Great Smoky Mountains (N.C. and Tenn.)—Guidebooks.
3. Appalachian Region, Southern—Guidebooks.
4. Great Smoky Mountains (N.C. and Tenn.)—Guidebooks.
I. Title. II. Series.
GV1045.5.A55J65   1999
796.6'3'0974—dc21
99–13586
CIP

Photos by the author unless otherwise credited
Maps by Steven Jones
Cover and text design by Suzanne Holt
Cover photo by Dennis Coello

Menasha Ridge Press
700 South 28th Street
Suite 206
Birmingham, Alabama 35233

All the trails described in this book are legal for mountain bikes. But rules can change—especially for off-road bicycles, the new kid on the outdoor recreation block. Land access issues and conflicts between bicyclists, hikers, equestrians, and other users can cause the rewriting of recreation regulations on public lands, sometimes resulting in a ban of mountain bike use on specific trails. That's why it's the responsibility of each rider to check and make sure that he or she rides only on trails where mountain biking is permitted.

CAUTION

Outdoor recreational activities are by their very nature potentially hazardous. All participants in such activities must assume the responsibility for their own actions and safety. The information contained in this guidebook cannot replace sound judgment and good decision-making skills, which help reduce risk exposure, nor does the scope of this book allow for disclosure of all the potential hazards and risks involved in such activities.

Learn as much as possible about the outdoor recreational activities in which you participate, prepare for the unexpected, and be cautious. The reward will be a safer and more enjoyable experience.

CONTENTS

AMERICA BY MOUNTAIN BIKE MAP LEGEND

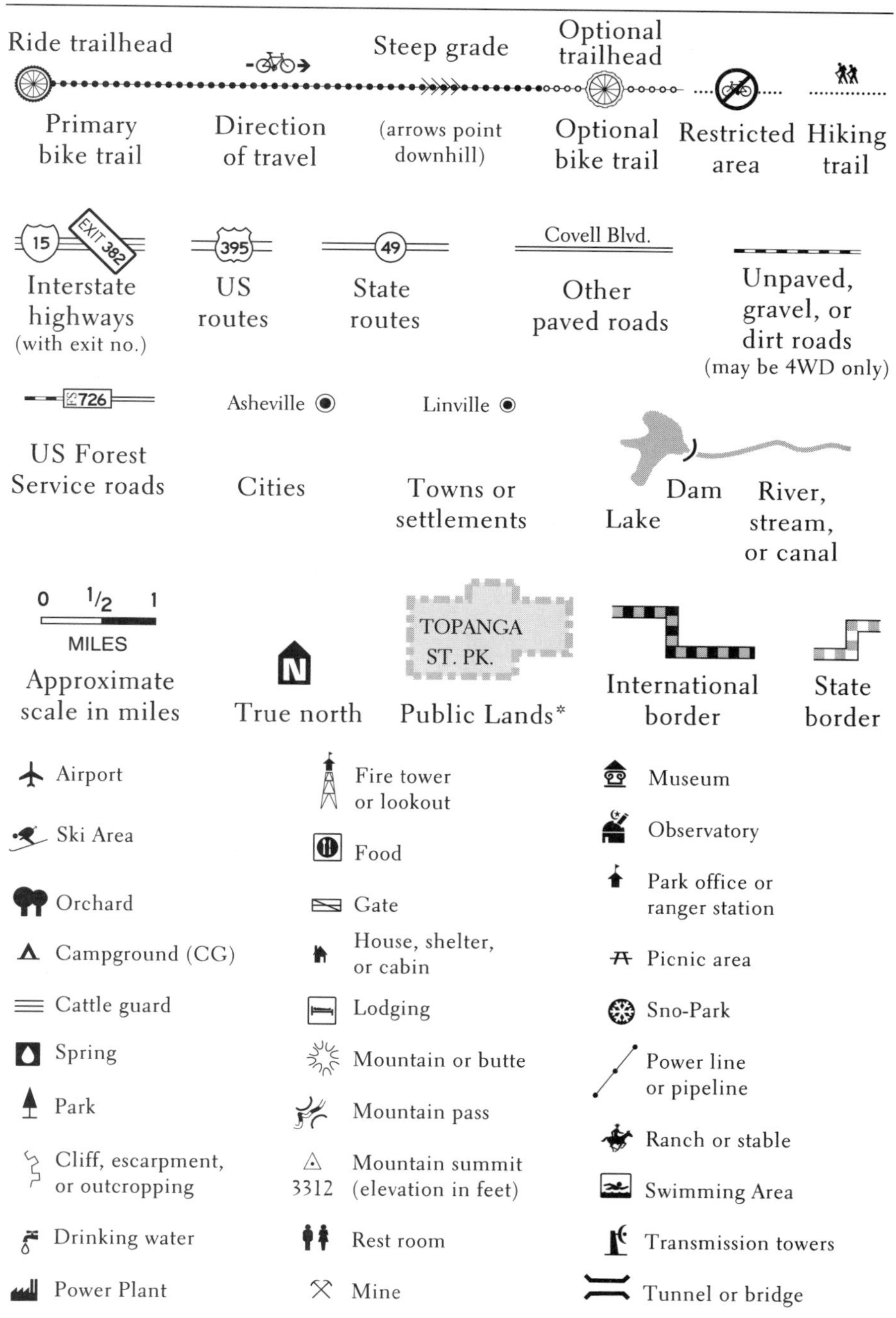

Ride trailhead — **Steep grade** — Optional trailhead

Primary bike trail | Direction of travel | (arrows point downhill) | Optional bike trail | Restricted area | Hiking trail

Interstate highways (with exit no.) | US routes | State routes | Covell Blvd. Other paved roads | Unpaved, gravel, or dirt roads (may be 4WD only)

US Forest Service roads | Asheville ● Cities | Linville ● Towns or settlements | Dam / Lake | River, stream, or canal

0 1/2 1
MILES
Approximate scale in miles | N True north | TOPANGA ST. PK. Public Lands* | International border | State border

✈ Airport

⚡ Ski Area

🌳 Orchard

▲ Campground (CG)

≡ Cattle guard

◘ Spring

🚰 Park

Cliff, escarpment, or outcropping

Drinking water

Power Plant

Fire tower or lookout

Food

Gate

House, shelter, or cabin

Lodging

Mountain or butte

Mountain pass

△ Mountain summit
3312 (elevation in feet)

Rest room

✕ Mine

Museum

Observatory

Park office or ranger station

⊼ Picnic area

Sno-Park

Power line or pipeline

Ranch or stable

Swimming Area

Transmission towers

Tunnel or bridge

*Remember, private property exists in and around our national forests.

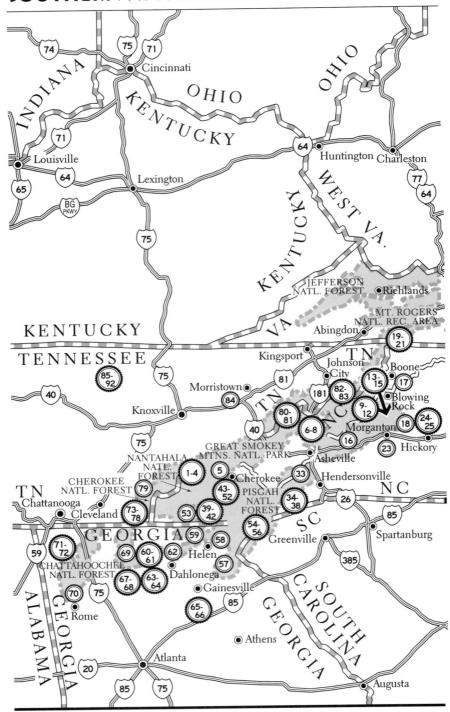

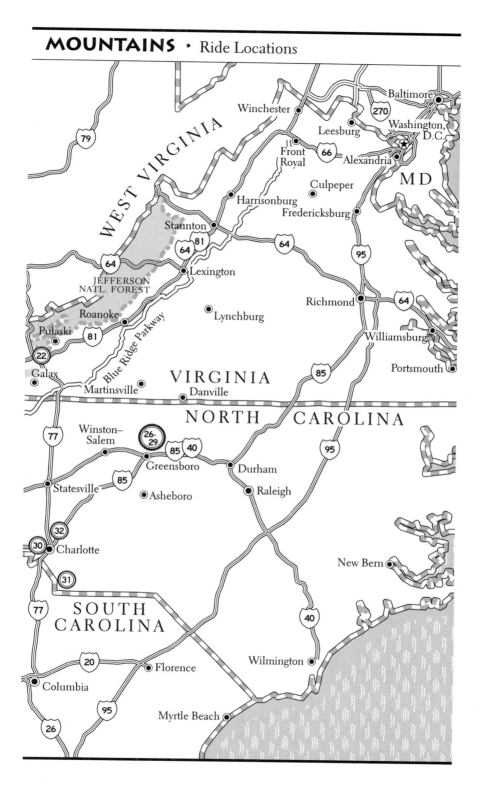

LIST OF MAPS

ACKNOWLEDGMENTS

This book is the third one I've written in the past four years, so I knew what I was getting myself into when editor Dennis Coello asked, "How about writing the guide for the Southern Appalachians?" The guide. I liked the way that sounded.

My first move was to acquire the information already out there—eight different collections. Therefore, my first thanks goes to all the hard-charging riders and researchers who have already published the whereabouts of many trailheads.

I also want to thank my editor, Dennis Coello, and publisher, Molly Burns, for their support in getting this guide started and finished. Also, the rest of the crew at Menasha, especially Holly Cross, have my sincere thanks for their long days spent getting the details right. Mountain biking, as most of us know, is in the details.

My family continues to give me their unflagging support as I pursue this strange career. My wife, Pam, and my son, Jared, deserve extra special thanks for their help in making sure I not only packed my bike, but also loaded the other tools and supplies required to get there and back.

Others, like the kind folks at bike shops and bike clubs I have called on the phone, but haven't met, stopped what they were doing to answer my odd questions. In this group, there are some people who have gone above and beyond simple kindness. Bill Devendorf, Craig Franz, and Woody top the list.

I, along with Menasha Ridge Press, especially want to thank Steve Thompson and John Derry for contributing the following rides for this guide: Panthertown Valley, Canaan Land Loop, Blue Valley, Pigeon Mountain, High Point on Pigeon Mountain, Indian Boundary, Hurricane Gap, Poplar Cove, Buffalo Mountain, and Pinnacle Tower.

There are others, of course. Most of them are people like you I met on the trail and asked, "So . . . do you know much about this trail?" Based on such conversations, I've discovered that people who ride a bike in the woods are special: friendly, clean, quiet, hardworking, and honest, not to mention strong, and for the most part, humble. But you already knew that. Thanks for the help.

FOREWORD

Welcome to *America by Mountain Bike*, a series designed to provide all-terrain bikers with the information they need to find and ride the very best trails around. Whether you're new to the sport and don't know where to pedal or an experienced mountain biker who wants to learn the classic trails in another region, this series is for you. Drop a few bucks for the book, spend an hour with the detailed maps and route descriptions, and you're prepared for the finest in off-road cycling.

My role as editor of this series is simple: First, find a mountain biker who knows the area and loves to ride. Second, ask that person to spend a year researching the most popular and very best rides around. And third, have that rider describe each trail in terms of difficulty, scenery, condition, elevation change, and all other categories of information that are important to trail riders. "Pretend you've just completed a ride and met up with fellow mountain bikers at the trailhead," I told each author. "Imagine their questions, be clear in your answers."

As I said, the *editorial* process—that of sending out riders and reading the submitted chapters—is a snap. But the work involved in finding, riding, and writing about each trail is enormous. In some instances our authors' tasks are made easier by the information contributed by local bike shops or cycling clubs, or even by the writers of local "where-to" guides. Credit for these contributions is provided, when appropriate, in each chapter, and our sincere thanks goes to all who have helped.

But the overwhelming majority of trails are discovered and pedaled by our authors themselves, then compared with dozens of other routes to determine if they qualify as "classic"—that area's best in scenery and cycling fun. If you've ever had the experience of pioneering a route from outdated topographic maps, or entering a bike shop to request information from local riders who would much prefer to keep their favorite trails secret, or if you know how it is to double- and triple-check data to be positive your trail info is correct, then you have an idea of how each of our authors has labored to bring about these books. You and I, and all the mountain bikers of America, are the richer for their efforts.

You'll get more out of this book if you take a moment to read the Introduction explaining how to read the trail listings. The "Topographic Maps" section will help you understand how useful topos will be on a ride, and will also tell you where to get them. And though this is a "where-to," not a "how-to" guide, those of you who have not traveled the backcountry might find "Hitting the Trail" of particular value.

In addition to the material above, newcomers to mountain biking might want to spend a minute with the glossary, page 313, so that terms like *hardpack, single-track,* and *waterbars* won't throw you when you come across them in the text.

All the best.

Dennis Coello
St. Louis

PREFACE

The mountains making up the southern range of the Appalachians are among the world's oldest. Worn away by wind and water, and covered by thick forests, the tips of the tallest mountains are elevational babies compared to the rocky tops out West. For example, North Carolina's Mount Mitchell commands the eastern high ground of the United States, reaching only 6,684 feet above sea level. But a place so green you've never seen.

What the Appalachians lack in size, they more than make up for with the look—and feel—of antiquity. If mountain biking is a spiritual experience for some (and I assure you it is), then these forests are the Notre Dames and Basilicas, and their trails are pews where we pedaling supplicants come to renew all that is vital within us.

The center of it all is, of course, the Great Smoky Mountains. It is here that the wild places of eastern America remain. The crumpled folds of granite have been pushed and squeezed into a mountainous line of high country overlooking valleys and coves lying thousands of feet below. It is a land of mystery, and the Indians who first lived here named it for the clouds that often drape its peaks.

Mountain chains no less impressive are connected to the Smokies, preserved in the national forests named Nantahala, Cherokee, Pisgah, and Chattahoochee. These forests lie in a nearly unbroken area covering western North Carolina, eastern Tennessee, and north Georgia. You want wild mountain biking? Then you've found it in the Appalachians. Load your bike and pick a spot on the map. Any spot. I guarantee you'll find no better place to ride off-road—no matter which side of the Mississippi you come from. Live long and pedal.

THE LAND

Green. Wet. Shady. The sensations of the Appalachians can be discovered in its creek coves and pure pine ridges, along quiet lakes and crashing rivers. The forest trails lead the mountain biker to these places. On single-track and fire roads, this world of incredible diversity opens up and reveals a truly wonderful and magical land. I don't believe this because I was born here (although that does

The sharp horizon of the Appalachians reflects its ancient history in the waters of a mountain lake.

give me a certain, incorrigible weakness for most things Appalachian). I believe it because it's true.

Geologically, the land under your fat tires emerged as soon as conditions on the young Earth allowed. The Hubble telescope points skyward and tells us of the cosmic past, while the Appalachians serve as Earth's museum of its earliest days. The tallest mountains in the Appalachians only reach about a mile and a quarter above sea level. Compared to the rock monsters out West whose peaks regularly reach two jagged miles and higher, North America's eastern range is a collection of smooth bumps.

But what a collection. Beginning in the south, in Georgia and northeast Alabama, the thousand-foot-tall rolling ridges are the remnants of Himalayan ranges. Over time, a billion years or so, these mountains eroded as Earth's atmosphere rubbed them down like a sandblaster. Blizzards, tornadoes, landslides, running water, and freezing temperatures—they all cracked the stone and carried it back into the sea.

Generally, the soils at higher elevations tend to have better structure and hold up better in wet conditions than those found at lower ones. Likewise, the soils on the western side of the Appalachians (Tennessee and Kentucky) tend to be sandier and thus hold up relatively well in wet conditions. However, it courts massive erosion to ride wet trails on some eastern slopes (especially areas in North Carolina and Georgia), which tend to have a higher concentration of clays.

When in doubt about whether or not to ride a trail after it's rained, wait it out. You'll find plenty of all-season rides—fire and service roads—described in this

Some days, the sky hangs low, like a gray ball caught in the claws of trees.

guide. Stow your disappointment about not getting to ride the single-track, and do the only decent thing a caring mountain biker will do and let the trail dry. The consequence of riding a trail that's too wet is, at the least, that the trail becomes rutted and dangerous to those who will ride it later. At the worst, the trail can be closed to mountain biking forever.

FOREST FLORA AND FAUNA

The diversity of plant and animal life in Appalachia is surpassed by few other places in the world. Much of it is as harmless as it is beautiful. Whether you're watching deer, birds, dragonflies, snakes, or spiders, the result is a world that never stands still. A world that welcomes you on your two fat tires. Just steer clear of leaves, teeth, stingers, and fangs and you'll never carry back anything more than fond memories of Appalachia's animals and plants.

Most of what you see will be green. Trees in a mixed hardwood forest of oaks, maples, and hickories blend with stands of evergreen—pines, laurels, hollies, and hemlocks. They all keep a high, dense ceiling overhead, from mid-April until late October. The most noticeable benefit to the immediate health for the off-road biker comes in the form of sweet, blessed shade, which makes even the most stifling summer days bearable. Another benefit, which may not be noticed as quickly, comes from the clean air produced by the trees. Examples of old man's beard, lichen, moss, and even fern can be found growing in branches and

A swath of blooming Indian ghost pipe turns the forest floor white.

on trunks, indications of the air's pristine health. Where they grow most thickly is where the air is cleanest. Breathe deep and enjoy.

Most forest plants are small and blend into the background, sporting tiny blooms of yellow, red, pink, orange, white, and blue. Unless you're on a slow climb, head down, and lucky, you will seldom see the rattlesnake plaintain's spike of tiny white orchids, or wintergreen's curved white bell. But hop off for a short walk into the understory, and you'll see them and more. Some plants, however, like poison ivy, saw briar, and blackberry, should be avoided for their obvious dermatological hazards.

Many trails cut through thickets of laurel, native azalea, or rhododendron, called "slicks," or "hells." These are found throughout Appalachia, blooming in spectacular displays from early May through early July. And unlike the smaller plants whose blooms lurk in forest shadow, a laurel thicket at peak bloom will catch even the quickest hammerhead's eye.

But what bikers will notice most about the plants and trees of the Appalachian forest is how their dynamic forces shape the trail, placing special demands on the biker's skill, strength, and preparation. Soil washes away from roots, exposing a surface that last week may have been easy but now gets slick when wet. Freezes and roots heave up rocks, which can find their way into the middle of a fast downhill. Deadfall blocks trails, requiring creative reroutes under, over, or around, on bike and off.

The animals of the forest, at least those of the Mammalian order, have far less impact on trail conditions and riding style. But I've never seen a rider who didn't get excited seeing a deer whip its white tail vertical before bounding away through the forest. In fact, for many bikers, it is this more intimate connection to the wild things in the woods that adds a unique dimension to mountain biking.

Under the heading of "Sightings—Four Legs and Fur," besides the ever present deer (whose population now exceeds that of the Pilgrim landing party), you may observe as many as 50 different genera. The intelligent and engaging squirrels and chipmunks are the other most frequently sighted examples, at least by this biker. Both are active year-round, and their barks add to the sounds heard on single-track. But riders beware: I've heard reports of the crafty critters sneaking into saddlebags and making off with a bag of nuts or a chocolate bar.

The rest of the Warm Bloods will offer fewer chances of direct observation, especially by the biker in motion. Their movements occur most commonly at night, but the dusky rider (either at first light or last) will make the occasional sighting of coons, opossums, and skunks returning from or heading into a night of omnivorous foraging. A solitary fox, bobcat, or coyote may suddenly appear on the trail ahead, then disappear just as quickly. Trees bear the nocturnal gnawings of another common mammal, the beaver. Moles and voles sometimes cross trails, leaving behind telltale tunnels on the surface where they have searched for meals of worms and grubs.

By far, birds make up the most numerous animals in the woods—at least, among those with backbones. Turkeys have made a comeback from their previous small populations of 30 years ago and exist in large numbers in some areas of the Appalachian Mountains. Each sighting of these "flying bowling balls" rekindles in me the admiration Ben Franklin must have felt when he suggested making them America's bird. In the same category, yet far less common, watching a grouse explode off its perch will make even the most stoic cyclist exclaim in awe.

But for the most part, especially after the trees have woven their summer canopy, birds will be like bad little children, heard and not seen. I'm always reminded of Tarzan and the jungle when the piercing call of a pileated woodpecker wrecks the calm of morning. Other songbirds—chickadees, virioles, nuthatches, finches, jays, buntings, doves, and cardinals—move in large flocks, trilling and whistling with indescribable complexity and beauty.

It is a special ride when I hear the shriek of a red-tailed hawk as it spirals high above me. Sometimes, I am lucky enough to catch its cousin, the sharp-shinned hawk, floating silently among the branches. Another big bird, the eagle, is making a comeback, and the sharp-eyed biker will sometimes be rewarded with the sight of its wide wings against the sky. Owls are seldom seen during daylight, but look up in the limbs and you may catch sight of one sleeping on its roost. Our family's favorite winter bird to watch, though, is the turkey vulture, or buzzard. Despite the disgust people associate with its eating habits and looks, its ability to sail the thermals has no equal among land birds.

Although the four-legged and two-legged creatures of the forest have little impact on how a mountain biker prepares for a trip, that changes when the number of legs jumps to six. The cool weather of late fall and winter keeps the insects at a much more manageable number, so much so that no extra preparation is required during these months. Beginning, however, in early March, trips into the woods will likely bring an encounter with buffalo gnats. They buzz incessantly around your head, looking to tap the fluid from your eyes. I've found that wearing glasses works best at thwarting their attempts to sip from my eyelid; eventually I still wind up with one lodged up my nose or in the back of my throat (and definitely in my ears), but at least I'll be able to see to find the tissues, swabs, and water bottle.

The tiny midge, or no-see-um, packs more pain per pound than any other nonstinging insect. A bloodsucker by design, it can quickly turn a rest stop into a leg-slapping and neck-whacking dance. Fortunately, repellent works and comes highly recommended for extended periods outside. Should you forego the chemical defense in lieu of "taking it like a mountain biker," be prepared for bites leaving an intense sensation, lasting approximately 10 to 15 minutes.

Mosquitoes search for warm-blooded meals nearly year-round in some parts of Appalachia, but they cannot fly fast enough to keep up with a moving bike, even on a slow climb. Yellow flies and horseflies are different, at least on the uphills. It's not 100 percent effective, but if it's horsefly season—mid-June to mid-July (before the dragonflies hatch)—I put a dab of repellent behind my ears, and on my legs and back. You might submit, as I've seen some do, and administer a complete body fogging, just to keep biting flies at bay.

Bees and wasps, however, are nearly impervious to the effects of repellent. Once they mount an attack, they become single-minded in their defense of the nest. That's the bad side. The good side lies in knowing these insects don't sting unless provoked. The most common attack comes from the yellow jacket, whose nest entrance has been smashed by an unwitting fat tire. Although one direct hit on the nest will trigger a response, it is usually the third or fourth biker back in a line who gets nailed. A quick application of ammonia hydroxide (sold under brand names like Sting Stick) or some other after-bite remedy will not only bring the intense pain under some control, it also speeds healing. Benadryl, likewise, can help diminish the reaction and is generally a wise precaution, while epinephrine is necessary for some to counter the effects from anaphylactic shock, a potentially fatal condition. Both Benadryl and epinephrine are good precautions for those allergic to insect bites and stings. Pedaling head-down into a bald-face hornet's low-hung nest (I've seen some bigger than picnic baskets) or unwisely swatting at a giant hornet will surely provoke a bite, but bees and wasps are generally pretty tough to provoke and will go about their business with no malevolent intent toward even the most deserving among us.

Of the eight-legged forest dwellers, spiders make up the bulk. And except for getting webbed and inadvertently injected with spider venom (it's only happened to me once, and I was on foot), the mountain biker should have little concern for Charlotte's descendants. A far more insidious threat to a biker's good time takes shape in the ugly little head of a tick. Yes, repellent works . . . most of the time. It will sometimes sweat its effectiveness away and leave a vulnerable path. If you find one on you, especially early in the year during the heavy, first hatch, chances are good another tick or two will be found slowly crawling up to some soft spot to suck your blood. Yes, it's gross and I'm sure I'll never get used to it, but don't call 911 on the cell phone. Just check yourself over carefully. By following standard tick removal procedure (grab the sucker firmly behind the head with tweezers and give it a good yank), chances are slim to none that you'll get ill as a result of the first six to eight hours of a tick's attachment.

Don't let all this bug information alarm you. Most bug-biker interactions will either take place unnoticed or become a special memory. Likewise with the rest of the animals in the forests of Appalachia. They blend into the plants and trees, all going about their business of feeding and breeding with seldom a notice from their two-legged cousin who rolls on rubber and pedals steel—Cyclus montanea.

THE PEOPLE

Mountain bikers' ancestors landed in Appalachia thousands of years ago. Small bands of what New World explorers called Indians roamed the climax forests, living hand-to-mouth off the land. They tended to have summer homes in the mountains and winter retreats at lower spots, mostly near rivers. The men made hunting trips and traded with other groups, while the women and children stayed home and did chores. Many women of modern Appalachia will tell you little has changed since those earliest days. Beginning, however, with de Soto's discovery of this mountainous region, things never were the same for its first people. The search for gold drew de Soto and others, and its discovery 300 years later sent the natives packing. The time in between, thought largely to be an unbroken period of Indian wars and unceasing conflict between the two races, was actually an era of much sharing and assimilation.

The names of places are the most noticeable legacy left from this time. You will never travel more than a few miles before seeing another river, mountain, or town bearing an Indian name—Amicalola, Tallulah, Nantahala, Tsali, Chattooga, Chattanooga, Chattahoochee. The names roll off the tongue like bikes on a downhill. Even the name for the great mountain range itself—Appalachia—comes not from the King's English, but from the tribe that lived near its southern slopes.

A trip into the heart of this region, however, still carries with it the mystique grown up around the people who live here. Few trailheads, no matter how remote, can be reached without passing by a solitary home or tiny community tucked back in a steep-sided draw. Images of *Deliverance* may surface for the mountain biker unfamiliar with Appalachia's people the first time a backwoods ride is planned. Or they may start telling jokes that begin with, "You know you're a redneck when . . ." Those who take the time to get beyond these easy stereotypes will find in the people of Appalachia hearts big and sweet as watermelons. Still, it might be a good idea to practice your drawl and obeisance just in case you ever lose the trail and wind up in someone's backyard at dusk, or in the middle of a redneck camping trip. That is, if you can't pedal away like a scalded dog.

Mountain biking brings people closer together, but in the case of the group above—
maybe a bit too close.

Still, given half a chance, the majority of people from Appalachia will treat
even a lost, Lycra-clad cyclist with metropolitan tolerance, if not downright hos-
pitality. I've traveled by myself into some of the most remote and secluded areas
in the South. Although some will call it luck, I have never had a bad personal
experience with the people I've met in the woods, whether hunters, horseback
riders, campers, hikers, law enforcement officers, or other bikers. Of course, if
someone does approach you, crowbar in hand (like what happened to my friend
Craig when he took a bike trip out West), don't stick around to see if he needs
help changing his tire.

TRAIL SELECTION

The area discussed in this guide covers roughly 25,000 square miles, from southwest Virginia, through Tennessee and North Carolina, down to north Georgia.
The center of it all is the Great Smoky Mountains. It is not only a large area, it
contains at least as many trails per square mile than any other place in America.
For every ride described in this guide, I would not be surprised to hear of at least
three or four more either waiting to be found or being quietly ridden by locals
only. If that sounds hard to believe, consider this: nearly every ridge has a road
or a remnant of one, logging's legacy to mountain bikers. And the rule is simple:
if it is within a national forest and not posted otherwise, guess what? It's mountain bike–legal. Ride on, ride on, ride on.

So with literally hundreds of trails to choose from, how did we decide which trails to include? Of course, we could do like others and describe a smaller area. Or we could make the number of rides fewer. But both ways seem like a cop-out in an area you can drive tip-to-tip in about six easy hours. So we compromised.

In areas where many trails can be connected in a variety of combinations, like Pisgah National Forest and Cherokee National Forest, either a representative trail or a centrally located trailhead has been included.

You will find few trails mentioned that require biking on blacktop. We all ride on asphalt at some time or another, and enjoy it. But the focus of this guide is to present as many off-road, single-track routes as possible, because that's what we want to ride every time . . . if we could. But we can't. But you can avoid the pavement. Some riders also avoid double-track, for a variety of reasons: too straight, too smooth, or too wide. But not me. As long as it doesn't have traffic on it, I love it. I still like it even when I have to share the road with those infernal combustion engines, which is why you'll find some trails described in this guide on which vehicles and bikes must ride together. The trails are just too good to leave out, pickup trucks or not.

Some riders also say "no" to riding horse trails. Too chewed up and too pooped up. Both good reasons, when they apply. But did you know Tsali, probably the East's most popular destination, is also a horse trail?

Almost every trail open to bikes is open to hikers as well. I have read about the uneasy relationship in some other parts of the country involving hikers and bikers, and it is unfortunate, being an occasional hiker myself. But it seems that Appalachian trails that have seldom seen heavy foot traffic have been pretty much taken over by bikes, at least unofficially. What I have found is that hikers generally stick to those trails open to foot travel only, leaving the multiuse trails to the horses and bikes. There are exceptions, of course. So don't assume that just because there's never been a hiker around that blind curve, there won't be one the next time.

Another factor used in deciding which trails to include is purely subjective. If I didn't like it, it didn't get included. I recall the time I rode an hour to the trailhead of a route in Florida. I took a look at the physical setting and immediately decided I would never want someone to walk up to me one day and ask, "Why would you ever send anyone to a place like that?"

Every effort has been made to ensure the trails described in this guide are designated and legal trails for mountain bike use. Therefore, no outlaw trails have been recommended, although most of us know of at least one trail where bikers ride illegally. And, finally, despite my inquisitive nature and exhaustive research, I'm sure I have simply not heard of all the trails. If you know of a trail that should have been included but was left out, I would like to hear from you. You can snail-mail me c/o the publisher, or send e-mail to me at sjones@stc.net. Enough talk. Let's ride.

Single-Track—Rides in this category have a significant length of single-track.

11 Upper Wilson
19 Iron Mountain Trail to Damascus
24 Greenway Mountain Bike Trail
27 Owl's Roost Trail
28 Bald Eagle Trail
29 Reedy Fork Trail
35 Slate Rock–Pilot Cove
37 Buckwheat Knob
46 Shell Stand Creek
51 Knobscorcher
52 Fontana Village
57 Lady Slipper at Lake Russell
60 Turner Creek Loop, No-Tell Trail
61 Black Branch Loop

63 Bull Mountain
65 Chicopee Woods
66 Tumbling Creek
67 Rich Mountain WMA
68 Ridgeway
69 Bear Creek
70 Berry College
73 Clear Creek
74 Clemmer Trail
75 Benton Falls
76 Slickrock
78 Iron Mountain
84 Panther Creek State Park

Double-Track—Rides in this category are entirely (or almost entirely) double-track.

1 Cades Cove
2 Rich Mountain Road
3 Parson Branch Road
4 Heintooga
6 French Broad River Route
7 Laurel River Trail
8 Mill Ridge
9 Yancey Ridge
13 Benson Hollow
14 Buckeye Trail
15 Spencer Hollow
17 18-Mile Ride
20 Grayson Highlands State Park
21 Virginia Creeper
22 New River
23 South Mountains
26 Bur-Mil Runner's Trail
31 Cane Creek Park
32 Beech Spring Mountain Bike Park
33 Bent Creek
38 Thrift Cove
39 Right Loop
40 Left Loop

41 Mouse Branch
42 Thompson Loop
43 Lemmons Branch
44 Calfpen Gap
45 Shell Stand Road–Swim Bald
47 Meetinghouse
48 Wauchecha Bald
49 Stecoah Gap
50 Cheoah Bald
58 Unicoi
59 Davenport Mountain
62 Little Sal Mountain Loop
64 Amicalola Falls State Park Trail
77 Old Copper Road Trail
85 Collier Ridge
86 Duncan Hollow
87 Big Ridge Rock Trail
88 White Oak Overlook
89 O & W Rail Trail
90 O & W Overlook
91 Leatherwood Overlook
92 Gernt Road

Adventure—These are rides remotely situated, and/or they offer many areas for exploration and discovery.

 9 Yancey Ridge
10 Schoolhouse Ridge
11 Upper Wilson
12 Woodruff Branch
13 Benson Hollow
15 Spencer Hollow
16 Woods Mountain
19 Iron Mountain Trail to Damascus
20 Grayson Highlands State Park
23 South Mountains
35 Slate Rock–Pilot Cove
37 Buckwheat Knob
44 Calfpen Gap
45 Shell Stand Road–Swim Bald

46 Shell Stand Creek
60 Turner Creek Loop, No-Tell Trail
61 Black Branch Loop
62 Little Sal Mountain Loop
67 Rich Mountain WMA
68 Ridgeway
69 Bear Creek
70 Berry College
73 Clear Creek
74 Clemmer Trail
76 Slickrock
78 Iron Mountain
89 O & W Rail Trail
92 Gernt Loop

Loops

 1 Cades Cove
 8 Mill Ridge
 9 Yancey Ridge
10 Schoolhouse Ridge
11 Upper Wilson
13 Benson Hollow
14 Buckeye Trail
16 Woods Mountain
18 Lower China Creek
23 South Mountains
24 Greenway Mountain Bike Trail
26 Bur-Mil Runner's Trail
30 Catawba Riverfront Mountain
   Bike Park
32 Beech Spring Mountain Bike Park
33 Bent Creek
34 Fletcher Creek Trail
36 The Pink Beds
37 Buckwheat Knob
38 Thrift Cove
39 Right Loop
40 Left Loop

41 Mouse Branch
42 Thompson Loop
46 Shell Stand Creek
51 Knobscorcher
52 Fontana Village
57 Lady Slipper at Lake Russell
58 Unicoi
59 Davenport Mountain
60 Turner Creek Loop, No-Tell Trail
61 Black Branch Loop
62 Little Sal Mountain Loop
63 Bull Mountain
64 Amicalola Falls State Park Trail
65 Chicopee Woods
66 Tumbling Creek
67 Rich Mountain WMA
68 Ridgeway
69 Bear Creek
70 Berry College
76 Slickrock
78 Iron Mountain
84 Panther Creek State Park

Out-and-Backs

 5 Clingmans Dome
 6 French Broad River Route
 7 Laurel River Trail
15 Spencer Hollow
20 Grayson Highlands State Park
25 Hilton Park

27 Owl's Roost Trail
28 Bald Eagle Trail
29 Reedy Fork Trail
31 Cane Creek Park
34 Fletcher Creek Trail
43 Lemmons Branch

Out-and-Backs (continued)

44 Calfpen Gap
45 Shell Stand Road–Swim Bald
47 Meetinghouse
48 Wauchecha Bald
49 Stecoah Gap
50 Cheoah Bald
73 Clear Creek
74 Clemmer Trail
75 Benton Falls

77 Old Copper Road Trail
85 Collier Ridge
86 Duncan Hollow
87 Big Ridge Rock Trail
88 White Oak Overlook
89 O & W Rail Trail
90 O & W Overlook
91 Leatherwood Overlook
92 Gernt Road

Advanced Only—A high degree of technical expertise is required.

16 Woods Mountain
46 Shell Stand Creek

Just for Starters—These rides are suitable for anyone comfortable on a saddle.

1 Cades Cove
6 French Broad River Route
14 Buckeye Trail
21 Virginia Creeper
22 New River
26 Bur-Mil Runner's Trail
28 Bald Eagle Trail
31 Cane Creek Park
33 Bent Creek
36 The Pink Beds

39 Right Loop
43 Lemmons Branch
62 Little Sal Mountain Loop
65 Chicopee Woods
66 Tumbling Creek
77 Old Copper Road Trail
85 Collier Ridge
86 Duncan Hollow
87 Big Ridge Rock Trail
90 O & W Overlook

Short Rides—Rides in this category are generally under 5 miles, but recent construction may have added significant mileage.

8 Mill Ridge
12 Woodruff Branch
14 Buckeye Trail
18 Lower China Creek
24 Greenway Mountain Bike Trail
25 Hilton Park
26 Bur-Mil Runner's Trail
28 Bald Eagle Trail
38 Thrift Cove

43 Lemmons Branch
52 Fontana Village
66 Tumbling Creek
75 Benton Falls
77 Old Copper Road Trail
85 Collier Ridge
86 Duncan Hollow
87 Big Ridge Rock Trail
90 O & W Overlook

Long Rides—Rides in this category are generally over 10 miles.

2 Rich Mountain Road
3 Parson Branch Road
4 Heintooga
5 Clingmans Dome
9 Yancey Ridge
16 Woods Mountain
17 18-Mile Ride

19 Iron Mountain Trail to Damascus
21 Virginia Creeper
22 New River
23 South Mountains
30 Catawba Riverfront Mountain
   Bike Park
34 Fletcher Creek Trail

Long Rides (continued)

35 Slate Rock–Pilot Cove
37 Buckwheat Knob
39 Right Loop
40 Left Loop
44 Calfpen Gap
45 Shell Stand Road–Swim Bald
46 Shell Stand Creek
47 Meetinghouse

48 Wauchecha Bald
50 Cheoah Bald
57 Lady Slipper at Lake Russell
63 Bull Mountain
64 Amicalola Falls State Park Trail
78 Iron Mountain
89 O & W Rail Trail

Difficult Fords—Rides in this category could possibly require a potentially hazardous stream or river crossing, produced by big, slick rocks and/or high water.

4 Heintooga
13 Benson Hollow
18 Lower China Creek
20 Grayson Highlands State Park
23 South Mountains
34 Fletcher Creek Trail

46 Shell Stand Creek
62 Little Sal Mountain Loop
69 Bear Creek
78 Iron Mountain
89 O & W Rail Trail

Traffic—There is a possibility of meeting vehicles somewhere on the trail.

1 Cades Cove
2 Rich Mountain Road
3 Parson Branch Road
4 Heintooga
6 French Broad River Route
9 Yancey Ridge
17 18-Mile Ride
35 Slate Rock–Pilot Cove
36 The Pink Beds

37 Buckwheat Knob
46 Shell Stand Creek
59 Davenport Mountain
60 Turner Creek Loop, No-Tell Trail
61 Black Branch Loop
62 Little Sal Mountain Loop
64 Amicalola Falls State Park Trail
78 Iron Mountain
91 Leatherwood Overlook

Shuttle Rides—These trips have a shuttle recommended.

2 Rich Mountain Road
3 Parson Branch Road
4 Heintooga
17 18-Mile Ride

19 Iron Mountain Trail to Damascus
21 Virginia Creeper
22 New River

MOUNTAIN BIKE!
The Southern Appalachian and Smoky Mountains

INTRODUCTION

Each trail in this book begins with key information that includes length, configuration, aerobic and technical difficulty, trail conditions, scenery, and special comments. Additional description is contained in 11 individual categories. The following will help you to understand all of the information provided.

Trail name: Trail names are as designated on United States Geological Survey (USGS) or Forest Service or other maps, and/or by local custom.

At a Glance Information

Length/configuration: The overall length of a trail is described in miles, unless stated otherwise. The configuration is a description of the shape of each trail — whether the trail is a loop, out-and-back (that is, along the same route), figure eight, trapezoid, isosceles triangle, decahedron . . . (just kidding), or if it connects with another trail described in the book. See the Glossary for definitions of *point-to-point* and *combination*.

Aerobic difficulty: This provides a description of the degree of physical exertion required to complete the ride.

Technical difficulty: This provides a description of the technical skill required to pedal a ride. Trails are often described here in terms of being paved, unpaved, sandy, hard-packed, washboarded, two- or four-wheel-drive, single-track or double-track. All terms that might be unfamiliar to the first-time mountain biker are defined in the Glossary.

   Note: For both the aerobic and technical difficulty categories, authors were asked to keep in mind the fact that all riders are not equal, and thus to gauge the trail in terms of how the middle-of-the-road rider — someone between the newcomer and Ned Overend — could handle the route. Comments about the trail's length, condition, and elevation change will also assist you in determining the difficulty of any trail relative to your own abilities.

Scenery: Here you will find a general description of the natural surroundings during the seasons most riders pedal the trail and a suggestion of what is to be found at special times (like great fall foliage or cactus in bloom).

Special comments: Unique elements of the ride are mentioned.

Category Information

General location: This category describes where the trail is located in reference to a nearby town or other landmark.

Elevation change: Unless stated otherwise, the figure provided is the total gain and loss of elevation along the trail. In regions where the elevation variation is not extreme, the route is simply described as flat, rolling, or possessing short steep climbs or descents.

Season: This is the best time of year to pedal the route, taking into account trail conditions (for example, when it will not be muddy), riding comfort (when the weather is too hot, cold, or wet), and local hunting seasons.

   Note: Because the exact opening and closing dates of deer, elk, moose, and antelope seasons often change from year to year, riders should check with the local fish and game department or call a sporting goods store (or any place that sells hunting licenses) in a nearby town before heading out. Wear bright clothes in fall, and don't wear suede jackets while in the saddle. Hunter's-orange tape on the helmet is also a good idea.

Services: This category is of primary importance in guides for paved-road tourers, but is far less crucial to most mountain bike trail descriptions because there are usually no services whatsoever to be found. Authors have noted when water is available on desert or long mountain routes and have listed the availability of food, lodging, campgrounds, and bike shops. If all these services are present, you will find only the words "All services available in . . ."

Hazards: Special hazards like steep cliffs, great amounts of deadfall, or barbed-wire fences very close to the trail are noted here.

Rescue index: Determining how far one is from help on any particular trail can be difficult due to the backcountry nature of most mountain bike rides. Authors therefore state the proximity of homes or Forest Service outposts, nearby roads where one might hitch a ride, or the likelihood of other bikers being encountered on the trail. Phone numbers of local sheriff departments or hospitals are hardly ever provided because phones are usually not available. If you are able to reach a phone, the local operator will connect you with emergency services.

Land status: This category provides information regarding whether the trail crosses land operated by the Forest Service, Bureau of Land Management, or a city, state, or national park; whether it crosses private land whose owner (at the time the author did the research) has allowed mountain bikers right of passage; and so on.

Note: Authors have been extremely careful to offer only those routes that are open to bikers and are legal to ride. However, because land ownership changes over time, and because the land-use controversy created by mountain bikes still has not completely subsided, it is the duty of each cyclist to look for and to heed signs warning against trail use. Don't expect this book to get you off the hook when you're facing some small-town judge for pedaling past a Biking Prohibited sign erected the day before you arrived. Look for these signs, read them, and heed the advice. And remember there's always another trail.

Maps: The maps in this book have been produced with great care and, in conjunction with the trail-following suggestions, will help you stay on course. But as every experienced mountain biker knows, things can get tricky in the backcountry. It is therefore strongly suggested that you avail yourself of the detailed information found in the 7.5 minute series USGS (United States Geological Survey) topographic maps. In some cases, authors have found that specific Forest Service or other maps may be more useful than the USGS quads and tell how to obtain them.

Finding the trail: Detailed information on how to reach the trailhead and where to park your car is provided here.

Sources of additional information: Here you will find the address and/or phone number of a bike shop, governmental agency, or other source from which trail information can be obtained.

Notes on the trail: This is where you are guided carefully through any portions of the trail that are particularly difficult to follow. The author also may add information about the route that does not fit easily in the other categories. This category will not be present for those rides where the route is easy to follow.

ABBREVIATIONS

The following road-designation abbreviations are used in *Mountain Bike! The Southern Appalachian and Smoky Mountains:*

CR	County Road	I-	Interstate
FR	Farm Route	IR	Indian Route
FS	Forest Service Road	US	United States highway

State highways are designated with the appropriate two-letter state abbreviation, followed by the road number. Example: TN 1 = Tennessee State Highway 1.

Postal Service two-letter state codes:

AL	Alabama	AZ	Arizona
AK	Alaska	AR	Arkansas

CA	California	NV	Nevada
CO	Colorado	NH	New Hampshire
CT	Connecticut	NJ	New Jersey
DE	Delaware	NM	New Mexico
DC	District of Columbia	NY	New York
FL	Florida	NC	North Carolina
GA	Georgia	ND	North Dakota
HI	Hawaii	OH	Ohio
ID	Idaho	OK	Oklahoma
IL	Illinois	OR	Oregon
IN	Indiana	PA	Pennsylvania
IA	Iowa	RI	Rhode Island
KS	Kansas	SC	South Carolina
KY	Kentucky	SD	South Dakota
LA	Louisiana	TN	Tennessee
ME	Maine	TX	Texas
MD	Maryland	UT	Utah
MA	Massachusetts	VT	Vermont
MI	Michigan	VA	Virginia
MN	Minnesota	WA	Washington
MS	Mississippi	WV	West Virginia
MO	Missouri	WI	Wisconsin
MT	Montana	WY	Wyoming
NE	Nebraska		

RIDE CONFIGURATIONS

Combination: This type of route may combine two or more configurations. For example, a point-to-point route may integrate a scenic loop or an out-and-back spur midway through the ride. Likewise, an out-and-back may have a loop at its farthest point (this configuration looks like a cherry with a stem attached; the stem is the out-and-back, the fruit is the terminus loop). Or a loop route may have multiple out-and-back spurs and/or loops to the side. Mileage for a combination route is for the total distance to complete the ride.

Loop: This route configuration is characterized by riding from the designated trailhead to a distant point, then returning to the trailhead via a different route (or simply continuing on the same in a circle route) without doubling back. You always move forward across new terrain but return to the starting point when finished. Mileage is for the entire loop from the trailhead back to trailhead.

Out-and-back: A ride where you will return on the same trail you pedaled out. While this might sound far more boring than a loop route, many trails look very different when pedaled in the opposite direction.

Point-to-point: A vehicle shuttle (or similar assistance) is required for this type of route, which is ridden from the designated trailhead to a distant location, or endpoint, where the route ends. Total mileage is for the one-way trip from the trailhead to endpoint.

Spur: A road or trail that intersects the main trail you're following.

Ride Configurations contributed by Gregg Bromka

TOPOGRAPHIC MAPS

The maps in this book, when used in conjunction with the route directions present in each chapter, will in most instances be sufficient to get you to the trail and keep you on it. However, you will find superior detail and valuable information in the 7.5 minute series United States Geological Survey (USGS) topographic maps. Recognizing how indispensable these are to bikers and hikers alike, many bike shops and sporting goods stores now carry topos of the local area.

But if you're brand new to mountain biking you might be wondering "What's a topographic map?" In short, these differ from standard "flat" maps in that they indicate not only linear distance, but elevation as well. One glance at a topo will show you the difference, for "contour lines" are spread across the map like dozens of intricate spider webs. Each contour line represents a particular elevation, and at the base of each topo a particular "contour interval" designation is given. Yes, it sounds confusing if you're new to the lingo, but it truly is a simple and wonderfully helpful system. Keep reading.

Let's assume that the 7.5 minute series topo before us says "Contour Interval 40 feet," that the short trail we'll be pedaling is two inches in length on the map, and that it crosses five contour lines from its beginning to end. What do we know? Well, because the linear scale of this series is 2,000 feet to the inch (roughly 2 3/4 inches representing 1 mile), we know our trail is approximately 4/5 of a mile long (2 inches × 2,000 feet). But we also know we'll be climbing or descending 200 vertical feet (5 contour lines × 40 feet each) over that distance. And the elevation designations written on occasional contour lines will tell us if we're heading up or down.

The authors of this series warn their readers of upcoming terrain, but only a detailed topo gives you the information you need to pinpoint your position exactly on a map, steer yourself toward optional trails and roads nearby, plus let you know at a glance if you'll be pedaling hard to take them. It's a lot of information for a very low cost. In fact, the only drawback with topos is their size — several feet square. I've tried rolling them into tubes, folding them carefully, even cutting them into blocks and photocopying the pieces. Any of these systems is a pain, but no matter how you pack the maps you'll be happy they're along. And you'll be even happier if you pack a compass as well.

In addition to local bike shops and sporting goods stores, you'll find topos at major universities and some public libraries where you might try photocopying the ones you need to avoid the cost of buying them. But if you want your own and can't find them locally, contact:

USGS Map Sales
Box 25286
Denver, CO 80225
(800) HELP MAP (435-7627)

VISA and MasterCard are accepted. Ask for an index while you're at it, plus a price list and a copy of the booklet *Topographic Maps*. In minutes you'll be reading them like a pro.

A second excellent series of maps available to mountain bikers is that put out by the United States Forest Service. If your trail runs through an area designated as a national forest, look in the phone book (white pages) under the United States Government listings, find the Department of Agriculture heading, and then run your finger down that section until you find the Forest Service. Give them a call and they'll provide the address of the regional Forest Service office, from which you can obtain the appropriate map.

TRAIL ETIQUETTE

Pick up almost any mountain bike magazine these days and you'll find articles and letters to the editor about trail conflict. For example, you'll find hikers' tales of being blindsided by speeding mountain bikers, complaints from mountain bikers about being blamed for trail damage that was really caused by horse or cattle traffic, and cries from bikers about those "kamikaze" riders who through their antics threaten to close even more trails to all of us.

The authors of this series have been very careful to guide you to only those trails that are open to mountain biking (or at least were open at the time of their research), and without exception have warned of the damage done to our sport through injudicious riding. All of us can benefit from glancing over the following International Mountain Bicycling Association (IMBA) Rules of the Trail before saddling up.

1. *Ride on open trails only*. Respect trail and road closures (ask if not sure), avoid possible trespass on private land, obtain permits and authorization as may be required. Federal and state wilderness areas are closed to cycling.

2. *Leave no trace*. Be sensitive to the dirt beneath you. Even on open trails, you should not ride under conditions where you will leave evidence of your passing, such as on certain soils shortly after rain. Observe the different types of soils and trail construction; practice low-impact cycling. This also means staying on the trail and not creating any new ones. Be sure to pack out at least as much as you pack in.

3. *Control your bicycle!* Inattention for even a second can cause disaster. Excessive speed can maim and threaten people; there is no excuse for it!

4. *Always yield the trail.* Make known your approach well in advance. A friendly greeting (or a bell) is considerate and works well; startling someone may cause loss of trail access. Show your respect when passing others by slowing to a walk or even stopping. Anticipate that other trail users may be around corners or in blind spots.

5. *Never spook animals.* All animals are startled by an unannounced approach, a sudden movement, or a loud noise. This can be dangerous for you, for others, and for the animals. Give animals extra room and time to adjust to you. In passing, use special care and follow the directions of horseback riders (ask if uncertain). Running cattle and disturbing wild animals is a serious offense. Leave gates as you found them, or as marked.

6. *Plan ahead.* Know your equipment, your ability, and the area in which you are riding—and prepare accordingly. Be self-sufficient at all times. Wear a helmet, keep your machine in good condition, and carry necessary supplies for changes in weather or other conditions. A well-executed trip is a satisfaction to you and not a burden or offense to others.

For more information, contact IMBA, P.O. Box 7578, Boulder, CO 80306; (303) 545-9011.

HITTING THE TRAIL

Once again, because this is a "where-to," not a "how-to" guide, the following will be brief. If you're a veteran trail rider these suggestions might serve to remind you of something you've forgotten to pack. If you're a newcomer, they might convince you to think twice before hitting the backcountry unprepared.

Water: I've heard the questions dozens of times. "How much is enough? One bottle? Two? Three?! But think of all that extra weight!" Well, one simple physiological fact should convince you to err on the side of excess when it comes to deciding how much water to pack: a human working hard in 90-degree temperature needs approximately ten quarts of fluids every day. Ten quarts. That's two and a half gallons—12 large water bottles, or 16 small ones. And, with water weighing in at approximately 8 pounds per gallon, a one-day supply comes to a whopping 20 pounds.

In other words, pack along two or three bottles even for short rides. And make sure you can purify the water found along the trail on longer routes. When writing of those routes where this could be of critical importance, each author has provided information on where water can be found near the trail—if it can be found at all. But drink it untreated and you run the risk of disease. (See *Giardia* in the Glossary.)

One sure way to kill the protozoans, bacteria, and viruses in water is to boil it. Right. That's just how you want to spend your time on a bike ride. Besides, who wants to carry a stove or denude the countryside stoking bonfires to boil water?

Luckily, there is a better way. Many riders pack along the inexpensive and only slightly distasteful tetraglycine hydroperiodide tablets (sold under the names Potable Aqua, Globaline, and Coughlan's, among others). Some invest in portable, lightweight purifiers that filter out the crud. Unfortunately, both iodine *and* filtering are now required to be absolutely sure you've killed all the nasties you can't see. Tablets or iodine drops by themselves will knock off the well-known *Giardia*, once called "beaver fever" for its transmission to the water through the feces of infected beavers. One to four weeks after ingestion, *Giardia* will have you bloated, vomiting, shivering with chills, and living in the bathroom. (Though you won't care while you're suffering, beavers are getting a bum rap, for other animals are carriers also.)

But now there's another parasite we must worry about—*Cryptosporidium*. "Crypto" brings on symptoms very similar to *Giardia*, but unlike that fellow protozoan it's equipped with a shell sufficiently strong to protect it against the chemical killers that stop *Giardia* cold. This means we're either back to boiling or on to using a water filter to screen out both *Giardia* and crypto, plus the iodine to knock off viruses. All of which sounds like a time-consuming pain but really isn't. Some water filters come equipped with an iodine chamber, to guarantee full protection. Or you can simply add a pill or drops to the water you've just filtered (if you aren't allergic to iodine, of course). The pleasures of backcountry biking—and the displeasure of getting sick—make this relatively minor effort worth every one of the few minutes involved.

Tools: Ever since my first cross-country tour in 1965 I've been kidded about the number of tools I pack on the trail. And so I will exit entirely from this discussion by providing a list compiled by two mechanic (and mountain biker) friends of mine. After all, since they make their livings fixing bikes, and get their kicks by riding them, who could be a better source?

These two suggest the following as an absolute minimum:

tire levers
spare tube and patch kit
air pump
Allen wrenches (3, 4, 5, and 6 mm)
six-inch crescent (adjustable-end) wrench
small flat-blade screwdriver
chain rivet tool
spoke wrench

But, while they're on the trail, their personal tool pouches contain these additional items:

channel locks (small)
air gauge
tire valve cap (the metal kind, with a valve-stem remover)
baling wire (ten or so inches, for temporary repairs)
duct tape (small roll for temporary repairs or tire boot)
boot material (small piece of old tire or a large tube patch)
spare chain link
rear derailleur pulley
spare nuts and bolts
paper towel and tube of waterless hand cleaner

First-aid kit: My personal kit contains the following, sealed inside double Ziploc bags:

sunscreen
aspirin
butterfly-closure bandages
Band-Aids
gauze compress pads (a half-dozen 4" × 4")
gauze (one roll)
ace bandages or Spenco joint wraps
Benadryl (an antihistamine, in case of allergic reactions)
water purification tablets / water filter (on long rides)
moleskin / Spenco "Second Skin"
hydrogen peroxide, iodine, or Mercurochrome (some kind of antiseptic)
snakebite kit

Final considerations: The authors of this series have done a good job in suggesting that specific items be packed for certain trails—raingear in particular seasons, a hat and gloves for mountain passes, or shades for desert jaunts. Heed their warnings, and think ahead. Good luck.

Dennis Coello

AND NOW, A WORD ABOUT CELLULAR PHONES . . .

Thinking of bringing the Flip-Fone along on your next off-road ride? Before you do, ask yourself the following questions:

- Do I know where I'm going? Do I have an adequate map? Can I use a compass effectively? Do I know the shortest way to civilization if I need to bail out early and find some help?

- If I'm on the trail for longer than planned, am I ready for it? Do I have adequate water? Have I packed something to eat? Will I be warm enough if I'm still out there after dark?

- Am I prepared for possible injuries? Do I have a first-aid kit? Do I know what to do in case of a cut, fracture, snakebite, or heat exhaustion?

- Is my tool kit adequate for likely mechanical problems? Can I fix a flat? Can I untangle a chain? Am I prepared to walk out if the bike is unrideable?

If you answered "yes" to *every* question above, you may pack the phone, but consider a good whistle instead. It's lighter, cheaper, and nearly as effective.

If you answered "no" to *any* of these questions, be aware that your cellular phone does little to reduce your risks in the wilderness. Sure, being able to dial 911 in the farthest corner of the White Mountains sounds like a great idea, but this ain't downtown, friend. If disaster strikes, and your call is routed to some emergency operator in Manchester or Bangor, and it takes awhile to figure out which ranger, sheriff, or search-and-rescue crew to connect you with, and you can't tell the authorities where you are because you're really not sure, and the closest they can come to pinpointing your location is a cellular tower that serves 62 square miles of dense woods, and they start searching for you but dusk is only two hours away, and you have no signaling device and your throat is too dry to shout, and meanwhile you can't get the bleeding stopped, you are out of luck. I mean *really* out of luck.

And when the battery goes dead, you're on your own again. Enough said.

Jeff Faust
Author of Mountain Bike! New Hampshire

GREAT SMOKY MOUNTAINS

No other single region defines Appalachia better than the Great Smoky Mountains. Formed in the Earth's earliest days, it remains the heart of an unbroken wilderness, stretching north from the Chattahoochee National Forest in north Georgia to the Monongahela National Forest in West Virginia. It doesn't take a trained botanist to see the diversity growing on the rich mountain slopes. There are nearly 150 tree species growing on the park's slopes. (For comparison, all of Europe has fewer than 100.) And not just any trees, mind you. There are over 200,000 acres of virgin hardwood and red spruce, not to mention the king tulip poplar at 200 feet tall with a 9-foot diameter. You say you like grapes? How about eating a fistful from a vine whose circumference is five feet? Has mountain laurel always been your favorite? Then check out some of the 40-foot-tall monsters growing in these woods.

This ancient land is also the center of attention for thousands of campers, hikers, and plain old sightseers who live east of the Mississippi. And, as expected, with all the people who come here hoping to see a black bear ambling among the brambles, or a deer grazing in the meadow, or a turkey strutting through the understory, the wilderness that attracts us to this place is threatened.

Already officials have begun taking a long, hard look at what the balance should be among the environment, the visitors, and the businesses built around the Great Smoky Mountains. Restrictions affect hikers who want to camp overnight on the trail—only so many per night, per trail are allowed, and those by permit only. Vehicles have not been limited . . . yet. But as use grows and traffic snarls, it's only a matter of time before the Forest Service or another agency says, "Okay. Enough. This land can't accommodate everyone who wants to come here without destroying what they're coming here for."

As pressure builds to do something to save the beauty of our national parks from the crush of our admiration, more and wider options will be made available to those who want to take a more athletic approach to experiencing places like the Smokys. What this implies for the future are more opportunities for the self-propelled traveler to our national parks in general, and the Smokys in particular. As of now, the official restrictions placed on bikes are few: basically, any road open to vehicles is open to bikes as well. However, only bikers willing to run a gauntlet of gas fumes and bumpers will explore the Smokys astride a saddle.

There are several rides inside this magnificent park that hint at what the entire Appalachian mountain range looked like long ago. Turn the page and read why mountain biking in the Smokys has no equal.

Source of additional information:

Superintendent
Great Smoky Mountains National Park
107 Park Headquarters Road
Gatlinburg, TN 37738
(423) 436-1200

RIDE 1 · Cades Cove

AT A GLANCE

NC

Length/configuration: An 11-mile paved loop

Aerobic difficulty: An occasional hill will get the lungs drawing deep

Technical difficulty: Deer, bears, and turkeys make up most of the trail obstacles you may encounter

Scenery: A broad meadow that was once a farm

Special comments: Despite this ride's paved surface, a trip to the Great Smoky Mountains is not complete without making this loop; park officials recognize this by restricting trail use at certain times to bikes only—dawns on Wednesdays and Saturdays, plus specially arranged full-moon rides

Hundreds of thousands of tourists come to the Great Smoky Mountains National Park each year, and almost every one of them takes the 11-mile paved Cades Cove Loop Road, either by car, truck, bus, or van. With so much vehicular congestion, why take this popular route by bike, and mountain bike at that?

The answer is as obvious as air in your tires. Sixteen (16!) different bodies of water cross under your fat tires: Feezell, Tater, and Cooper Branches, just to name a few. With all the water and wide open pasture, you're likely to see deer by the herds and turkeys by the flocks. The black bears love it in Cades Cove as well, so don't be surprised to catch a rumbling bundle of fur making its (or their) way into the forest slopes rising around you. But, please, don't feed them your Powerbar.

RIDE 1 • Cades Cove
RIDE 2 • Rich Mountain Road
RIDE 3 • Parson Branch Road

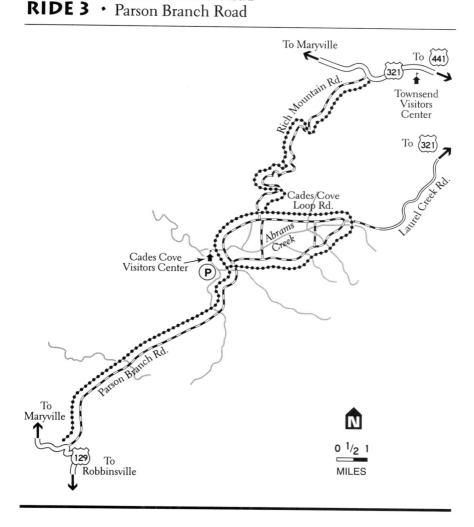

Besides the natural beauty, Cades Cove has an operating gristmill and some restored farm buildings where you can stop and admire both form and function.

It is possible, and likely, that you'll have a great ride at any time of the day or week, regardless of the traffic, but the preferred times for coming to bike Cades Cove are on Wednesdays and Saturdays, from dawn to 10 A.M., beginning in early May and lasting until late September. All other traffic is restricted then, giving early rising bikers the road all to themselves. And what a road.

Photo by Dennis Coello.

General location: In the western portion of the Great Smoky Mountains National Park.

Elevation change: Noticeable but negligible.

Season: Winter may bring periods of ice and snow, closing the loop and associated roads leading to and surrounding it.

Services: The Cades Cove Visitor Center at the westernmost end of the loop has water and rest rooms; there is a camping area on the left before you enter the one-way loop. Bryson City and Sylva have the special services required by bikers: repairs, supplies, and trail information.

Hazards: This is a popular route for cars. If you ride when it is open for their use, be prepared to ride defensively. Otherwise, you only have to prepare to let the bears and other wildlife have the right of way.

Rescue index: Getting to you will be easy; however, getting you anywhere else will take some time due to the curvy, twisty nature of the roads in the area.

Land status: In the Great Smoky Mountains National Park.

Maps: This route can be found on the Great Smoky Mountains Trail Map, on sale in any of the park's visitor centers.

Finding the trail: Leave Cherokee, North Carolina, headed north on US 441. Turn left on Little River Road (past Clingmans Dome Road) and left again on Laurel Creek Road. Cades Cove Loop Road begins at the end of Laurel Creek Road.

Sources of additional information:

Superintendent
Great Smoky Mountains National Park
107 Park Headquarters Road
Gatlinburg, TN 37738
(423) 436-1200

Cades Cove District Ranger
107 Park Headquarters Road
Gatlinburg, TN 37738
(423) 448-4105

Notes on the trail: Start the loop at the ranger station at the entrance to Cades Cove. After turning left back onto Cades Cove Loop Road from the parking lot, look for the gravel connector on the left, a little over a mile. A smaller (counterclockwise) loop can be ridden by taking this road nearly a mile to the other side of the pavement. From there, turn left again onto the road. It's another 1.5 miles back to the ranger station, giving a total ride of nearly 4 miles. If you ride past that first left, look for another gravel connector on the left. It, too, leads across to the other side of the loop, making an 8-mile trip back to the ranger station. By continuing straight past the two gravel connectors, the Cades Cove Visitor Center will be seen on the right a little over halfway through the ride. Forge Creek Road turns to the right just beyond the visitor center. The only other intersections occur on the left: the other side of the gravel roads mentioned earlier, leading back to the other side of the loop. By taking the first road back across, the ride is lengthened by 5 more miles; the second left after the visitor center reconnects to the paved loop for an additional 8 miles.

RIDE 2 · Rich Mountain Road

AT A GLANCE
———————

Length/configuration: An out-and-back, 7.7 miles one way (15.4 miles total)

Aerobic difficulty: You'll do some serious huffing and puffing on this ride

Technical difficulty: The lightly graveled road (with primarily a dirt base) takes most of the technical requirement out of this ride

Scenery: Cades Cove, Cades Cove Mountain, Rich Mountain, and Hesse Creek

Special comments: This route is open to vehicles during the peak-use months of May through late September; at those times, bikes must travel one way only and use a shuttle for the return trip

This out-and-back called Rich Mountain Road (7.7 miles one way, 15.4 miles total) curves more times than a black snake climbing a tree. The first half of this ride over lightly graveled surface climbs Cades Cove Mountain. At the top of the climb, you can look back to the south where the large bowl of Cades Cove sprawls like a giant's cupped palm. Rich Mountain squats to the east, its bulk hiding many of the Smokys' tallest peaks from view.

If you reach this trailhead in the summer, plan to share the road with cars and other vehicles. However, if you arrange to be trailside at dawn on a Wednesday or Saturday from early May to late September, you can ride without the intrusion of combustion engines clattering by. You are likely to catch sight of a big buck crossing the road ahead, velvet shedding from a freshly grown rack of horns. Or you may come by, as I did, just in time to see the tail end of a hawk's dive onto a truly mourning dove.

General location: In the western portion of the Great Smoky Mountains National Park.

Elevation change: You'll be gaining somewhere in the neighborhood of 800 feet—about 100 feet per mile—but it'll seem like more.

Season: During the summer, you'll need to leave a vehicle on the shoulder of the road at the end of the one-way, at the park's northern boundary on Rich Mountain Road where traffic again becomes two way. You could also leave your car farther north, at Townsend or in the parking lot at Tuckaleechee Caverns, which will make for a significantly longer (yet downhill and paved) ride. Traffic is one way only from the beginning on Cades Cove Loop Road until the end at Rich Mountain Road, and bikes must follow the laws governing other vehicles. From late September until early May (dates vary, so call to make sure), this route is officially closed to motorized vehicles due to the possibility of large amounts of snow and ice, which could lay on the road until the spring thaw. But it is possible that an unusually warm or late winter could leave this road open to mountain bikes for a few days or weeks, while other traffic is restricted all day long.

Services: The Cades Cove Visitor Center at the westernmost end of the loop has water and rest rooms; there is a camping area on the left before you enter the one-way loop. Depending on where you're coming from, it might be easier to attain special services from the Maryville-Knoxville direction, or from the south, Sylva or Bryson City.

Hazards: During the summer, other vehicles using this road could be a problem. Other than that, no significant hazards exist, unless you attempt this route when ice and snow cover the road.

Rescue index: This road is monitored regularly and often (during the summer months), making a rescue easier. A ride here during winter months, when the road is closed to traffic, however, will make any rescue much more difficult and time consuming.

Land status: In the Great Smoky Mountains National Park.

Many trails in Appalachia
follow tiny creeks and
streams, each with its
own special place.

Maps: The Great Smoky Mountains Trail Map, on sale in any of the park's visitor centers, shows this route plus the many hiking trails.

Finding the trail: Leave Cherokee, North Carolina, headed north on US 441. Turn left on Little River Road (past Clingmans Dome Road) and left again on Laurel Creek Road. Cades Cove Loop Road begins at the end of Laurel Creek Road. Take Cades Cove Loop until you reach the parking lot at the visitor center. Rich Mountain Road is on the right just after passing the second gravel road to the left, about 4 miles from the beginning of the Cades Cove Loop.

Source of additional information:

Superintendent
Great Smoky Mountains National Park
107 Park Headquarters Road
Gatlinburg, TN 37738
(423) 436-1200

Notes on the trail: There's not much tricky navigation required for this ride. Starting at Cades Cove Visitor Center, it's about a 4-mile climb up to Cades Cove Mountain, followed by the drop into the Hesse Creek watershed. Still headed north, climb once more to reach the gap near Rich Mountain, where the park's northern boundary lies.

RIDE 3 · Parson Branch Road

AT A GLANCE

NC

Length/configuration: An out-and-back gravel double-track, 12 miles one way (24 miles total)

Aerobic difficulty: The climbs over Hannah Mountain and Chilly Spring Knob are challenging

Technical difficulty: The lightly graveled road (with a dirt base) makes this a technically easy ride

Scenery: Cades Cove, Forge Creek, Parson Branch, surrounded by Hannah Mountain, Chilly Spring Knob, Bunker Hill, and Hickory Top

Special comments: This route is open to vehicles during the peak-use months of May through late September; at those times, bikes must travel one way only, so riders should leave a vehicle; Parson Branch Road stayed closed all of 1997 so that flood damage to it could be repaired

The perfect camping trip can take place anywhere inside the Great Smoky Mountains National Park. But since we're mountain bikers, it would be preferable to pitch the tents at Cades Cove, which is where a majority of the park's bike rides begin, like this 12-mile out-and-back (up to 24 miles total) along the lightly graveled Parson Branch Road. The ride starts south, heading upstream on the unpaved Forge Creek Road, a two-way road. Once reaching Parson Branch Road, traffic is one way only from early May until late September (call for specific dates, as these change from year to year), so be sure to plan ahead to leave a vehicle at the other end of US 129. This road can be ridden as an out-and-back only when it is closed to motorized traffic.

The climb to Hannah Mountain stops high above Cades Cove, below and behind you to the north. A good place to take a break, especially if you haven't had one already, comes at the intersection with Gregory Bald Trail and Hannah

Mountain Trail. Don't worry about drying those socks and shoes you got wet crossing the creek. You'll have plenty more creek crossings through low-water bridges on the section down Parson Branch and to US 129, a good reason not to ride here on a bitterly cold day. Another good reason is that snow sometimes gets saddle-high in places. But it wasn't snow that kept this road closed for nearly five years. It was water, and a flood of it at that, which washed out the bridges at several locations.

General location: In the western portion of the Great Smoky Mountains National Park.

Elevation change: As you stand at the Cades Cove Visitor Center (1,750 feet), look at the mountains rising all around. You'll be going up and over the ones to the south, roughly 1,000 feet change in elevation. The trip to US 129 takes you all the way down to 1,295 feet, but not before climbing the northern shoulder of Gregory Bald.

Season: During the summer, it is recommended that you leave a shuttle vehicle at the end of the one-way, at US 129, a few miles north of Deals Gap.

Traffic is one way only from the beginning of Parson Branch Road to its intersection with the highway, and bikes must follow the laws governing other vehicles. Be prepared to get your feet wet anytime of the year. Also, keep in mind that despite the high elevation, flash floods can and do occur, making a creek crossing at those times a potentially dangerous affair. During the winter, when Parson Branch Road is closed to vehicles and the water's low, ride it as the great out-and-back it is, providing, of course, you don't mind the possibility of having some ice and snow.

Services: The Cades Cove Visitor Center at the westernmost end of the loop has water and rest rooms; there is a camping area on the left before you enter the one-way loop. Bryson City and Sylva have the special services required by bikers.

Hazards: During the summer, vehicles using this road could be a problem; other than that, no significant hazards.

Rescue index: This road is monitored regularly and often during the times when traffic is allowed, making any rescue easier. But during the times when traffic is restricted, rescue becomes much more difficult.

Land status: In the Great Smoky Mountains National Park.

Maps: The Great Smoky Mountains Trail Map, on sale in any of the park's visitor centers, shows this route plus all the other bike routes.

Finding the trail: Leave Cherokee, North Carolina, headed north on US 441. Turn left on Little River Road (past Clingmans Dome Road) and left again on Laurel Creek Road. Cades Cove Loop Road begins at the end of Laurel Creek Road. Take Cades Cove Loop until you reach the visitor center. Parson Branch Road is reached by taking the right turn onto Forge Creek Road. You can shorten the ride 4 miles by beginning at the intersection of Parson Branch Road and Forge Creek Road.

Source of additional information:

Superintendent
Great Smoky Mountains National Park
107 Park Headquarters Road
Gatlinburg, TN 37738
(423) 436-1200

Notes on the trail: Begin by riding the 4-mile-long approach on Forge Creek Road. Bear right onto Parson Branch Road. The climb to Hannah Mountain takes place over the next 3 miles. It's a 5-mile trip from there to US 129.

RIDE 4 · Heintooga

AT A GLANCE

Length/configuration: A lightly graveled (with a dirt base) and pavement road that can be ridden as a 46.5-mile loop, 42-mile-or-less (total) out-and-back, or anywhere from a 17- to a 21-mile one-way, using a shuttle

Aerobic difficulty: The loop and out-and-back require maximum effort to gain (or regain) 3,500 feet up to the high point at Heintooga Picnic Area; the ride downhill is practically a no-pedaler for more than 17 miles

Technical difficulty: The lightly graveled road should not pose problems to bikers with any experience, provided they stay below the posted speed limit, which is difficult to do in places

Scenery: Balsam Mountain, numerous creeks feeding Raven Fork, and the Cherokee Indian Reservation

Special comments: The route is open to vehicles. Fortunately, they travel one way (downhill) for most of the road. Approximately 5 paved miles of the ride cuts across the Cherokee Indian Reservation. Some riders elect to set the shuttle where the pavement turns to gravel, to avoid traveling on the busier Big Cove Road.

RIDE 4 · Heintooga

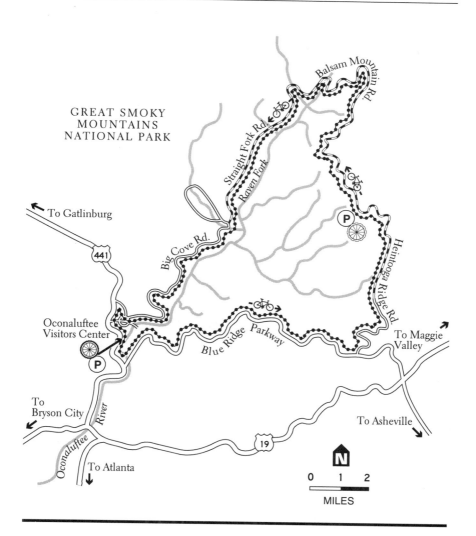

GREAT SMOKY
MOUNTAINS
NATIONAL PARK

Balsam Mountain Rd.

Straight Fork Rd.

Raven Fork

To Gatlinburg

441

Big Cove Rd.

Heintooga Ridge Rd.

Oconaluftee
Visitors Center

P

Blue Ridge Parkway

To Maggie
Valley

To
Bryson City

River

To Asheville

Oconaluftee

To Atlanta

19

N

0   1   2
MILES

Springtime is a great time to visit the Great Smoky Mountains National Park and enjoy the mountain road along Heintooga Ridge, in the park's eastern region. Depending on how you'd like to ride it, Heintooga can be a 46.5-mile loop, which incorporates a small section of the Blue Ridge Parkway; or you can tailor the route to make up either an out-and-back (anywhere from 34 to 42 miles on an out-and-back), or you can set a shuttle at Heintooga Picnic Area at the top of Balsam Mountain Road. On my last visit, my friends Dennis, Sandy,

Photo by Dennis Coello.

and Joe and I set a shuttle and then set off on a 17-mile, downhill-only, cheek-flapping extravaganza.

Whichever way you choose, you'll be following the old route of narrow-gauge rail cars, which were used to haul out the virgin timber felled from the slopes. Several overlooks provide comfortable spots to stop and take a break while looking across Balsam Mountain Cove. You may feel like you're riding in a tunnel at times, with rhododendron and mountain laurel growing like crooked fingers over the road. The gravel road (primarily a dirt base with only a small scattering of stones) begins a narrow and even more steeply pitched descent on its way to Raven Fork, a wide white-water creek. Traffic becomes two way here. On that ride I took with Dennis, Sandy, and Joe, our feet became uncomfortably cold and wet from the creek crossing, but we were distracted from our discomfort at the sight of two small Cherokee girls, laughing and playing barefoot in the shoals.

General location: Oconaluftee Visitor Center, Great Smoky Mountains National Park.

Elevation change: 3,500 feet in approximately 17 miles.

Photo by Dennis Coello.

Season: The gravel road is closed to motorized vehicles during the winter. Call ahead to see if there has been too much snow even for cycling at the higher elevations.

Services: An entire industry has grown up around the Great Smoky Mountains National Park. Most services for the average vacationer can be found nearby, but for biking services, you'll need to head to Nantahala Outdoor Center in Wesser, North Carolina, south on US 74, or on to Sylva.

Hazards: Bikers ride at different paces and cars full of sightseers often creep along, too, so be prepared to overtake them. Also, watch your speed on the descents. You can easily go too fast and hit one of the larger rocks in the road, which could throw you off balance.

Rescue index: Rescue is easy on this route, as long as you stay on the road. It's nearly impossible if you slide down the side of the mountain. If this ride is taken when the road is closed to motorized traffic, a rescue becomes extremely difficult.

Land status: Mostly the Great Smoky Mountains National Park; however, a 5-mile swath cuts through the Cherokee Indian Reservation.

Maps: You can buy the Great Smoky Mountains Trail Map for a nominal fee at the Oconaluftee Visitor Center.

Finding the trail: Take US 441 north out of Cherokee, North Carolina, and park at the Oconaluftee Visitor Center. For an out-and-back or loop, use this spot as the low trailhead. For the shuttle, leave one vehicle here. Leave the other vehicle at the trailhead; find it by following the directions below in Notes on the Trail.

Sources of additional information:

Superintendent
Great Smoky Mountains National Park
107 Park Headquarters Road
Gatlinburg, TN 37738
(423) 436-1200

Oconaluftee Visitor Center
US 441 North
Cherokee, NC 28719
(828) 497-1900

Notes on the trails: Take the loop in a counterclockwise direction by heading south on US 441 until you come to the intersection with the Blue Ridge Parkway; head north on the parkway for approximately 8 miles. Turn left onto Heintooga Ridge Road, which changes to Balsam Mountain Road at Heintooga Picnic Area. If you're setting a shuttle, leave a vehicle here. The upper trailhead begins here. Prepare for a downhill of epic proportions. The road is one way at this point, for approximately 12 miles down to the gate that marks where the road becomes two way again. Travel along the two-way section for about 3 more miles, to where the pavement begins. Turn left at the stop sign at the intersection with Big Cove Road. Be on the lookout for a right turn through Park Housing, approximately 8 miles after you turn onto Big Cove Road. You may want to scout this turn beforehand by car; otherwise, if you miss the turn you'll have to go the extra mile to the intersection with US 441 in downtown Cherokee. If this happens, turn right toward the Oconaluftee Visitor Center. If you make the turn through Park Housing, turn left after reaching US 441. The parking lot is less than a mile up on the left.

RIDE 5 · Clingmans Dome

AT A GLANCE

Length/configuration: A paved out-and-back, 7 miles one way (14 miles total)

Aerobic difficulty: It's a huffer and puffer at an elevation where the air is thin

Technical difficulty: The paved surface takes care of any really technical difficulties

Scenery: The ride begins at Newfound Gap and ends near the peak of Clingmans Dome; when you look in the dictionary for a definition of scenery, this is what you'll find

Special comments: I recommend riding Clingmans Dome when traffic is prohibited, December 1 through March 31; otherwise, the vehicles make it unsafe

If the Great Smoky Mountains National Park has a drawback for mountain bikers, it is the lack of single-track trails where bikes are allowed. But it is too beautiful a place to see only from behind a windshield or plodding along on two feet, which is why I'm recommending this 7-mile one-way (14 miles total) paved ride to Clingmans Dome. There isn't any site east of the Mississippi River where a mountain biker can ride any higher.

For most bikers, the thin air will be more than a minor inconvenience. Few bikers are acclimated to the diminished amount of oxygen found at higher elevations, and care should be taken not to overestimate your ability to make the transition. But breathlessness is an integral part of this ride. The climb takes you near the top of the world's oldest mountains, smoothed somewhat by their exposure to the elements for billions of years, but still obviously wild and rugged. After you've gained the summit, let your eyes fly across the heart of the Appalachian Mountains.

General location: In the middle of the Great Smoky Mountains National Park.

Elevation change: Begin at 5,046 feet and nearly reach the top of Clingmans Dome: 6,643 feet.

Season: Attempt this ride only during those times when the road is closed to vehicles, generally the winter. But therein lies the rub, as they say. There will be precious few days when the roads are closed to motorized traffic and there isn't yet an unrideable layer of snow covering the road.

RIDE 5 · Clingmans Dome

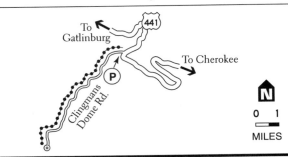

Services: Since you're pretty much in the middle of the park, all services are a long drive away to either the Oconaluftee or the Sugarlands Visitor Center. Bikers can acquire those special services by heading north to the Maryville-Knoxville area, or south to Bryson City or Sylva.

Hazards: If you ride when no other vehicles besides bikes are allowed, the only danger you face is running out of breath or maybe fainting from the sheer beauty of it all. If you ride on the snow, be sure before you go too far up to check your traction on the snow so you'll be sure you can stop on the way down.

Rescue index: It could be a long time before you're missed and before help reaches you.

Land status: In the Great Smoky Mountains National Park.

Maps: The Great Smoky Mountains Trail Map, on sale in any of the park's visitor centers, shows this route.

Finding the trail: Leave Cherokee, North Carolina, headed north on US 441. Or you can leave Gatlinburg headed south on US 441. Once you reach Newfound Gap, park in the lot and begin riding into the southwest.

Source of additional information:

> Superintendent
> Great Smoky Mountains National Park
> 107 Park Headquarters Road
> Gatlinburg, TN 37738
> (423) 436-1200

Notes on the trail: No turns required; just stay on the road and ride the ridge up, up, and away. Check your brakes before the trip back down. Repeat as necessary.

PISGAH NATIONAL FOREST: FRENCH BROAD DISTRICT

The Pisgah National Forest is divided into four different districts: Toecane, French Broad, Grandfather, and Pisgah. The French Broad District, named for a wide and powerful river, lies in a remote section of the Appalachians adjoining the Tennessee state line. The French Broad River, the region's principal waterway, drains a huge water basin northwest of Asheville. It first flows over 70 miles due north on its way through a gap, then west to Tennessee. People from all over the world paddle, raft, and fish in and along this river. Mountain bikers, however, have only recently begun riding the surrounding trails, which explains why you'll find bait stores in Hot Springs, but no bike shops.

You'll also find stores (but not many) in Hot Springs catering to the large number of hikers who come each year to walk the nearly 75 miles of the Appalachian Trail in the French Broad District. Hot Springs first gained attention from the white man when thermal springs were discovered nearby. A soak in the 100-degree springs (North Carolina's only natural mineral water hot springs) can still be arranged downtown at the Hot Springs Spa (camping and rustic cabins as well), not far from the French Broad Ranger District office. And for a fine meal, head to the Smoky Mountain Diner. Other than that, the out-of-towner has to head to Asheville or Knoxville for more specialized biking services, although Bluff Mountain Outfitters on Main Street in Hot Springs may have some basic supplies.

Sources of additional information:

French Broad Ranger District
U.S. Forest Service
P.O. Box 128
Hot Springs, NC 28743
(828) 622-3202

Bluff Mountain Outfitters
152 Bridge Street
Hot Springs, NC 28743
(828) 622-7162

Breakaway Bicycle Shop
127 Charlotte Highway
Asheville, NC 28803-9673
(704) 299-8770

Carolina Fatz Mountain Bike
1500 Brevard Road
Asheville, NC 28806-9561
(704) 665-7744

Liberty Bicycles
1987 Hendersonville Road
Asheville, NC 28803-2122
(704) 684-1085

Pro Bikes
793 Merrimon Avenue
Asheville, NC 28804-2448
(704) 253-2800

Bike Zoo
4445 Kingston Pike
Knoxville, TN 37919-5226
(423) 558-8455

West Hills Bicycle Center
5113 Kingston Pike
Knoxville, TN 37919-5152
(423) 584-2288

RIDE 6 · French Broad River Route

AT A GLANCE

Length/configuration: An out-and-back gravel road with a short section of pavement, 6 miles one way (12 miles total)

Aerobic difficulty: Although it's flat, you can pedal like the dickens and get a good workout

Technical difficulty: The lightly graveled road (primarily on a hard-packed surface) and pavement are easily ridden

Scenery: The entire length goes along the French Broad River, stopping at the Tennessee state line

Special comments: The city of Hot Springs has naturally occurring heated springs, ideal for a spell in the spa after riding one of the area's three mountain bike trails (see Rides 7 and 8)

This out-and-back (6 miles one way, 12 miles total) follows the French Broad River, an important landmark in this isolated area of extreme western North Carolina. The surface of Paint Rock Road—pavement for the first mile and a half, gravel the rest of the way—lies on top of an ancient trading route used by Native Americans.

After following the gentle grade along the river for a few minutes, you'll understand why people have long been drawn to the French Broad. Halfway through the ride, on the right, Murray Branch crosses under the road and joins the wide river, its banks shaded by beech and maple trees. Across the road on the left, Murray Branch Day Use Area has picnic tables and rest rooms (not to mention convenient parking) to go along with a panoramic view of the French Broad.

RIDE 6 · French Broad River Route

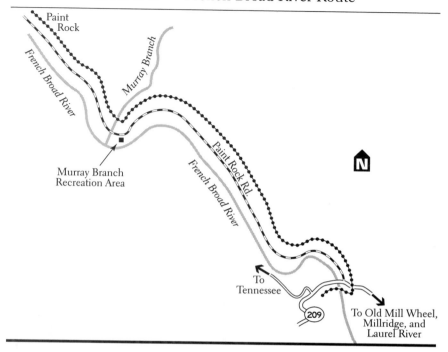

The turnaround on the ride comes at Paint Rock, where the borders of three counties (Madison, Cocke, and Greene) and two states (North Carolina and Tennessee) touch. Judging by the graffiti left behind on the sides of the famous rock wall, I'd say a great many cultures have come together here as well.

General location: In Hot Springs, North Carolina.

Elevation change: Little change.

Season: An all-season route.

Services: Hot Springs has all the basics but few of the specialties. The National Forest Service office is located downtown. Murray Branch Recreation Area has rest rooms and water.

Hazards: The biggest hazard will come from sharing the road with motorized vehicles. Be on alert.

Rescue index: Should you need it, rescue would come quickly. A good, strong yell can carry all the way back to town.

Land status: Paint Rock Road is maintained by Madison County.

Maps: The forest office in Hot Springs has the *Guide to Hiking, Biking, and Horseback Riding Trails in the Hot Springs Area,* which shows this route. It is also shown on the Pisgah National Forest—Grandfather, Toecane, and French Broad Ranger Districts Map.

Paint Rock marks where the French Broad River leaves North Carolina and enters Tennessee.

Finding the trail: Leave Hot Springs headed northeast on US 25/70. Paint Rock Road is the first road on the left after you cross the French Broad River.

Source of additional information:

French Broad Ranger District
U.S. Forest Service
P.O. Box 128
Hot Springs, NC 28743
(828) 622-3202

Notes on the trail: If you're beginning from town, the best bet may be to park at the ranger office, about a mile south on the left from the trailhead, and pedal the short stretch north, cross the river, and take the left onto Paint Rock Road. The other option is to park at Murray Branch Recreation Area for an out-and-back of approximately 5 miles total. An adjoining forest service road, FS 468 (located near Murray Branch Recreation Area), can be taken for an additional 2 miles one way (4 miles total) to explore the upper watershed of Davis Creek. On the other side of the Tennessee state line (at Paint Rock), FS 54 and FS 41 fork to the left and right, respectively. The left onto FS 54 leads to Lone Pine Gap, on the way to Tennessee SR 107 (a 5-mile trip one way); the right fork (more like straight) onto FS 41 follows Paint Creek and eventually reaches Hurricane Gap, covering approximately 7 miles one way (14 miles total).

RIDE 7 · Laurel River Trail

AT A GLANCE

NC

Length/configuration: 3.6 miles one way (7.2 miles total) on a riverside out-and-back double-track

Aerobic difficulty: There is little elevation change and little aerobic demand

Technical difficulty: Some sections require extraordinary skill in riding over rocks or along tight and narrow treadways

Scenery: This section of river is a rush, both physically and emotionally

Special comments: The ruins of an old logging town, Runion, are at the end of the trail

If you've ever wanted to get an intense rock-riding experience, the 3.6 miles along the Laurel River (7.2 miles total for the out-and-back) will provide the perfect setting. The trail narrows down to single-track for most of the way, weaving through a landscape of laurel, rock cliffs, and rhododendron. That's on one side. On the other is the crashing sound of roaring white water.

The area had received a lot of rain just before I visited, and the river was churning at what was obviously a high watermark. The sound of so much water—so close—charged my ride with extra excitement. Small streams ran along and into the trail before dropping into the current below. About midway through the first leg comes what I call the Half Mile of Pile, a jumbled collection of river rocks that would serve better as a creek bed than a bike trail. Just a little farther, the road widens where the former sawmill settlement of Runion served an earlier era's lumber needs. The railroad tracks mark the end of the route. On the other side of the tracks, the Laurel joins the French Broad.

General location: Located 5.5 miles northeast of Hot Springs, North Carolina, on US 25/70.

RIDE 7 • Laurel River Trail
RIDE 8 • Mill Ridge

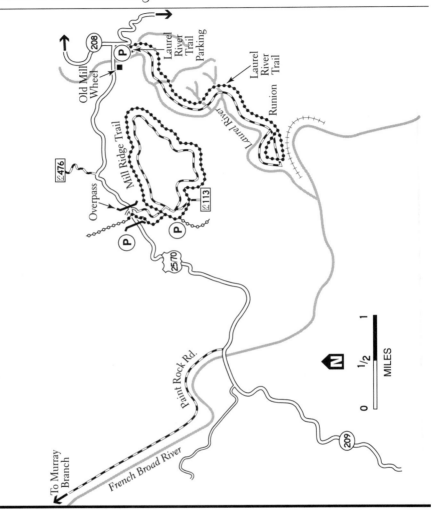

Elevation change: Negligible elevation change on this route, as long as you don't run off the trail and into the river, a 10- to 15-foot sudden drop.

Season: An all-season trail.

Services: Hot Springs has the basics, but the trailhead has naught but a parking lot.

Hazards: An abundance of poison ivy grows into the trail; avoid being switched by it as you pass. Large rocks (small boulders) present serious—but rideable—obstacles. If you ride on the railroad tracks, keep an eye and ear out for trains.

The Laurel River makes its whitewater way to the abandoned rail town of Runion.

Rescue index: You could be stranded for quite some time if you were unlucky. The best suggestion is to ride prepared for self-rescue. Make special note of the precautions mentioned in the Introduction on pages 9–10. But on the whole, it is not a difficult place to reach.

Land status: The trail remains on Pisgah National Forest land.

Maps: The *Guide to Hiking, Biking, and Horseback Riding Trails in the Hot Springs Area* contains the detailed information for riding this trail.

Finding the trail: Leave Hot Springs headed northeast on US 25/70. After approximately 5.5 miles, an intersection has US 25/70 going to the right. Turn right here (past the water wheel) and park in the long gravel lot on the right of the highway, almost immediately after making the turn.

Source of additional information:

French Broad Ranger District
U.S. Forest Service
P.O. Box 128
Hot Springs, NC 28743
(828) 622-3202

Notes on the trail: The first quarter-mile follows single-track and dead-ends into a gravel road. Turn right. You'll notice signs announcing "Private Property" and "Foot Travel Only." Do not be daunted. You are on the right trail; the signs are for adjoining property. Watch for the right fork about a half mile away. Another right fork occurs about a hundred yards on down. There are no more intersections until you reach a double-track coming in from the left; this is a shortcut to the train tracks and the ruins of Runion.

By continuing straight another three-quarters of a mile, you'll reach the train tracks and a trestle over the Laurel River. Should you want to ride the tracks for a short distance, take a left for about a half mile, where a double-track comes in on the left. Turn left and follow it until it rejoins the main trail. A final note: the Forest Service map shows the trail continuing west, or by turning right at the tracks. I did not investigate on bike, but the map shows a connector leading up to Mill Ridge. If so, you'd have about a 25-mile loop by using Mill Ridge (FS 113) and the paved US 25/70.

RIDE 8 · Mill Ridge

AT A GLANCE

Length/configuration: A 3.5-mile loop, with double-track and single-track

Aerobic difficulty: Surprisingly, there's only one significant climb, barely a half mile

Technical difficulty: This is an easy trail to ride

Scenery: A spectacular overlook occurs at the top of FS 113

Special comments: Taken in a clockwise direction, this loop seems like it's mostly downhill; don't ask me how

This 3.5-mile loop of single- and double-track is one of only three officially designated mountain bike trails in the French Broad District of the Pisgah National Forest. By parking down at the lot before FS 113 crosses the bridge, an additional 2 miles can be ridden on the climb up to Lover's Leap Ridge (really), which follows a narrow road barely clinging to the steeply pitched mountain.

It is possible that you'll see some motorized traffic traveling along portions of this road, but you are much more likely to see deer disappearing into the tangle of laurel thickets growing on the steep slopes. I saw plenty of signs indicating bobcats and coyotes use the bike trail as well.

The most unusual aspect of this trail is its seeming lack of uphill, at least in a clockwise direction, a curious feature for a loop, especially one with such a screaming downhill section. At the end of the loop, take time for the short climb

Some days that tight double-track just can't be beat.

to the overlook where the Appalachian Trail intersects, and where a wide view opens to the south, showing the French Broad River in the valley below.

General location: This trail is located approximately 3 miles northeast of Hot Springs, North Carolina, on US 25/70.

Elevation change: There is only one short hill, just as the single-track cuts off the gated service road. Although it is fairly steep, it is over soon.

Season: An all-season trail.

Services: Hot Springs has the basics; the trailhead has only a sign and parking.

Hazards: Possible oncoming bike traffic could occur; other than that, no hazards exist out of the ordinary.

Rescue index: This is a fairly easy place to get rescued due to the nearby service roads and the short, easy walk out.

Land status: Pisgah National Forest property.

Maps: The forest office in Hot Springs has the *Guide to Hiking, Biking, and Horseback Riding Trails in the Hot Springs Area.*

Finding the trail: Leave Hot Springs headed northeast on US 25/70. Approximately 3 miles up, you'll see a road to the right, FS 113. Take it, then turn left on and over the bridge crossing US 25/70 (if you pass under US 25/70, you've gone too far). Go all the way up until FS 113 dead-ends at an overlook—that is, if you don't want to tack on the additional three-quarters of a mile from the parking lot near the bridge. If you want the extra length, park in the lot before you cross the bridge. You'll see FS 113A (gated and normally closed) turning off to the left after you reach the top.

Source of additional information:

French Broad Ranger District
U.S. Forest Service
P.O. Box 128
Hot Springs, NC 28743
(828) 622-3202

Notes on the trail: Wanting to extend the length of the basic loop, I parked on the other side of the bridge and made my slow way up the side of Lover's Leap Ridge. By the time I reached the top I was warmed up with the three-quarters of a mile climb. It made me feel like I had earned the nearly 3-mile-long falling grade, which doesn't end until the single-track splits off to the right. It's a relatively short climb to where the trail dead-ends into FS 113. Taking a left at this intersection leads to an overlook, and the right leads back to the trailhead.

PISGAH NATIONAL FOREST: GRANDFATHER DISTRICT

Grandfather Mountain stands as the most frequently painted and photographed natural feature in the Linville Gorge area. A friend of mine in Blowing Rock has one room with a photo of the grand mountain centered on each wall, with each photo showing a different season. Another friend can walk a hundred yards to his parents' house and see the mountain itself, with its broad brow of granite defining the horizon. Most people view its sharp crags up close for the first time via the Blue Ridge Parkway. The approach from the north is especially dramatic: one final, sharp curve and the face of the mountain jumps into view. The effect is so impressive that a pull-off into the conveniently located parking area nearly becomes mandatory. While stopped, look off to the left, where the steep slopes of the Wilson Creek drainage hold enough mountain bike trails to keep a body bike-bound every day for a month.

As prominent as Grandfather is, its towering neighbor, Mt. Mitchell, gets all the attention in record books as the highest point in the eastern United States. With all the obvious peaks rising nearby, it is not surprising to discover this area is among the most popular destinations for skiers. One such resort, Beech Mountain, has begun to tap into the potential for opening up its off-season descents to mountain bikers. As remarkable and extensive as the mountain biking opportunities in the Grandfather area are, the trails are hardly a fraction of what they could be. Part of the reason why this district of the Pisgah National Forest has remained relatively undeveloped for biking comes from its overall rugged and remote setting. Another reason may come from the current status of a large tract of potential biking trails, which is slated to become a wilderness area in the near future. Still, as the following trail descriptions will show, local bike clubs and volunteers have been actively adding to and maintaining over a hundred miles of off-road routes. But don't come here expecting 5 percent grades and groomed wide single-track, although the Boone Fork Recreation Area has a few miles of trail in that category. Instead, come prepared for an intense aerobic workout on trails demanding strength, fitness, and a high degree of technical skill, all in a setting of unsurpassed beauty. Some of us need no more reason than that to hit the trail.

Grandfather Mountain
looms over the trails near
Wilson Creek.

Sources of additional information:

Boone Bike & Touring Company
899 Blowing Rock Road
Boone, NC 28607-4865
(828) 262-5750

Magic Cycles
208 Faculty Street #1
Boone, NC 28607-4190
(828) 265-2211

Rock & Roll Sports
280 East King Street
Boone, NC 28607-4042
(828) 264-0765

High Country Mountain Bike Association
P.O. Box 22
Blowing Rock, NC 28605
(828) 295-3496

RIDE 9 · Yancey Ridge

Length/configuration: A long 8-mile loop of double-track

Aerobic difficulty: This one will make you wish you had an extra set of lungs

Technical difficulty: Although it's double-track, you will need sharp skills to keep your balance in places

Scenery: The slow climb up parallels Gragg Prong, a small but energetic stream

Special comments: There's an out-and-back of up to 3 miles one way (6 miles total) at the turn toward Marks Mountain that many bikers tack on, making the entire ride a 14-miler

Perhaps the best ride in the Wilson Creek area is this eight-mile-plus double-track loop. But don't let the double-track tag fool you. It's not smooth and well maintained. Big rocks and ruts in the road are waiting to upset the inattentive biker. Coupled with the speed gained on the downhill, Yancey Ridge (often referred to as Yancey Short, as opposed to Yancey Long) has all the features of the classic mountain bike experience: scenery, taxing climbs, technical sections, and a jowl-flapping fast downhill.

The long climb up to Old House Gap follows Gragg Prong for most of the 40 minutes it will take to reach the turn onto Yancey Ridge. It is a scenic and loud body of water rushing down to join—like every other creek and stream this side of Grandfather Mountain—Wilson Creek. Chances are good you will need a break before topping out at the gap, and it's so pretty, there's no reason why you shouldn't. At least let the bike rest.

Yancey Ridge is as scenic as they come, but you'll need to stop in order to appreciate it. From the top, it's a pure screamer. All the elevation is lost pretty quickly in two main stages. Once you reach Paul's Pool, a large boggy area of potholes, only one final drop remains along the much busier and better maintained FS 981.

General location: Located 6 miles southeast of Linville, North Carolina.

Elevation change: It's pretty much a straight climb-and-drop of slightly more than a thousand feet.

RIDE 9 • Yancey Ridge

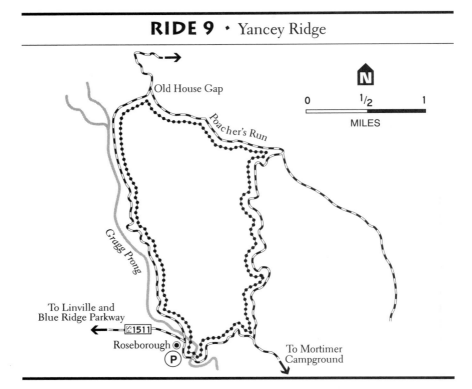

Season: The nice part about this ride comes from its relative safety even during hunting season. It's a year-round ride.

Services: No services are found at the trailhead. The closest water and rest room can be found at Mortimer Campground, but it might be just as quick to head back to Linville or Blowing Rock for these and all other basic services. Boone provides the specialized services.

Hazards: There are some notable obstacles on this double-track. First, although you may go years before seeing a vehicle on any part of this trail, it *is* open to vehicles, at least to those that can make it. And, on the day I rode it, a truck was parked in the middle of the road with its two passengers digging around suspiciously in the woods above.

"Poachers," my buddy Craig said.

Another hazard you will want to avoid (other than the numerous rocks and ruts) is the rather long mudhole just before the intersection with FS 981. Craig told me about a rider known for his eccentric tendency to ride straight through mudholes in order to prevent further erosion. On the Yancey Ridge trail, Craig said, he rode straight through the long, deep pothole. The result? A spectacular endo with rider landing smack on his back—unhurt, but needing assistance to get unstuck from the goo. When you see it, you'll know which one I mean.

Craig takes a banked turn on the back side of Yancey Ridge.

Rescue index: Although the road is open to vehicles, rescue could be difficult and time consuming. Ride this one prepared for self-rescue.

Land status: In the Pisgah National Forest.

Maps: Three sources are recommended for this area: Pisgah National Forest—Grandfather, Toecane, and French Broad Ranger Districts Map; Wilson Creek Area Trail Map; plus, a set of maps produced by High Country Mountain Bike Association, all of which can be purchased or ordered from local bike shops and the Grandfather District office in Nebo, North Carolina. Also, High Country's map set can be picked up at the Blowing Rock Chamber of Commerce.

Finding the trail: From Linville, head south on US 221/181 and take the third street on the left (SR 1545). Travel a little less than 2 miles before you reach the stop sign at an otherwise unmarked intersection with the Blue Ridge Parkway. Continue straight across the parkway on what is called Roseborough Road. Travel approximately 5 miles before you reach a bridge over Gragg Prong. Cross the bridge and park on the right. FS 192 goes up the right side of Gragg Prong.

Source of additional information:

District Ranger
Grandfather Ranger District
Route 1, Box 110A
Nebo, NC 28761
(828) 652-2144
To find the office, take exit 90 from Interstate 40 (Nebo–Lake James) and follow the signs.

Notes on the trail: It's a 3-mile climb up to Old House Gap where you turn right and continue the climb. It's downhill from there until the intersection where a right turn leads down and eventually to the intersection with FS 981. However, a left turn at this point begins about a 3-mile out-and-back (6 miles total). If you take this out-and-back portion, it is advisable to turn around once the trail begins to descend sharply. After returning from the out-and-back, bear left at the intersection this time. The ride downhill is fast, with a really nice banked curve. It dead ends into FS 981 after going through a boggy area. Take a right turn here for the fast 1.3 miles back to the parking area at Gragg Prong.

RIDE 10 · Schoolhouse Ridge

AT A GLANCE
_____

Length/configuration: A 10-mile loop of mostly lightly graveled service road, with some single-track

Aerobic difficulty: This is a moderate workout, with periods of extended exertion

Technical difficulty: Some of the single-track coming down Schoolhouse Ridge is washed out, and riding is very difficult; most of the trail, however, is only moderately challenging at best

Scenery: Schoolhouse Ridge and the Wilson Creek area—overlooks and creek bottoms

Special comments: The steepest sections of Schoolhouse Ridge, lasting less than a half mile, have switchbacks built off to the right, which are easy to miss if you are concentrating too much on staying upright

RIDE 10 • Schoolhouse Ridge
RIDE 11 • Upper Wilson

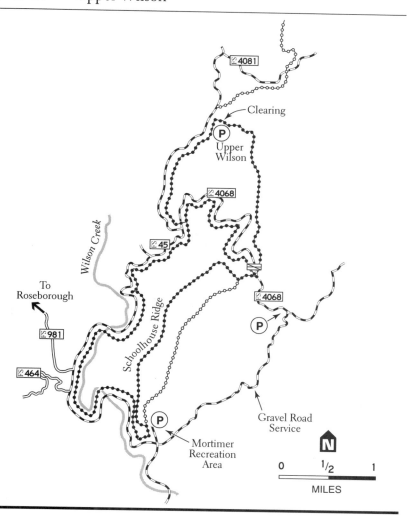

This ten-mile loop uses a two-and-a-half-mile section of single-track to connect two gravel roads near the Mortimer Campground. The single-track was originally designed with hikers in mind, and some of the steeper sections, which lose 600 feet in little over a half mile, provided all the challenge I could handle. It was only later that I heard switchbacks had been put in place around the worst of the washouts and ruts.

Back on the gravel road and climbing up Wilson Creek, it is interesting to remember the Great Flood of Forty, earlier this century. After a drought had

Craig studies the trail on
Schoolhouse Ridge.

baked this mountainous area for many weeks, a hurricane moved inland, spreading torrential rains that lasted for days.

Instead of soaking in as most of it normally would have, the rain ran off Grandfather Mountain, into Laurel Creek and Wilson Creek. The creeks jumped their banks in a wall of water high and strong enough to destroy an entire garment plant. Locomotives used in transporting material were washed away and have not been seen since. In fact, you will nearly reach the intersection with FS 45 before achieving the same elevation the flood did.

General location: Located about 10 miles southeast of Linville, North Carolina.

Elevation change: Approximately a thousand feet of difference between the highest and lowest points on the trail, most of which occurs on the descent to and climb away from Mortimer.

Season: Stay off the trail during wet weather and during hunting season (especially during what's known as "gun season," which occurs during the late fall and lasts until the New Year). North Carolina's hunting season does not allow hunting on Sunday, which makes it a good day to ride. Call for specific hunting season dates.

Services: Many services can be obtained at either Blowing Rock or Linville, only a half hour away. All other services are located a good 45 minutes away in Boone. Water, rest rooms, and camping are found at Mortimer Campground; a small store is located near its entrance.

Hazards: The rutty sections on the single-track descent to Mortimer will likely cause you to dismount, planned or not. You may encounter cars and trucks on the gravel road, especially during high-use periods like the opening weekend of hunting season, but only rarely during off-peak times.

Rescue index: You will experience no region more rugged and remote than Pisgah National Forest's Grandfather District. Always ride prepared for self-rescue.

Land status: In the Pisgah National Forest.

Maps: Three sources are recommended for this area: Pisgah National Forest— Grandfather, Toecane, and French Broad Ranger Districts Map; Wilson Creek Area Trail Map; plus, a set of maps produced by High Country Mountain Bike Association, all of which can be purchased or ordered from local bike shops and the Grandfather District office in Nebo, North Carolina. Also, High Country's map set can be picked up at the Blowing Rock Chamber of Commerce.

Finding the trail: Leave Blowing Rock, North Carolina, on US 221 headed southwest to Grandfather Mountain. Approximately 8 miles out of town, look on the left for Edgemont Road and turn. If you pass the Blue Ridge Parkway, you've gone too far. Turn around and take the first road on the right after passing back across the parkway. Stay on Edgemont Road for 10 miles. FS 4068 begins on the left. Pull off on the side of Edgemont Road and park or turn onto FS 4068 and park.

Source of additional information:

District Ranger
Grandfather Ranger District
Route 1, Box 110A
Nebo, NC 28761
(828) 652-2144
To find the office, take exit 90 off Interstate 40 (Nebo–Lake James) and follow the signs.

Notes on the trail: Head down FS 4068, taking in some rollers in the first 2.5 miles. At the top of a climb, as the road bends left, look for the single-track going into the woods on the right. A single-track connector back up to Wilson Ridge is on the left as well. The first mile and a half of single-track is fairly moderate in both pitch and difficulty. At the top of the second climb, the trail turns left at Dead Man's Point, 2,240 feet above sea level. The next section loses more than 600 feet in slightly more than a half mile. Check your brakes, and your nerve. On the bottom, or nearly so, look to the left for the single-track turning toward the campground. It's a short but sweet section that narrows to a thin line of trail barely 18 inches wide in places. It ends inside the campground. Turn right on the campground service road, which leads to FS 90 a quarter mile away. Take the right out of the campground and begin the 4.5-mile climb back up to FS 4068.

RIDE 11 · Upper Wilson

AT A GLANCE

Length/configuration: A 6.5-mile loop, with nearly equal sections of single-track, double-track, and service road

NC

Aerobic difficulty: Plenty of reasons to breathe hard, but only a moderate workout overall

Technical difficulty: The single-track has a short section of root steps—difficult to ride in either direction

Scenery: Rolling ridge lines, with a descent into the Upper Wilson Creek watershed

Special comments: This route uses the upper section of what the Forest Service calls Wilson Ridge Trail, an out-and-back 14.7 miles long one way (29.4 total). Lower Wilson offers a more rugged and challenging experience, with numerous carries and hikes.

The 6.5 miles of Upper Wilson loop are made up of a two-mile section of single-track, two and a half miles of gated fire road, and two miles of open gravel road. It's called Upper Wilson from its position on the Wilson Ridge trail, 14.7 miles one way (29.4 total), an out-and-back open for biking. The overall rugged nature of Lower Wilson makes it a less popular destination. Upper Wilson, though, is everything a trail should be. The trail's good condition has been kept that way through a lot of hard work by High Country Mountain Bike Association. The most noteworthy feature of the entire ride comes right after you clear the trailhead. The single-track starts its descent off Wilson Ridge over a series of waterbars, spaced every 30 to 40 yards, it seems. These waterbars have been carefully designed to give the acrobatic biker plenty of chances at big air. After five to ten waterbars, the first significant descent is complete.

Wilson Ridge itself is a series of rollers, with the trail having four different climb-and-drops in the first two miles, each offering an ideal aerobic workout. The climbs are relatively steep, pushing the pulse quickly up into the head-pounding stage. But just before the climb gets too strenuous, it's over and followed by a fast-as-you-want-it downhill. Another special feature of this trail is its location in the middle of a large network of trails. Some trails are maintained, while others are abandoned logging roads just waiting for an adventurous biker to explore.

When Wilson Creek
flooded in the early
twentieth century, its
waters would have
covered Craig's helmet.

General location: Located about 16 miles southeast of Linville, North Carolina.

Elevation change: There's only 400 feet between the highest point and lowest point on the trail, but that distance is swapped several times over the course of the loop.

Season: Hunting season is usually from late October through mid-December. It is a good idea to stay out of the woods between those dates. But note that hunting is not allowed on Sundays in North Carolina, making it a good day for biking. Also, periods of heavy rainfall can wreak havoc on this area, causing flash floods of consequence to both biker and car driver. Remember to stay off the trails after heavy rains; riding on muddy trails damages them.

Services: Many services can be obtained at Blowing Rock or Linville, only a half hour away. All services are located a good 45 minutes away in Boone. Mortimer Campground has water, camping, and rest rooms, as well as a nearby store.

Hazards: Some ruts and rocks lie in the middle of the single-track. Cars and trucks may be encountered on the gravel roads, although the remoteness makes meeting a vehicle unlikely except during hunting season and summer weekends.

Rescue index: You will experience no region more rugged and remote than Pisgah National Forest's Grandfather District. Always ride prepared for self-rescue.

Land status: In the Pisgah National Forest.

Maps: Three sources are recommended for this area: Pisgah National Forest— Grandfather, Toecane, and French Broad Ranger Districts Map; Wilson Creek Area Trail Map; plus, a set of maps produced by High Country Mountain Bike Association, all of which can be purchased or ordered from local bike shops and the Grandfather District office in Nebo, North Carolina. Also, High Country's map set can be picked up at the Blowing Rock Chamber of Commerce.

Finding the trail: Leave Blowing Rock, North Carolina, on US 221 headed southwest to Grandfather Mountain. Approximately 8 miles out of town, look on the left for Edgemont Road and turn. If you pass the Blue Ridge Parkway, you've gone too far. Turn around and take the first road on the right after passing back across the parkway. Stay on Edgemont for 8 miles. A parking area is on the left. The trail begins behind the gate, on the right, before crossing the wildlife opening.

Source of additional information:

District Ranger
Grandfather Ranger District
Route 1, Box 110A
Nebo, NC 28761
(828) 652-2144
To find the office, take exit 90 off Interstate 40 (Nebo–Lake James) and follow the signs.

Notes on the trail: The single-track takes a fairly straight line, staying on top of Wilson Ridge. Several trails cut away from the main trail on top, and the trail isn't blazed yet. So stay on top where the well-worn trail is easy to follow. Do that and you'll have no trouble finding the descent to FS 4068. At the intersection with FS 4068, ride past a steel barrier and turn right onto the gravel road. Several more rollers follow in the 2.5 miles between this intersection and the final climb onto FS 45. Turn right at the intersection of FS 4068 with FS 45. After a steady, slow, 2-mile climb, the trailhead will be on the right.

RIDE 12 · Woodruff Branch

AT A GLANCE

NC

Length/configuration: Although it was originally designed as an out-and-back single-track 2.4 miles long (4.8 miles total), it is described here as a challenging 3-mile loop using a gated service road, forest service road, and single-track

Aerobic difficulty: There are no easy aerobic rides in the Grandfather District, but this one is less strenuous than most

Technical difficulty: Assuming you do not ride the extremely technical and dangerous north half, the other mileage is less than daunting and can be safely handled by an intermediate biker

Scenery: Although Grandfather Mountain is hidden from view on this ride, the end of FS 4081 is a good place to take an overlook break

Special comments: This route has some relatively short but extremely technical mileage in places

The day I arrived at the Woodruff Branch trailhead (a taxing three-mile loop on single-track and gravel road) was a day lifted from a Hitchcock movie. Sure that something odd would happen, I groped my way off the foggy Blue Ridge Parkway and onto Roseborough Road, a narrow road that drops away quickly. It was also a road scheduled to be scraped that day. The road crew had plowed up a big mound of dirt approximately two-thirds of the way across the road, which forced oncoming traffic to meet head-on with no room to maneuver. It was a long, brake-tapping way to FS 45.

I was beginning to feel a little better when I saw the carsonite post planted by the gate on FS 4081. The sign proclaimed that I had, indeed, reached Woodruff Branch bicycle trail, maintained courtesy of High Country Mountain Bike Association. However, as I unloaded my bike and put on my gloves, a government vehicle pulled up to the gate and a man in green fatigues got out lugging a large radio.

Not wanting to intrude, but eavesdropping intently, I caught enough of the radio transmission to know there was trouble. As the army ranger returned to his vehicle, I asked him if anything was wrong. "Are you getting ready to ride this road?" the ranger asked, indicating FS 4081.

RIDE 12 · Woodruff Branch

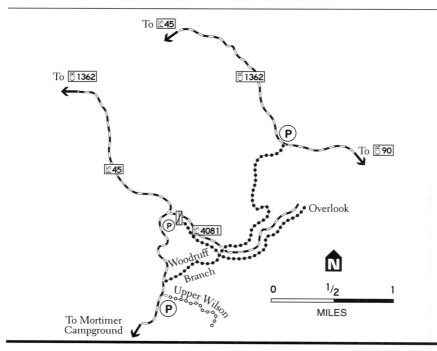

When I told him I was, he said, "Will you do me a favor? We lost a guy down there somewhere. He answers to Delta-6. If you see him, will you tell him to turn his radio on?" Yessir.

Unfortunately for me, I didn't get the chance to tell Delta-6 anything. He was found unharmed—or at least until his sergeant caught up with him. But what I did find on this short trail was even more fun than finding the missing trooper.

On the way down the thickly graveled road, I missed the turn onto the single-track, which I didn't realize until I got to the bottom of a long descent . . . and the road and everything stopped at the edge of an overlook. I was beginning to develop a case of the "where-am-I's," but I managed to control myself enough to enjoy the spectacular view here. The section of single-track I found on the way back up (on the right from this direction) turned out to be extremely steep, so steep I had to also walk it most of the way down. The single-track on the left, however, turned out to be a great little ride, reaching a ridge before bumping down some major but rideable washouts.

General location: Located about 16 miles southeast of Linville, North Carolina.

Elevation change: Roughly 1,200 feet are lost one way over the course of 2.5 miles. Whoosh! Most of it, however, is lost on the northern half, where walking is advised in many places.

This overlook at the end of FS 4081 shows where Delta-6 lost his way.

Season: Hunting season is usually from late October through mid-December. It is a good idea to stay out of the woods between those dates. However, note that hunting is not allowed on Sundays in North Carolina, making it a good day to ride. Also, periods of heavy rainfall can wreak havoc to this area, causing flash floods. Remember to stay off the trails after heavy rains; riding on muddy trails will damage them.

Services: Many services can be obtained at either Blowing Rock or Linville, only a half hour away. All other services are located a good 45 minutes away in Boone. Water, camping, rest rooms, and a small store can be found at or near Mortimer Campground.

Hazards: The steep descent to SR 1362 should be attempted—at least on bike—only by advanced riders. The southern half was pretty well rutted but required no more than moderate technical skills. The rate of descent on FS 4081 is swift so it is possible to miss the turnoff to both parts of the trail. No problem. The road stops at the cliffs of Barn Ridge a little over a mile from the trailhead, requiring a slow pedal back up. The turnoffs for the single-tracks will come *slowly* into view.

Rescue index: You will experience no region more rugged and remote than Pisgah National Forest's Grandfather District. Always ride prepared for self-rescue.

Land status: In the Pisgah National Forest.

Maps: Three sources are recommended for this area: Pisgah National Forest— Grandfather, Toecane, and French Broad Ranger Districts Map; Wilson Creek

Area Trail Map; plus, a set of maps produced by High Country Mountain Bike Association, all of which can be purchased or ordered from local bike shops and the Grandfather District office in Nebo, North Carolina. Also, High Country's map set can be picked up at the Blowing Rock Chamber of Commerce.

Finding the trail: Leave Blowing Rock, North Carolina, on US 221 headed southwest to Grandfather Mountain. Approximately 8 miles out of town, look on the left for Edgemont Road and turn. If you pass the Blue Ridge Parkway, you've gone too far. Turn around and take the first road on the right after passing back across the parkway. Stay on Edgemont for 7 miles. The gated FS 4081 will be on the left.

Source of additional information:

> District Ranger
> Grandfather Ranger District
> Route 1, Box 110A
> Nebo, NC 28761
> (828) 652-2144
> To find the office, take exit 90 off Interstate 40 (Nebo–Lake James) and follow the signs.

Notes on the trail: Ride past the gate and down the wide fire road. Look for the right turn off the road and onto single-track a long half mile farther. It's signaled by a carsonite post. But leave the turn for later and head straight on down the road. It's only another half mile or so, and the view is more than worth it. On the way back up, the right turn down the steep and technical section of Woodruff Branch comes first. Be prepared for some extreme biking opportunities if you take it. Plus, you'll either be pushing back the same ridge or taking a long section of gravel road via SR 1362 up Anthony Creek and onto FS 45. That's why I recommend leaving the techno stuff for later (or never) and making a small loop with another Woodruff Branch single-track section, which will be on the left on the way up. It climbs a ridge before falling into some large washouts and ruts, but nothing overly demanding of intermediate skills. A small climb ends on FS 45, less than a quarter mile from the Upper Wilson trailhead. Turn left to continue a longer ride on Upper Wilson Ridge, or head right to return to the trailhead at FS 4081.

RIDE 13 · Benson Hollow

AT A GLANCE

Length/configuration: A 5.5-mile loop of mostly gated double-track, with the rest single-track

Aerobic difficulty: This is not a strenuous ride

Technical difficulty: With the exception of creek crossings (4), which require a dismount and carry, this trail has only token technical requirements

Scenery: A circumnavigation of the bowl of Benson Hollow, with an exceptional display of creeping cedar

Special comments: Stronger riders may combine Buckeye Trail for a figure-eight ride

My friend Craig and I showed up at the trailhead of this 5.5-mile loop inside Boone Fork Recreation Area determined to piece together some trails that bisect the main loop. The double-track portion of the loop (about three and a half miles) has at least two other sections of single-track, which at one time or another Craig had been temporarily discombobulated on. He wasn't exactly lost; he just didn't know where he was at the moment.

Always ready to bushwhack, I followed Craig's lead as we wound through the first lap without a hitch, stopping at each intersection with single-track. "Now that one," Craig explained as we reached the first trail to the left (riding counterclockwise), "goes over the berm and comes to a boggy area where it fades away. You can hike through, but it's not fun. Eventually, it hits the main loop."

It was late December and the trees had lost their leaves, except for some oaks and a few scattered beeches. Craig set a quick pace, rolling up the small ridge overlooking Deep Cove. We came to another piece of trail to the left. "That's the other end of the first trail I pointed out. Don't go down there."

After getting back to Craig's truck, we decided to take another gated road we had seen on the left. It is marked 106 with a carsonite post and begins with promise. However, it soon narrows with a steep climb up to a ridge, overgrown with small pines and littered with blowdown.

"Hey," Craig said when we stopped at a small trail leading to the left, "I know that trail. I forget where it leads, but I know where we are now. We'll return to the main loop soon."

True to his word, we hit the trail and finished another lap, coming to the second creek crossing where, just before, we had seen another trail going off to the

RIDE 13 • Benson Hollow
RIDE 14 • Buckeye Trail

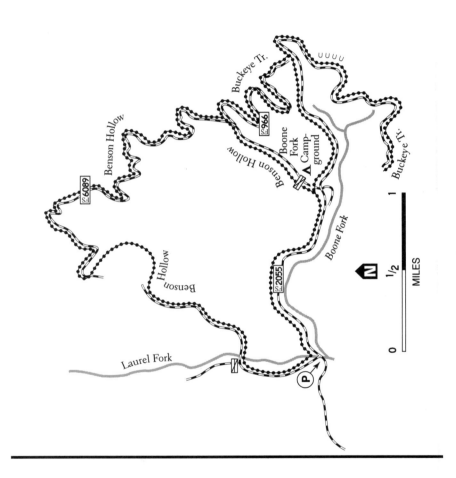

left. "Let's see where that goes," we both said. And off we went to complete a day of bike exploration at its best. Benson Hollow. Remember that name.

General location: Located about 13 miles south of Blowing Rock, North Carolina.

Elevation change: Less than 200 feet separates the lowest from the highest points on the trail; however, several small rollers occur in between.

Season: It's hunting season usually from late October through mid-December.

Biking in Benson Hollow is enough to make any-one smile—even this grizzled gearhead. Photo by Craig Franz.

It is a good idea to stay out of the woods between those dates. But note that hunting is not allowed on Sundays in North Carolina, making it a good day to bike.

Services: During the warmer months, you will find water at the campground, and there is a pit toilet. All other services are located a good 45 minutes away in Boone, although many basic services can be obtained at Blowing Rock, only 20 minutes away.

Hazards: The only significant hazard will be crossing the creeks, and they offer little trouble so long as you don't try to ride across; dismount and carry your bike over.

Rescue index: It's pretty easy to get rescued on the Benson Hollow trail; at worst, it would be a walk-out of 3 miles over fairly even terrain.

Land status: In the Pisgah National Forest.

Maps: The Pisgah National Forest—Grandfather, Toecane, and French Broad Ranger Districts Map plus a set of maps produced by High Country Mountain Bike Association are recommended. Both can be purchased or ordered from local bike shops and the Grandfather District office in Nebo, North Carolina.

Also, High Country's map set can be picked up at the Blowing Rock Chamber of Commerce.

Finding the trail: Leave Blowing Rock, headed south on US 321. Approximately 13 miles from Blowing Rock, look for Roby Martin Road on the right and turn. It dead ends into the paved Globe Mountain Road/Mulberry Church Road. Turn right and follow it for about 4 miles, turning right again at the sign for Boone Fork Recreation Area campground. Park at the campground.

Source of additional information:

> District Ranger
> Grandfather Ranger District
> Route 1, Box 110A
> Nebo, NC 28761
> (828) 652-2144
> To find the office, take exit 90 off Interstate 40 (Nebo–Lake James) and follow the signs.

Notes on the trail: Begin riding the double-track (a gated service road, FS 6089), following the creek on the right. You will see another gated road on the left marked "Benson Hollow" on a carsonite post. Ride past two single-tracks coming in from the left. After passing them, look for the marked left turn, a little over 2 miles from the campground. (If you miss the turn and go straight, it will be only 50 yards or so before the trail dies in a clump of weeds.) About a quarter mile farther, turn hard to the right down a section leading to the first creek crossing. It originally had a log bridge, but that was washed out. There are plans to install a culvert. About a hundred yards farther, note another trail crossing the creek on the left. This is not the trail back to the trailhead. Continue straight for the creek crossing about 30 yards farther. After 2 more creek crossings (a total of 4), a straightaway comes immediately before a cattle crossing, a gate, and a road going off to the right. Turn left at the road for the final quarter mile or so.

RIDE 14 · Buckeye Trail

AT A GLANCE

Length/configuration: A 3-mile loop (mostly double-track) with a 1-mile out-and-back (2 miles total) attached to the loop, making a total possible length of 5 miles

Aerobic difficulty: A moderate to easy workout

Technical difficulty: All but a half-mile section of single-track is smooth fire road or gravel road

Scenery: Boone Fork Recreation Area, creek crossings, and open views on Benson Hollow and Hayes Knob

Special comments: Tentative plans have Buckeye Trail (via the out-and-back) connecting Benson Hollow Loop to Spencer Hollow Loop

Trail guru Bill Devendorf told me, "Buckeye was built with the whole family in mind." He was referring to Boone Fork Recreation Area's tiny Buckeye Trail, a short three-mile loop with an out-and-back that is a mile long one way (two miles total). The trail was built by High Country Mountain Bike Association in collaboration with national forest officials.

Elevation is gained slowly for the most part. Long, slow switchbacks follow the contours of a mature forest of oaks, hemlocks, and maples shading dark green "hells" of laurel and rhododendron. If you don't know why these thickets are called hells, you've never tried to make your way through one, especially lugging a mountain bike.

Back at the campground, I met a hunter preparing to hunt one of the animals that travels easily through the hells of Benson Hollow. Otis Post told me, "I've been tracking a bear pushing 2-inch claws. He's a big one. The wildlife biologist with the Forest Service said he could weigh 600 pounds." Otis held out his hand about hip high and said, "He'd be this high at the shoulders. Let me know if you see him."

General location: Located 13 miles south of Blowing Rock, North Carolina.

Elevation change: Less than 200 feet separates the lowest from the highest points on the trail; however, several small rollers occur in between.

Season: An all-season trail.

Services: During the warmer months, you will find potable water at the campground, and there is a pit toilet. All other services are located a good 45 minutes

Jared takes off through
dappled sunlight.

away in Boone, although many basic services can be obtained at Blowing Rock, only 20 minutes away.

Hazards: There won't be many hazards encountered on this trail, outside of other trail users, one of whom may be the big bear Otis was hunting. A couple of creek crossings will challenge the beginning biker.

Rescue index: If rescue is required on Buckeye, it would be no big deal walking out.

Land status: In the Pisgah National Forest.

Maps: The Pisgah National Forest—Grandfather, Toecane, and French Broad Ranger Districts Map plus a set of maps produced by High Country Mountain Bike Association are recommended. Both can be purchased or ordered from local bike shops and the Grandfather District office in Nebo, North Carolina. Also, High Country's map set can be picked up at the Blowing Rock Chamber of Commerce.

Finding the trail: Leave Blowing Rock, headed south on US 321. Approximately 13 miles from Blowing Rock, look for Roby Martin Road on the right and turn. It dead ends into the paved Globe Mountain Road/Mulberry Church

Road. Turn right and follow it for about 4 miles, turning right at the sign for Boone Fork Recreation Area campground. Park at the campground.

Source of additional information:

District Ranger
Grandfather Ranger District
Route 1, Box 110A
Nebo, NC 28761
(828) 652-2144
To find the office, take exit 90 off Interstate 40 (Nebo–Lake James) and follow the signs.

Notes on the trail: Complete this loop by heading counterclockwise out of the campground and turning right onto the gated fire road (FS 6089), which follows a creek. Note that the left turn onto Benson Hollow Trail is blue-blazed. Continue past this turn, crossing over a creek in a sharp right curve. From there, three sharp left curves in the road come before a sharp right turn onto the single-track, marked by a carsonite post. However, the out-and-back continues straight at this point, ending at a clear-cut where the deep bowl of Benson Hollow lies below.

If you elect to ride the out-and-back, the turn onto the single-track will be on the left coming back. The single-track ends inside the easternmost area of the campground.

RIDE 15 · Spencer Hollow

AT A GLANCE

Length/configuration: A long 8-mile loop, mostly service road with some single-track

Aerobic difficulty: Prepare for a "grunt climb," and bring along an extra lung

Technical difficulty: Once on top, the single-track portion requires intermediate to advanced skill

Scenery: Tremendous views of Pisgah's outstanding mountains: Table Rock and Hawksbill, just to name two

Special comments: With some bushwhacking and advanced map reading, it is possible to connect this trail to Buckeye Trail (see Ride 14)

RIDE 15 · Spencer Hollow

Had I known what I was in for, I would've suggested to my biking buddy Craig that we hold off on this long 8-mile loop and try it another day. With a full day of riding already completed on nearby Benson Hollow and Buckeye (around 15 miles for me), we decided to take on the double-track climb up Spencer Branch Road with an hour or so of daylight left.

My aching legs carried me past incredible views on the steady climb toward Johnnys Knob and Whetstone Mountain. Looking a bonk squarely in the eyes, I had to hop off before reaching the top and coax my feet forward. Don't get me wrong. I was still having fun, just not as much fun as I'd been having.

Riding the high-banked double-track of Spencer Hollow.

Craig, still on his bike and looking fresh, encouraged me with, "Just a little way now." Of course, he'd already told me that three times, so I knew he was fudging some. I had it pictured that once we reached "the top," it would be a whoosh down to the bottom, which I thought I could handle without too much whining. I stood on my pedals, relieved to be headed downhill, when I looked ahead and saw a hill bigger than any I had climbed that day. Off the bike and push. My pride had departed 30 minutes earlier. I'm not sure how many rollers we had in between what became the final downhill rush, but rest assured there are plenty for even the most frolicsome of legs.

General location: Located 13 miles south of Blowing Rock, North Carolina.

Elevation change: The 4-mile-plus climb is steady, gaining somewhere in the neighborhood of a thousand feet. The ridge lines on top will add to that.

Season: Hunting season is usually from late October through mid-December. It is a good idea to stay out of the woods between those dates. However, note that hunting is not allowed on Sundays in North Carolina, making it a good day to ride.

Services: All services are located a good 45 minutes away in Boone, although many basic services can be obtained at Blowing Rock, only 20 minutes away.

Hazards: The single-track portion contains some rocks, roots, and loose soil from the recently graded clear cut; however, the soil will firm up. Other than that, a few sections are steep and twisting, requiring intermediate skills or better.

Rescue index: Spencer Branch Road is an easy road to get rescued from, providing you can get a vehicle up there. However, a rescue could require as much as a 4-mile walk out.

Land status: In the Pisgah National Forest.

Maps: The Pisgah National Forest—Grandfather, Toecane, and French Broad Ranger Districts Map plus a set of maps produced by High Country Mountain Bike Association are recommended. Both can be purchased or ordered from local bike shops and the Grandfather District office in Nebo, North Carolina. Also, High Country's map set can be picked up at the Blowing Rock Chamber of Commerce.

Finding the trail: Leave Blowing Rock, headed south on US 321. Approximately 13 miles from Blowing Rock, look for Roby Martin Road on the right and turn. Almost 3 miles farther, gated FS 189 (Spencer Branch Road) will be on the right. Begin here after parking off to the side near the gate.

Source of additional information:

District Ranger
Grandfather Ranger District
Route 1, Box 110A
Nebo, NC 28761
(828) 652-2144
To find the office, take exit 90 off Interstate 40 (Nebo–Lake James) and follow the signs.

Notes on the trail: The climb is a steady one for a little over 4 miles until it appears to level off at a meadow. (Don't take any of the spur roads you see on the way up.) Note the road going off to the right and downhill, but do not take it. Take instead the left turn (up . . . again), which begins the series of steep, short rollers. It all ends with a final, technical single-track descent back onto FS 189. Turn right to complete the 2 quick miles or so to the trailhead, or take a left for another lap of what is an approximate 4-mile loop.

RIDE 16 · Woods Mountain

AT A GLANCE

Length/configuration: A 21.7-mile loop of double-track and single-track

Aerobic difficulty: There aren't any more difficult

Technical difficulty: An advanced course with plenty of technical challenge

Scenery: Woods Mountain, Betsy Ridge, view of Mount Mitchell

Special comments: A portion of this trail follows the Mountains to the Sea Trail (MST), North Carolina's premier hiking trail

---

When I began research on this area of the Pisgah National Forest, I was told to contact Bill Devendorf for information on local bike trails. I've never received better advice. And this 21.7-mile loop of single-track and dirt road around Woods Mountain is proof. You see, Bill not only talks the talk on trail building and maintenance, he walks it. If it weren't for Bill's active involvement in trail construction (laying culverts and swinging a pulaski, wielding a chain-saw, etc.), it is doubtful Woods Mountain and many other area trails would be open for bikes.

When Bill told me about Woods Mountain, his eyes sparkled. "It starts with an 11-mile climb. No breaks. Just straight up. Over two thousand feet of vertical change. Single-track for advanced riders only." For those who are looking for a classic mountain bike adventure, it won't get any better than a day spent tackling these steep climbs and descents.

The westernmost portion of the trail comes within five miles of Mount Mitchell, the eastern United States' highest point at 6,684 feet above sea level; you will get a good look at it. The trail cuts through a wild section of forest where you're liable to see almost anything that has legs. Using an old roadbed in places, the trail also incorporates a long piece of the Mountains to the Sea Trail, a single-track of truly epic proportions. No skidding.

General location: Near Mount Mitchell, North Carolina.

Elevation change: The figure is officially given as 2,500 feet between the highest and lowest points on the trail, but my figures indicate closer to 2,000. At any rate, the elevation gained and lost will be enough to make your head swim and your lungs and thighs ache.

RIDE 16 · Woods Mountain

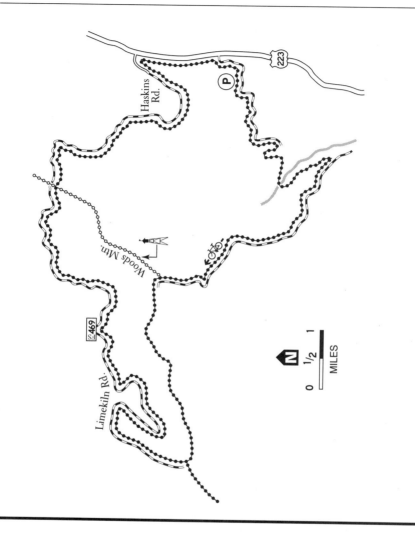

Season: This is an all-season trail. Caution is advised, however, during hunting season.

Services: Basic supplies can be picked up at local nearby stores, but the more specialized services will have to be obtained at Marion or Morganton.

Hazards: There are some hidden turns on downhill sections, and since this trail doesn't receive a great deal of use, they are easy to miss. Rocks, deadfalls, steep downhills, creek crossings, you name it. This is the ultimate mountain bike trip.

Rescue index: Don't expect a cell phone to get you out of a jam on this one. You're on your own, and it's a long walk out.

Land status: In the Pisgah National Forest.

Maps: The Pisgah National Forest—Grandfather, Toecane, and French Broad Ranger Districts Map plus a set of maps produced by High Country Mountain Bike Association are recommended. Both can be purchased or ordered from local bike shops and the Grandfather District office in Nebo, North Carolina. Also, High Country's map set can be picked up at the Blowing Rock Chamber of Commerce.

Finding the trail: Leave Boone headed south on NC 105 and take US 221 out of Linville until reaching Linville Falls. From the junction at US 221 and NC 183 keep heading south for 17.5 miles. Turn right onto a gravel road where you should see the parking lot on the left and the Woodlawn Work Station on the right.

Source of additional information:

District Ranger
Grandfather Ranger District
Route 1, Box 110A
Nebo, NC 28761
(828) 652-2144
To find the office, take exit 90 off Interstate 40 (Nebo–Lake James) and follow the signs.

Notes on the trail: Ride up the gravel road about a hundred yards and turn left onto the gated road. Approximately a mile and a quarter farther, turn right onto the single-track, which is marked by a white dot, signifying the Mountains to the Sea Trail. Ride straight on this trail for another mile before turning right again, then crossing a log bridge over the creek a tenth of a mile away. Follow the trail until it joins the logging road and turn left. In the next three quarters of a mile, the road crosses the creek. Look for the short, steep trail bearing to the right after a long half mile. After that, turn right onto a fire road for the climb up Betsy Ridge. Another mile brings you to where MST (white dot blaze) is rejoined. Follow it for half mile past where the double-track comes in back on the left, watching for a sharp right turn up the hill. Just beyond that, the trail splits—the left fork gaining the top of the knob, and the right staying level for a short distance before rejoining the left. Take the left fork up the hill after a mile and a half, still riding with the white blazes. After getting to the top of another knob (the view to the west is of Mount Mitchell), watch carefully for the sharp left turn off the downhill.

Don't pick up too much speed and you'll see the turn in time to make it safely, beginning a 2-mile ride along a ridge line. The next turn—a right—is equally easy to miss. Leave the MST by taking a two-o'clock turn into the rhododendron on some single-track. After a half mile, turn right at the service road (FS 469), Limekiln Road. The ride is approximately half over at this point. The rest of the ride stays on Limekiln until the intersection with Haskins Road 9 miles farther. Take a left onto Haskins, which turns to pavement in a half mile. Take extra care riding the busy US 221 back to the right toward Wood Lawn Work Station.

RIDE 17 · 18-Mile Ride

AT A GLANCE

Length/configuration: Despite its name, it's actually 17 miles one-way (34 miles total), out-and-back (gate-to-gate), on a forest service road

Aerobic difficulty: Plenty of long, tall rollers give the lungs a thorough workout

Technical difficulty: The entire length is gravel road, which has little technical difficulty attached to it

Scenery: Spectacular views to the northeast and southeast, the Johns River valley, plus mountains, mountains everywhere

Special comments: This ride is typically arranged with a shuttle; however, it can just as easily be ridden as an out-and-back with half done from one trailhead, and the other half done from the opposite trailhead—on different days, of course

Some mountain bikers disdain gravel road trips, preferring single-track or nothing. However, the remotely situated FS 187—17 miles one-way (34 miles total) gate-to-gate, or 21 miles for its entire length one-way (42 miles total)—may persuade even the staunchest single-tracker that some gravel roads must be ridden. My friend, Craig, warned me this ride is not 18 miles long—at least not between any recognized landmarks—saying it is closer to 16 miles. My odometer registered 17 miles, which would be beside the point if the ride wasn't known as "18-mile Ride." But you get the idea. The ride begins on the northern end in a small community near Maple Grove Church. There are some dogs living nearby who seem to enjoy chasing bikers, and for that reason, you may want to move farther on before parking and beginning the series of long, winding switchbacks. Although I lost count of the number of ridges this road traverses, I remember the number of roads (ten), both gated and not, that intersect with FS 187. Each is a promising route worthy of exploration.

General location: Southeast of Boone, North Carolina.

Elevation change: Although the elevation difference between the highest and lowest points on this ride is slightly more than 500 feet, it is misleading. This elevation is gained and lost more than just a few times.

Season: Since the gates on either end normally remain open, it is a good idea to plan for a time when traffic is likely to be lighter (not on the first day of hunt-

RIDE 17 · 18-Mile Ride

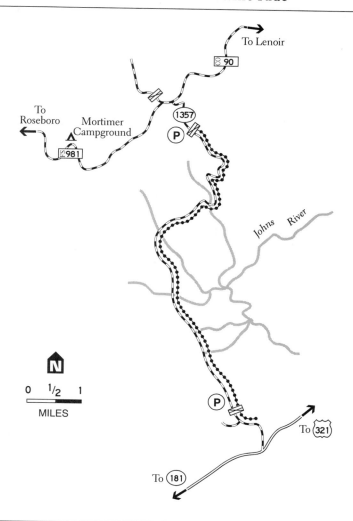

ing season, for example). The day I rode, I saw exactly one car, driven by a teenager who appeared to be looking for a place to park with her boyfriend.

Services: Lenoir may be the closest place to get the basics, but Morganton is the place to head for those special services bikers may require.

Hazards: Cars, trucks, and chasing dogs complete the list of hazards.

Rescue index: Although you may encounter some traffic on this road, it is wise to ride prepared for self-rescue.

Reaching a ridge-top curve brings with it a gratitude that is in direct proportion to the steepness of the climb.

Land status: This is land within the Pisgah National Forest.

Maps: The map recommended for this area is Pisgah National Forest—Grandfather, Toecane, and French Broad Ranger Districts.

Finding the trail: North trailhead—From Mortimer campground, head east on gravel road NC 90. Just over 3 miles (it will seem a lot longer due to the road's curves) look for a road on the right with a sign announcing Maple Grove Church. The road is signed SR 1357, Maple Grove Church Road. After going 2 miles farther, the gate will likely be open. Park on the side of the road wherever there's room.

South trailhead—Across from Mortimer Work Center (a half mile east of Mortimer campground), turn south onto SR 1328, which follows Wilson Creek over 8 miles down to its intersection with the paved Brown Mountain Beach Road (SR 1328). Turn left and take the next gravel road on the left (approximately 1.3 miles). About a mile and a half farther, turn right onto FS 187. The gate marking the opposite end of the ride is nearly a half mile farther. Park wherever there's room on the shoulder of the road.

Source of additional information:

District Ranger
Grandfather Ranger District
Route 1, Box 110A
Nebo, NC 28761
(704) 652-2144
To find the office, take exit 90 off I-40 (Nebo–Lake James) and follow the signs.

Notes on the trail: Beginning at the north trailhead, you will have few difficulties in navigating this out-and-back. Several roads (at least 10) go off FS 187 in 17 miles. Although they go off in both directions, the roads to the right (at least 6) will stay on national forest property longer. One road to the left, approximately 11 miles south of the north trailhead, winds for quite a ways along a creek.

RIDE 18 · Lower China Creek

AT A GLANCE

Length/configuration: An almost 4-mile loop, about half of it single-track

Aerobic difficulty: Only one grade will give much reason to breathe hard, and it's nearly over before the oxygen debt is realized

Technical difficulty: The section on the double-track service road is easy; however, the single-track, with its numerous creek crossings and cantaloupe-sized rocks scattered in the trail, can be daunting for a biker with little experience

Scenery: The ride along the creek is outstanding, and the view along the gravel road isn't bad either

Special comments: If you start your ride from Blowing Rock, the length of this ride can be nearly doubled, and the elevation change becomes significant. It's also a good ride to take along the fly rod.

My friend Bill had warned me about riding this four-mile loop of double-track and single-track in the winter. "How many pairs of shoes did you bring?" When I answered, "Three," he seemed satisfied. "You're gonna get wet," he went on to say. Sounds like fun, I said to myself. Just wish it were warmer than 20 degrees in the shade.

After reaching the trailhead on Globe Road, I pulled on my old shoes over wool socks. Sure would like a good long uphill at the start to put a glow in my bones, I thought. I tried to put ideas of wind chill out of my mind as my eyes watered from the wind. I could feel a deep-core chatter begin and regretted having left my extra layer back at the car.

The downhill ended quickly, though, and I listened to the sound of big water crashing over rocks on my left. "Hmm," I said, "must be China Creek." Actually,

RIDE 18 • Lower China Creek

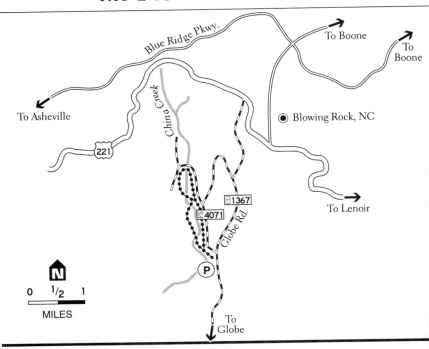

I found out later by studying the maps that what I heard was most likely Thunderhole Creek, formed by the confluence of China Creek and New Year's Creek, which subsequently forms the Johns River about three miles away.

Had it been in the good ole summer time, I would have tried each and every water crossing, probably falling in at least half of them and loving it. But I took advantage of the low water level and picked my way carefully across, using the strategically placed stones. Before I knew it, the last stream crossing had been made—with dry feet, thank you, Bill.

General location: Just outside of Blowing Rock, North Carolina.

Elevation change: There is little elevation change on the 4-mile loop—approximately 250 feet.

Season: Hunting season is a good time to ride elsewhere, plus it is also advised to check the water level before trying to cross the rip-roaring creeks below.

Services: Blowing Rock has many of the basics, and nearby Boone will be able to supply the rest.

Hazards: Obviously the creek crossings top this list, but the large rocks along the creek bank can be difficult to negotiate as well.

Steep slopes surround Thunderhole Creek, formed by the cold waters of New Year's and China Creeks, south of Blowing Rock.

Rescue index: Lower China Creek is a relatively easy place to get rescued from due to the short distance from Blowing Rock and the wide service road leading to the trailhead. The gated service road, which serves as half of the route, can be traveled easily by vehicles. Still, I advise riding prepared for self-rescue.

Land status: In the Pisgah National Forest.

Maps: The Pisgah National Forest—Grandfather, Toecane, and French Broad Ranger Districts Map plus a set of maps produced by High Country Mountain Bike Association are recommended. Both can be purchased or ordered from local bike shops and the Grandfather District office in Nebo, North Carolina. Also, High Country's map set can be picked up at the Blowing Rock Chamber of Commerce.

Finding the trail: Leave Blowing Rock at the intersection of US 321/221 and turn south onto Business 321. About a half mile down on the right, you will see the turn onto Johns River Road (also called Globe Road). Approximately 3.4 miles farther, after passing into Caldwell County, you will see FS 4071 on the right. Park where the road is wider and do not block the gate or the road.

Source of additional information:

District Ranger
Grandfather Ranger District
Route 1, Box 110A
Nebo, NC 28761
(828) 652-2144
To find the office, take exit 90 off Interstate 40 (Nebo–Lake James) and follow the
signs.

Notes on the trail: The road heads downhill, curving along the contours of
Rocky Knob and Little Rocky Knob. About 10 minutes into the ride, cross over
a cement bridge that spans New Year's Creek. About 5 minutes later, in a sharp
left curve, a road comes in on the right, dropping sharply from a tall knob. A
small creek goes under the road (if this creek is over the road, you are advised to
save this ride for another day), and on the left, amid a jumble of large rocks, the
single-track begins. About another minute later, at a **T** intersection, turn left.
(The right turn leads up the creek all the way back to Blowing Rock, but it is not
an easy ride. Plus, it winds up in someone's backyard.) A total of 5 creek crossings occur before the climb back up to the road, where it's about a 5-minute slow
climb up to the trailhead.

SOUTHWEST VIRGINIA AREA RIDES

This guide's northern boundary reaches the region just across the North Carolina border and into southwest Virginia. The extensive network of trails inside the Mount Rogers National Recreation Area supplies the bulk of destinations, with most routes using all or a part of either the Iron Mountain Trail (IMT) or the Virginia Highlands Horse Trail (VHHT).

Mount Rogers is Virginia's highest peak at 5,729 feet, but don't expect any bike routes at that height. As a part of the Lewis Fork Wilderness Area, the mountain is reserved for foot travel only. But slide down the slope a bit and you'll see that no fewer than 10 different trails have been opened for bike use, with the number growing quickly as local bike clubs and volunteers hammer out plans for future construction.

Grayson-Highlands State Park, which adjoins Mount Rogers National Recreation Area, also allows biking on a selection of its trails, but in practice it is actually a part of the Mount Rogers network. On the southern side and northern side of the recreation area are two of the country's most popular rail-trails, the Virginia Creeper and New River Trail. These former rail right-of-ways retain their wide cinder surface, making them ideal for riders of all abilities.

In addition to these and other developed off-road trails, the wandering biker can locate many public gravel and dirt roads that link small, secluded mountain communities. On one such ride, I had been pedaling for nearly an hour on a fairly well-maintained road. I would climb a steep hill and drop quickly into a heavily wooded creek basin. By the third such climb-and-drop, I had convinced myself I was heading deeper and deeper into the Virginia forests. On the fourth drop, I rounded a curve and met two young boys walking, fishing poles in hand. It turned out they were headed for their favorite fishing hole and had come from the tiny settlement I saw at the bottom of the descent, which, despite the 4×4s and manicured lawns, seemed like it had changed very little in the past hundred years.

Sources of additional information:

Highlands Ski & Outdoor Center
P.O. Box 1944
Interstate 81, Exit 19
Abingdon, VA 24210
(540) 628-1329

Cherry Creek Cyclery
107 South Main Street
Galax, VA 24333-3909
(540) 236-4013

Mountain Sports Ltd.
1021 Commonwealth Avenue
Bristol, VA 24201-3327
(540) 466-8988

Virginia Heights Bicycle Shop
1007 North Fourth Street
Wytheville, VA 24382-1005
(540) 228-8311

Boyd's Bicycle Shop
10 7th Street
Bristol, TN 37620-2214
(423) 764-4932

Larry's Cycle Shop
718 East Center Street
Kingsport, TN 37660-5200
(423) 247-2751

Piney Flats Bicycles
5585 Highway 11 East
Piney Flats, TN 37686-4454
(423) 538-9005

Blue Blaze Bike & Shuttle Service
P.O. Box 982
Damascus, VA 24236
(800) 475-5095 or (540) 475-5095

RIDE 19 · Iron Mountain Trail to Damascus

AT A GLANCE

Length/configuration: A nearly 8.5-mile one-way with shuttle or an out-and-back (17 grueling miles total without the shuttle) on single- and double-track

Aerobic difficulty: Show up expecting a thorough aerobic exercise

Technical difficulty: Plenty of challenges will keep even the most advanced rider on guard

Scenery: This ride lies within the Mount Rogers National Recreation Area, uses a section of the former treadway of the Appalachian Trail, and passes near Iron Mountain

Special comments: Many other sections of the Iron Mountain Trail can be ridden alone or in combination with other trails

Many, like me, will argue the best off-road biking destinations east of the Mississippi River are found in the Appalachian Mountains. Although there are numerous trails in the region deserving the "classic" label, the Mount Rogers National Recreation Area can lay claim to home of what many say "is the best they is," the Iron Mountain Trail. The IMT, as it is known by locals, uses closed service roads as well as single-track to make up the thoroughly challenging—both technically and physically—eight and a half miles in between FS 90 and Damascus.

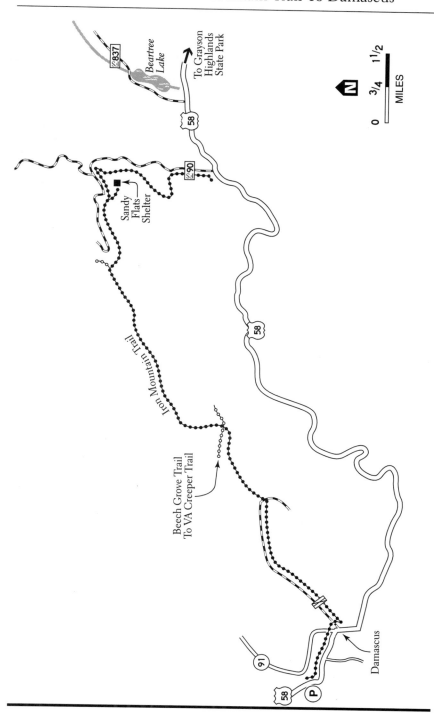

S.R. 837

Beartree Lake

To Grayson Highlands State Park

58

F.S. 90

Sandy Flats Shelter

Iron Mountain Trail

Beech Grove Trail To VA Creeper Trail

58

91

Damascus

58

P

N

0   3/4   1 1/2
MILES

Trees drive long roots into bare rock, returning a part of Appalachia to the sea.

It's fairly easy and inexpensive to leave your vehicle at the trailhead in Damascus and catch a shuttle up to FS 90. Several of the local stores provide shuttles. The initial mile-long climb will give you a great return on the speedy downhill that follows, and it's worth every labored breath. Double-track gives way to tight single-track; thick forest canopies break away into sky-wide overlooks. Creek crossings and narrow jumbles of stone that require careful maneuvering—it's all here.

By the time Damascus is reached, a fair share of mud, if not blood, will be caked to calves and forearms. (I was told once that if you didn't finish the ride scraped up a little, you weren't doing something right. I don't know about that, but I do know that you'll have a chance at least to lose some face color on the drop downhill.) Take a postride break in town at Cowboys where they've got pig skins and moon pies. And don't forget that RC.

General location: Located in Damascus, Virginia.

Elevation change: This is elevation country; expect it to change dramatically on this ride.

Season: Hunting season (mid-fall to early winter, but call for specific seasons) is less desirable than other times, but even then you're not likely to see bikers staying off the IMT. It takes high water in the creeks and deep snow on the ground to shut this trail down.

Services: Nearby Damascus has the basic services, plus many of the specialized ones required by visiting mountain bikers, such as shuttling and repairs.

Hazards: Hikers and horseback riders, as well as other bikers, will present occasional obstacles and hazards, along with sizable rocks in the middle of steeply pitched single-track.

Rescue index: The closer you are to Damascus, the easier the rescue; however, Mock Holler chute (on the last downhill leading to town) is the most likely site where assistance would be needed. This popular trail will likely have someone coming along shortly to render aid; however, the possibility of becoming stranded far from town makes it advisable to ride prepared for self-rescue.

Land status: In the Mount Rogers National Recreation Area.

Maps: I recommend two sources: the Jefferson National Forest Virginia map, and Tom Horsch's production, *1997 Mount Rogers National Recreation Area Trail Guide to Beartree/Damascus VA Area.*

Finding the trail: Head east out of Damascus on US 58 and go approximately 6 miles to where FS 90 begins on the left. Have the shuttle drop you off here, or, if you're biking to this point, turn left here.

Sources of additional information:

Mount Rogers National Recreation Area
Route 1, Box 303
Marion, VA 24354
(540) 783-5196 or (800) 628-7202

Blue Blaze Bike & Shuttle Service
P.O. Box 982
Damascus, VA 24236
(800) 475-5095 or (540) 475-5095

Notes on the trail: Begin the uphill climb and turn left onto the gated service road after about three quarters of a mile. The orange blazes of Beartree Bushwhacker Trail should be obvious. It's about a half-mile ride on this road to a big pile of rocks on the right, which is the point where the single-track turns right. Note the blaze about 20 yards in. Get off the bike and push a short distance. Once remounted, ride to the right across the creek. Some elevation is gradually gained but then lost on the way past Sandy Flats shelter on the left. Take a left onto FS 90 and ride about a quarter mile to where the yellow IMT blaze, along with the orange blaze, should be seen. The next intersection, at a **T** shows the yellow blazes going left. The single-track leads to an abandoned logging road; turn left here. It's nearly a half mile to a left turn into the forest (note the yellow blaze for IMT). Pass Beech Grove Trail on the left, which is marked by both an orange blaze and a yellow diamond. (A false turn here is not the end of the world, just a connector to the Virginia Creeper Trail; see Ride 21.) Take the IMT's sharp right turn onto what becomes double-track at this point. It's a downhill with a series of difficult creek crossings. The last section descends what is known as Mock Holler, a rough and rock-laden double-track that has caused the upset of more than one able-bodied biker. Ride around the gate and make the intersection with Fourth Street. Turn right on US 58 (Laurel Avenue) and ride to the red caboose to complete the one-way ride. If you started the ride at FS 90 and are taking this route as an out-and-back, reverse directions . . . but watch out for oncoming bikers screaming down Mock Holler.

RIDE 20 · Grayson Highlands State Park

AT A GLANCE

Length/configuration: 5.5 miles total, made up of a 2.5-mile loop at the end of a 1.5-mile out-and-back approach (3 miles total)—all double-track

Aerobic difficulty: It's not demanding, but there is one three-quarter-mile climb

Technical difficulty: The trail is wide and clear, though pock-marked by horse hooves; stream crossings, with large and hard-to-see stones, deserve caution

Scenery: Mountain meadows full of highbush blueberries, white water, old forest, and cattle are part of this ride

Special comments: The trails at Grayson Highlands can also serve as connectors and beginnings to many other trails in Mount Rogers National Recreation Area

I reached the trailhead for this five-and-a-half-mile ride at dusk one late spring day and decided to wait until morning before heading out. That evening I studied the map by campfire and traced the double-track's route. A one-and-a-half-mile (three miles total) approach trail would carry me to the intersection where I could take a two-and-a-half-mile clockwise loop. Not a long ride, but about as long as I could safely take if the predictions were right about the violent thunderstorms arriving later that morning.

I awoke to the sound of birds singing in the blend of maples and beech trees near my camp. Clouds had already appeared, and the air had a feel of rain to it. I stopped the park ranger as he made his rounds. He told me, "Yes, the trails are open and clear so far as I know." It never hurts to ask.

I set out on the trail as wisps of clouds moved through the treetops. I heard the sound of water crashing on boulders below as I made my way down to Quebec Branch, fording it easily. I got my feet wet on the next crossing, through the larger Big Wilson Creek, but it didn't dampen the fun I was having. During the long climb up to the Scales intersection, I could look out across a wide pasture where cattle were grazing among tall, broad highbush blueberries, unfortunately not quite ripe.

The rocky surface of the road was occasionally filled by a spring running down one rut or another. Ravens squawked an alarm at my coming so near their

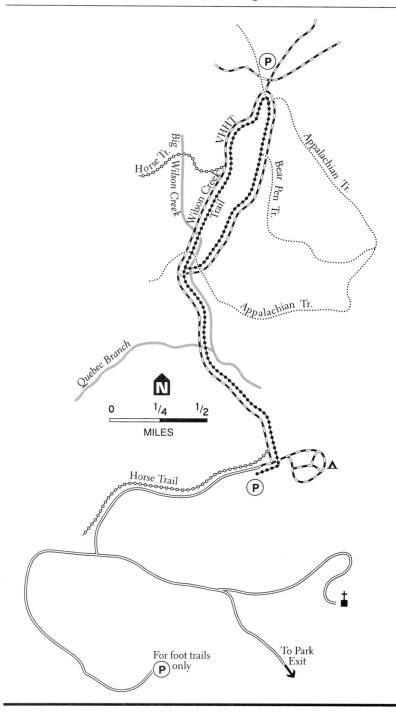

The wide, shallow ford across a creek near Grayson Highlands State Park.

foraging in cow pies. And at one point, I had to slow down and prod the cows out of the way with my front tire.

General location: Slightly east of where Tennessee's northeast tip touches Virginia.

Elevation change: About 750 feet of climbing for the entire trip—half of it coming on the climb away from Big Wilson Creek.

Season: This is an all-season trail. However, Grayson Highlands does allow hunting inside its boundaries, and—unlike North Carolina—Virginia does allow hunting on Sundays.

Services: Grayson Highlands State Park has all the modern facilities expected in a fine campground. There are few stores between trailhead and Damascus, a nearly 30-minute ride to the west, where the basic supplies and services can be obtained. A little farther to the northwest, Abingdon, Virginia, should provide the rest.

Hazards: Hunters, horses, cattle, rocks, and other riders present the only significant hazards.

Rescue index: Chances are good that assistance will quickly come from fellow trail users, especially on weekends. But remember, it is fairly remote country, and any major rescue could take a significant time to get organized.

Land status: Grayson Highlands is part of Virginia's state park system.

Maps: The best map is Mount Rogers High Country and Wilderness, complete with contour intervals. It can be bought at most area bike stores, but I got my copy at the Green Cove Visitor Center (see Ride 21).

Finding the trail: Take Interstate 81 north out of Bristol to Abingdon. Get off on US 58 heading southeast toward Damascus. After about 20 minutes of driving curvy US 58 east out of Damascus, Mount Rogers School is on the right. Continue straight approximately 3 more miles. The sign at the entrance to Grayson Highlands State Park is on the left. After paying an entrance fee, continue another 3 miles headed toward the campground on Wilburn Ridge. Park in the small lot on the right, where there's also a pay phone.

Source of additional information:

Grayson Highlands State Park
Route 2, Box 141
Mouth of Wilson, VA 24363
(540) 579-7092

Notes on the trail: Head west out of the campground and look for the double-track leading off to the right. After riding past the gate, you'll spot a trail to the left that leads back to the horse campground and is closed to bikes. A trail splits off to the right soon after, and is open to bikes. If you would like to take a diversion that is 1.7 miles one way (3.4 miles total), turn right; otherwise, continue straight on Seed Orchard Road. After Wilson Trail comes in on the right, a crossing of Quebec Branch comes next. In another half mile, Big Wilson Creek must be crossed. Scales Trail comes in on the right. Bear left for now on Wilson Creek Trail, but you'll be circling back to this same intersection. The Appalachian Trail crosses soon after. The next three quarters of a mile will gain nearly 400 vertical feet. Continue right at the intersection with the Virginia Highlands Horse Trail, and pick up Scales Trail at the next intersection, where you'll turn right. You'll go about another 1.5 miles before returning to the intersection near Big Wilson Creek. The trailhead is reached by returning on the road to the campground.

RIDE 21 · Virginia Creeper

AT A GLANCE

Length/configuration: 32.3 miles one way on an out-and-back (64.6 miles total) double-track, but as with all out-and-backs, you can ride shorter sections.

Aerobic difficulty: The grade is never very steep, but it's constant. At times you will feel like you are only creeping along.

Technical difficulty: This is a smooth, graveled surface, except for the trestles.

Scenery: Fantastic ride along (and over) a rushing mountain creek.

Special comments: This trail is a fine example of a rails-to-trails conversion.

If there was only one rails-to-trail, the nearly 33 miles (64.6 miles total) of the former Virginia-Carolina Railroad would have to be it. The scenery is beautiful to see as well as to hear. For much of the way, the grade follows water roaring over boulders in the stream bed. The most scenic of these, Whitetop Laurel Creek, offers bikers packing along a fly rod a great opportunity to fish.

No train has used the bed for over 20 years, so trees have begun growing over the trail to form a solid canopy in many places. You'll pass through farms, even yards. Cows graze nearby. Hikers and horseback riders share the trail. The trestles spanning the creeks are so high above the water that acrophobics should, perhaps, be led across with blinders.

You're not likely to see any beavers near the confluence of the two creeks below the longest and tallest of the trestles, but you just might. At least once in recent memory, a large lodge and dam was constructed just upstream from this trestle. Demolition experts were called in and sticks of dynamite placed at strategic points. Twice. The first explosion, although sending boughs and beavers in all directions, failed to remove the dam.

General location: Put your finger on a map where Tennessee, North Carolina, and Virginia come together, and you've got it.

Elevation change: This rail line was called the Virginia Creeper for the slow, steady climb up the mountain, "only a 2 percent grade."

Season: The gravel surface makes this a year-round ride. Spring is an especially beautiful time when the clusters of mountain laurel blooms hang out over the

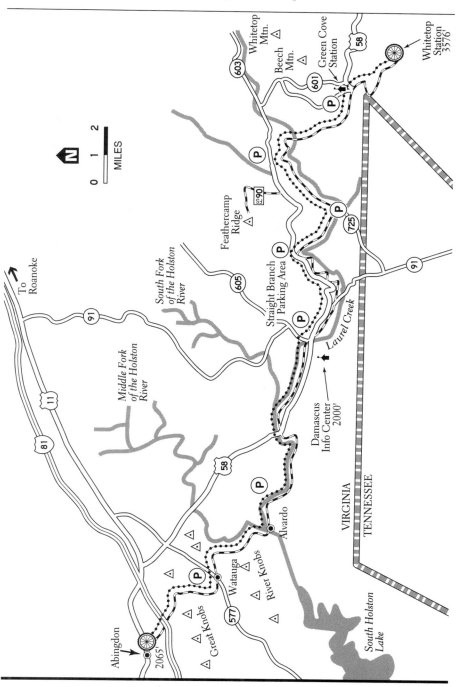

N

MILES
0 1 2

603

Whitetop Mtn.

Beech Mtn.

Green Cove Station

58

601

P

Whitetop Station
3576'

P

RT
90

Feathercamp Ridge

725

P

91

South Fork of the Holston River

605

Straight Branch Parking Area

P

P

To Roanoke

91

Laurel Creek

Middle Fork of the Holston River

Damascus Info Center 2000'

11

81

58

P

VIRGINIA

TENNESSEE

Alvardo

577

Watauga

River Knobs

P

Great Knobs

Abingdon
2065'

South Holston Lake

A barn along part of the Virginia Creeper.

trail. In winter, however, it's good to remember that bridges freeze before the trail does. My friend Bill performed an unexpected helmet test one frozen dusk when his front tire lost purchase. He's happy to report that the trestle railings can withstand the force of a 200-pound biker slamming into them.

Services: Water and rest rooms are provided at Green Cove Station, when it's open. However, it and other information stations are only open during the peak visitor seasons (late spring, summer, and early fall) and then only during normal business hours. The town of Damascus has the basic supplies (with some special services), and the city of Abingdon provides a full range of goods and services, including a bike shop.

Hazards: You'll have to cross roads and watch for motorized vehicular traffic at some intersections. You'll encounter horses and their riders, as well as hikers. Be polite and yield the trail; pass by only after giving a friendly greeting.

Rescue index: Rescue is easy on the Virginia Creeper Trail. Many homes lie near the trail, and there are frequent intersections either with or near major roads and highways.

Land status: Although it is perfectly legal for you to be on the trail in between Abingdon and Damascus, the actual ownership of the land remains in private hands. The trail is listed as a National Recreation Trail in Mount Rogers National Recreation Area.

Maps: A good map can be picked up at one of the information stations or local bike shops; ask for the Virginia Creeper National Recreation Trail.

Finding the trail: There are 9 parking and access areas for this trail. Although all are open and legal year-round, the primary ones are found in Damascus, Green Cove, and Abingdon. To reach the Damascus trailhead, stay on US 58 headed west out of town. Look for the red caboose on the left about a mile and a half farther. Park in the area provided. The Green Cove trailhead is reached by taking the winding US 58 (J.E.B. Stuart Road) about 9.5 miles (it'll seem a lot farther) east out of Damascus to the intersection with VA 603. Stay on US 58 for a little over 6 miles and turn right onto Fire House Road for 2 more miles to the Whitetop trailhead. In Abingdon, stay on US 58 to downtown and turn left at the light (Pecan Street) where the Virginia Creeper Trail sign has been posted. The trailhead is marked by the locomotive; parking is on the right, across the street.

Sources of additional information:

Mount Rogers National Recreation Area
Route 1, Box 303
Marion, VA 24354
(540) 783-5196 or (800) 628-7202

Blue Blaze Bike & Shuttle Service
P.O. Box 982
Damascus, VA 24236
(800) 475-5095 or (540) 475-5095

Highlands Ski and Outdoor Center
P.O. Box 1944
Abingdon, VA 24212
(540) 628-1329

Notes on the trail: This is a very easy trail to navigate. The problem comes from deciding which trailhead to use. It's simplest to begin in Abingdon and creep up the trail to Damascus, the approximate halfway point. From Abingdon, the distance to the next intersection (trailhead) is 2.9 miles, but parking is limited. From Abingdon to Alvardo is 8.5 miles. The distance from Abingdon to Damascus is 15.5 miles. It's 19.5 miles from Abingdon to the next parking, which is found at Straight Branch. It's 24 miles from Abingdon to Konnarock Junction. From Abingdon to the Junction to Green Cove is 29.3 miles (58.6 miles total). The last 3 miles of the trail come on the short trip from Green Cove to Whitetop Station, where the trail ends. For total mileage, simply double the distance. For some, the best way to ride this trail is to arrange for a shuttle service to take you to the top (Whitetop Station) and make the easy pedal down to Abingdon.

RIDE 22 · New River

AT A GLANCE

Length/configuration: 57 miles one way on an out-and-back double-track (114 miles total)—since this is an out-and-back, shorter rides can be planned easily

Aerobic difficulty: The old rail grade isn't aerobically demanding for most riders; however, by selecting a higher gear and quicker cadence, a thorough workout can be obtained

Technical difficulty: Crossing trestles and entering tunnels are the only technical challenges on this smooth trail

Scenery: An extended view of the New River and the narrow gorges leading to it

Special comments: A 2-mile section near SR 100, near Barren Springs, remains closed due to property rights negotiations

Linear Park. It has a nice ring to it, and New River Trail State Park is Virginia's only one, all 55 official miles of it. The route follows the rail bed of the old Norfolk and Western line, which specialized in hauling the lead, copper, and other minerals layered among the granite mountains. As a result, don't expect tight single-track; it is wide enough to take a train through, although in places, just barely.

If looking down into the churning white water of a mountain river hundreds of feet below weakens your grip on the handlebar, you'll need to dismount and walk across the trestles more than once. Likewise, if dark gives you anxiety attacks, you may want to travel prepared with a bike light. One tunnel is 229 feet long.

Although the state-run facility at Fosters Falls hasn't been completed, one day it will join the numerous privately owned campgrounds adjacent to the trail. The overall length makes riding the entire stretch in one day impractical for most. And the ride along America's second oldest river is too good to rush. So mount the panniers and stow the fly rod and camping equipment.

General location: The New River, between Galax and Pulaski, Virginia.

Elevation change: The gain on this trail is approximately 250 feet. Beginning in Pulaski the elevation is 1,900 feet. Over the first 3 miles the elevation rises to

Abandoned rail lines in Appalachia, some of which have been converted to bike trails, often stay within hearing distance of crashing rivers and streams.

2,150 feet and then is gradually lost in the next 7 miles. Much of the ride will seem on the level.

Season: An all-season trail.

Services: The park's headquarters are located at Shot Tower Historical State Park (midway through the ride) and has rest rooms, water, and parking. Numerous private campgrounds supply the basics. Either Galax or Pulaski will be able to provide a nearly complete list of services.

Hazards: Riding over trestles can be tricky and requires full concentration. Be alert for other trail users and vehicles at certain intersections.

Rescue index: Rescue is easy on this trail. There are plenty of intersections with paved roads, and many people use this trail.

Land status: Managed by Virginia's Department of Conservation and Recreation.

Maps: Newly updated maps of the trail can be obtained by request from the New River Trail State Park (see address page 90).

RIDE 22 · New River Trail State Park

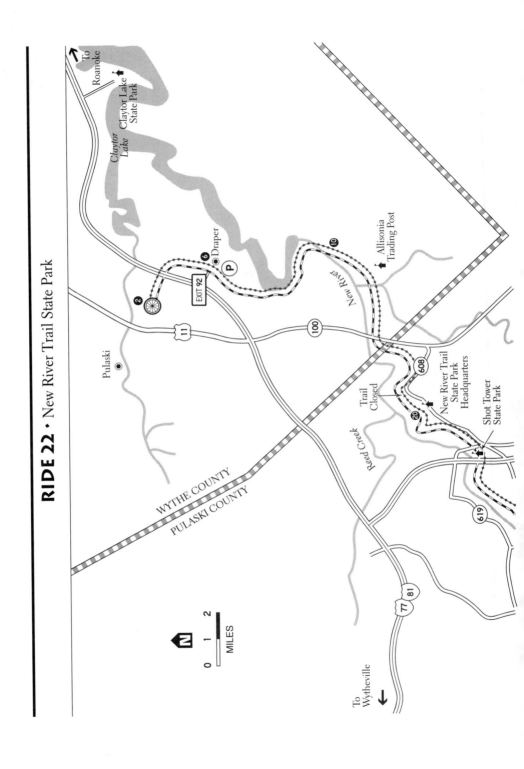

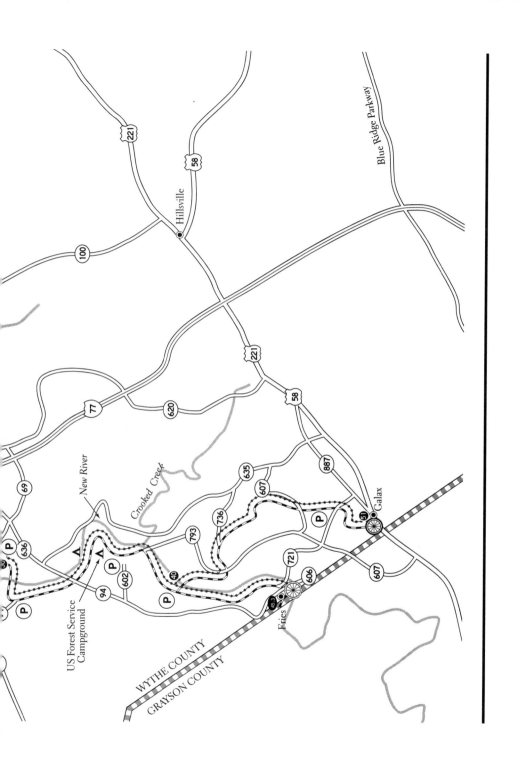

Finding the trail: Galax trailhead—Exit Interstate 77 onto US 58 (exit 14) and head west to Galax, approximately 10 miles away. The trailhead is on the right, just after you cross Chestnut Creek. Pulaski trailhead—Leave I-81 on exit 94 (VA 99) headed north. Two miles up, turn right onto Xaloy Way where a prominent sign has been posted. The trailhead lies on the right, a tenth of a mile farther in. There are, of course, many other access points along the way, which the maps show.

Source of additional information:

New River Trail State Park
Route 1, Box 81X
Austinville, VA 24312
(540) 699-6778

Notes on the trail: Beginning at the north trailhead, in Pulaski, pass over I-81 at the 3.6-mile mark. By the time the bridge at Hiwassee is reached, 6 trestles and bridges have been crossed in 10 miles or so. The detour around a Barren Springs piece of private property occurs near the 17-mile mark. Shot Tower, where lead "shot" was made by pouring the molten metal from the top of the tower, is 25 miles away from the Pulaski trailhead, and it is home to the park's headquarters. Fries Junction lies near the 40-mile mark. A visit to Fries (about 5.5 miles away—11 miles total) can be added to the ride before you return to complete the final 12 miles to the Galax parking lot.

FAMOUS FOOTHILL TRAILS

Even though the rides in Hickory, Greensboro, and Charlotte do not technically lie in the Appalachian Mountains, it just seemed right to include these places for this guide. Many of the same people I saw riding the mountain trails said they also ride these trails. For a very good reason. They live here. Another reason I've included these rides is that they're fun. Good beginner's trails with some challenges thrown in. Nothing too intense—that is unless you're making the very difficult climb at South Mountains State Park. And the scenery is mostly pretty, if not downright beautiful.

Sources of additional information:

Triad Wheelers Bicycle Club
P.O. Box 9812
Greensboro, NC 27429

Greensboro Velo Club
P.O. Box 29052
Greensboro, NC 27429
(336) 274-5959

Tarheel Trailblazers
P.O. Box 35273
Charlotte, NC 28235
(704) 559-8076

First Flight Bicycles
2435 North Center Street
Hickory, NC 28601
(828) 324- 9350

RIDE 23 · South Mountains

AT A GLANCE

NC

Length/configuration: An 18-mile loop, or a 9-mile one-way out-and-back (18 miles total) gravel road with a short paved section

Aerobic difficulty: The only time you'll be catching your breath on this one is when you're off your bike

Technical difficulty: For the most part, the technical skills required are moderate. One section, however, eroded by horseback traffic, will give a tough test

Scenery: South Mountains and plenty of open views to all points of the compass

Special comments: South Mountains is one of only two North Carolina state parks that allow mountain biking

My biking buddy Craig and I showed up at the trailhead of this 18-mile double-track loop expecting a grueling affair. We were not disappointed. We'd heard stories of the massive elevation changes over short distances. Some bikers told us they weren't sure it was worth it. Not exactly what you like to hear. Craig and I, though, were bolstered by the knowledge that we would be exploring new territory. After all, what's a forest for?

A couple of deer stood ahead of me on the first climb. I was almost close enough to touch them when they bolted down the slope. It was as if they'd seen such huffing and puffing before and knew there was nothing to fear from a creature in so much distress.

A few miles farther in, Craig and I caught up to a hiker taking a break. He looked like he belonged to the Civil War era, with his handmade boots, close-trimmed beard, and curious-looking knapsack. After we chatted a few minutes, he slung his gear over his shoulder, telling us, "Like Stonewall Jackson said, 'March the men an hour and rest 'em ten minutes.' "

The route (closed to vehicles, but not horses) retains a primitive atmosphere and is remarkably quiet. We enjoyed our ride all the way to Benn Knob, the highest point on the trail at 2,894 feet above sea level. From Benn Knob, though, the wilderness is broken by a paved road, which isn't so bad. The rapid paved descents were fun but too smooth for our liking. Electric wires are strung along the road to feed Pine Mountain Resort, which adjoins the state park, so you'll hear the hum of high voltage overhead on this part of the ride.

If you're like me and don't like to ride pavement, then turn around here and take the route as an out-and-back (nine miles out, nine miles back).

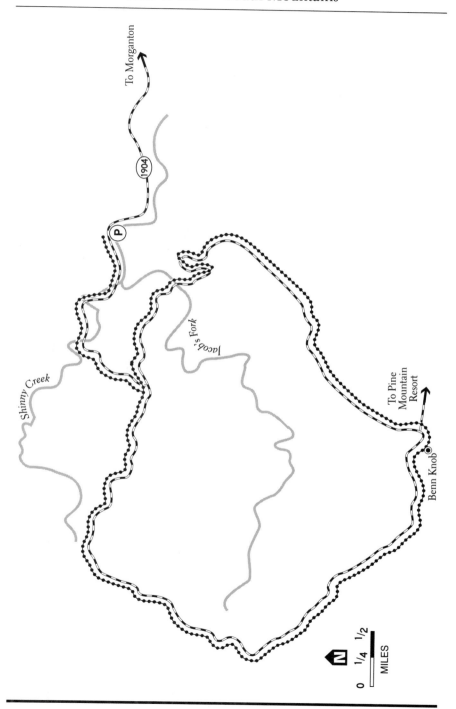

To Morganton

1904

P

Shinny Creek

Jacob's Fork

To Pine Mountain Resort

Benn Knob

N

0 ¼ ½

MILES

Craig is seen here hopping for joy at South Mountains State Park.

The route past Benn Knob, which leads to High Shoals Falls (South Mountains' featured natural attraction) and the creek crossing at Jacob's Fork, is badly eroded—another good reason to turn around at Benn Knob. Also, crossing the creek if the water levels are up isn't advisable.

General location: South Mountains State Park is located near Morganton, North Carolina.

Elevation change: The difference between the highest and lowest points on the trail is approximately 1,500 feet, but many rollers make up a significant additional amount of total elevation gained.

Season: Following heavy or sustained rain Jacob's Fork often floods, making it impassable; otherwise, this is an all-season trail.

Services: The state park has primitive camping year-round—and no hunting. A rest room is near the park office, and you can replenish your water supply there. Otherwise, head to Morganton, about 20 miles away, for a full range of services.

Hazards: Fording Jacob's Fork at high water is dangerous. You may encounter horseback riders on the trail; always yield to these skittish, unpredictable animals. You'll encounter hikers, too, and you should, as always, yield to them. The whoop-de-doos (actually waterbars) are plenteous and offer great fun but are potential hospital bills.

Rescue index: If you follow the required registration procedure, you'll likely be found by sundown. Otherwise, it could take an uncomfortably long time to be found. Ride prepared for self-rescue.

Land status: Managed by North Carolina's Division of Parks and Recreation, Department of Environment, Health, and Natural Resources.

Maps: A good map of South Mountains State Park can be picked up at the office or at the registration station.

Finding the trail: Exit Interstate 40 at Morganton and head south on SR 18 (exit 107). Drive 11 miles to Sugar Loaf Road (SR 1913) and turn right. After about 4 miles, at the **T** intersection with Old NC 18, turn left. Drive 2.8 miles and turn right onto SR 1901. Continue straight for about 1.4 miles and veer right onto the gravel road, heading uphill slightly. After about 2 miles, you'll go through the gate. It's another 1.8 miles to the parking lot. The marked trail begins by the registration station, in between the parking lot and office.

Sources of additional information:

South Mountains State Park
Old NC 18
Morganton, NC 28655
(828) 433-4772

Division of Parks and Recreation
Department of Environment, Health, and Natural Resources
P.O. Box 27687
Raleigh, NC 27611
(919) 733-4181

Notes on the trail: After registering, head up H.Q. Trail for over 2 miles to reach the intersection with Upper Falls Trail. Turn right and ride about 2.5 miles more to find the gate at Lower CCC Trail. Turn left. Stay on the road for 5.6 miles, skirting by to the left of Benn Knob. (I recommend turning around at Benn Knob, but should you want the full loop, instead of an out-and-back, read on.) Turn left past a yellow gate to get on the mostly paved Dogwood Trail (it begins as a dirt road). The paved road goes down and up at least two significant ridges, after which you'll quickly lose significant elevation on the way to Jacob's Fork where the road turns back to gravel. After crossing the creek, turn left at the junction with Raven Rock Trail. The climb up from Jacob's Fork is long and steep. It is rideable the entire way, but most riders will need to dismount at least once and push—no excuses necessary. Do not take Cut-Off Trail; it's an out-and-back (off limits to bikes) and not a shortcut to the trailhead. The way back requires taking a right onto H.Q. Trail and whoop-de-dooing all the way back.

RIDE 24 · Greenway Mountain Bike Trail

AT A GLANCE

Length/configuration: 2.4 miles of single-track plus a half mile of asphalt greenway make up this loop

Aerobic difficulty: Most sections require only moderate exertion, but parts demand a full-blown aerobic push

Technical difficulty: Tough, but not too tough; the route has been built with mountain bikers in mind and pushes intermediates to the edge, but not over

Scenery: It is pretty, like most North Carolina hill country, but not spectacular because of a section along a power line

Special comments: This showcase route is being built and managed by the fine folks at First Flight Bicycles in Hickory and Statesville; the 2.4 miles of single-track is just the beginning of what will be a more developed network

This custom-designed loop of 2.4 miles of single-track (plus a half mile of asphalt greenway), gives the Hickory off-road rider an ideal place to take a quick lap or two during a lunch break or after work. The route originally was set aside for hikers, but when the greenway opened, the off-road biking area was assigned to First Flight Bicycles for maintenance.

This partnership between the city and First Flight has resulted in a top-flight ride. Although it is currently short, I was told that the single-track is only the beginning phase. Plans for an additional four or so miles, squeezed into the remaining area inside the park, are in the works. It may take some time for the trail to be completed, but if the final result is anything like what is already in place, the wait will be worth it. But why wait? Call First Flight (or your local bike club) and volunteer for a trail-building party.

General location: Hickory City Park is located in Hickory, North Carolina, just east of US 321 and north of Interstate 40.

Elevation change: Some sections are steep, but most are moderate in both length and pitch.

Season: An all-season trail.

Services: Bathrooms and water sources are located inside the park, but a short trip into town can fill the full need of supplies and services.

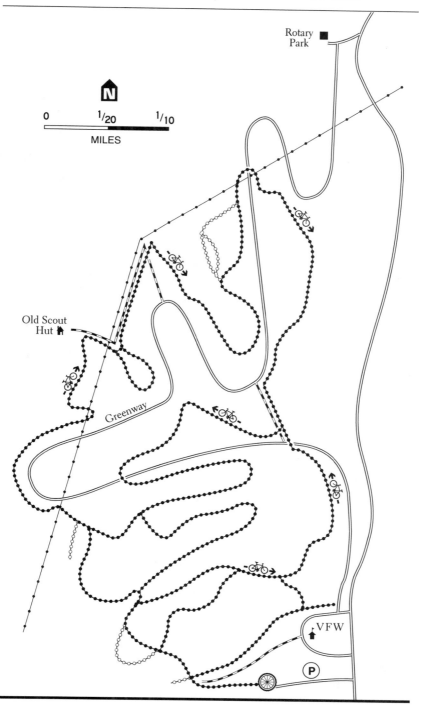

Rotary Park

N

0   1/20   1/10

MILES

Old Scout Hut

Greenway

VFW

P

A sample of the good
stuff on Greenway
Mountain Bike Trail.

Hazards: When I rode the trail, roots and rocks made up the bulk of potential hazards. I also saw broken glass on parts of the trail. But I saw signs advertising planned work parties, which will no doubt clean up these kinds of hazards.

Rescue index: This park's popularity and proximity to major roads make rescue fairly simple and quick.

Land status: Hickory City Park is owned and operated by the city government of Hickory, North Carolina.

Maps: An excellent map (Greenway Mountain Bike Trail) was drawn and provided to me by First Flight Bicycles.

Finding the trail: From I-40, take exit 123 to SR 127 North. Look for 16th Avenue NE (SR 127) on the left (you'll see Viewmont School at the intersection). Turn left, heading north on SR 127. Drive about a half mile and look for 6th Street cutting back sharply to the right under a flashing yellow light. Turn right on 6th Street and drive about 3 miles. Watch on the right for the sign to Hickory City Park. Turn here and park. Bike out of the parking lot and head toward the road. The paved greenway will be on the left. Take it and immediately turn left into the Veterans of Foreign Wars parking lot. Just before reaching the chain-link gate, look to the right for the single-track diving into the forest.

Sources of additional information:

First Flight Bicycles
2435 North Center Street
Hickory, NC 28601
(828) 324-9350

First Flight Bicycles
218 South Center Street
Statesville, NC 28677
(828) 878-9683

Notes on the trail: Yellow ribbons and red (paper) arrows mark each intersection, making it practically impossible to get lost. The recommended direction of travel is clockwise. There are creek crossings (two), power line right-of-ways (two), and intersections with the greenway (three). In order to complete the loop back to the parking lot, you'll have to take the greenway for a half mile. If you'd rather take the single-track approach back, turn right at the top of the double-track across from the old mulch facility (actually just a clearing) and repeat some of the single-track you rode earlier. Bear in mind, though, that the recommended direction of travel makes it likely that you'll encounter bikers coming from the other direction on this section of the ride. You'll have to cross the creek and ride up the hill in order to reconnect with the trail's quarter-mile section of single-track ridden at the start. Just before crossing the creek again, look to the right for a short connector leading to the VFW parking lot. Of course, if you're like me, one lap is not enough. It's a fun ride and shows how a mountain biking trail should be built. Plans also call for using the greenway to connect rides at nearby Hilton Park (see Ride 25) with those at Hickory City Park.

RIDE 25 · Hilton Park

AT A GLANCE

Length/configuration: 2 miles of small single-track loops connected to a 2-mile, one-way, double-track out-and-back (4 miles total)—approximately 6 miles total

Aerobic difficulty: Strenuous, plenty of steep climbs

Technical difficulty: A challenge at every level

Scenery: Pretty and neat inner-city park along water

Special comments: The maze of single-track trails makes this an interesting place to explore without fear of getting lost, but sharp bike-handling skills are required

RIDE 25 · Hilton Park

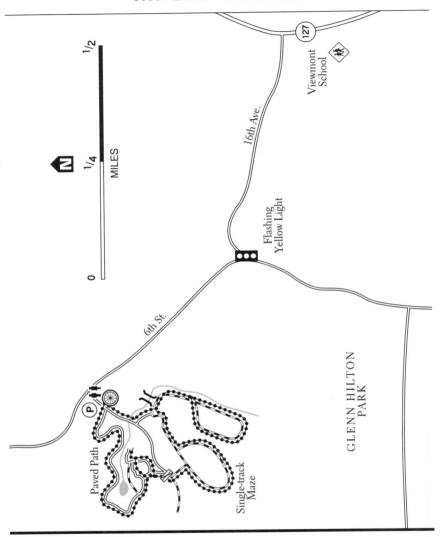

The combination of small loops connected to a double-track out-and-back make approximately six miles (total) of off-road riding in Hickory, North Carolina's Hilton Park. And the number of miles is growing. The result is a popular urban mountain biking destination for those who don't have time to make the trip west into the Pisgah National Forest.

This park is a good place to bring the entire family. The paved greenway path, which will ultimately connect this park to Hickory City Park (see Ride 24), is open to hikers, bikers, and rollerbladers. A nearly quarter-mile-long section of

A bridge inside Hilton Park.

the greenway passes along the creek, and some of the treadway has been board-walked. The three-foot-wide surface floating directly on top of the water undulates under the weight of bike and biker, giving a unique feel to biking I'd never experienced before. Note well: Inexperienced riders should dismount and walk their bikes across this part. But for those who can handle the tricky weight shifts required on this section, ride it. You'll like it.

General location: Located in Hickory, North Carolina.

Elevation change: The single-track network constantly falls or climbs. Nothing long, but the rolling hills will keep the lungs working hard.

Season: An all-season trail.

Services: The park has water and rest rooms. A short trip to downtown Hickory will be all that's necessary in order to acquire any other services.

Hazards: Lots of roots and rocks require concentration. Some extremely steep sections should be hiked—even down, unless you've been blessed by Saint Downhiller.

Rescue index: Rescue is only a short walk away; however, should someone have to walk up and find (after first missing) you, it could take some time if you're on the single-track section. Fortunately, this is a popular destination, and you should not be stranded long.

Land status: Owned and operated by the Hickory city government.

Maps: No maps of the park or the trails were available. The map included here is a result of my investigations and interrogations.

Finding the trail: From Interstate 40, take exit 123 to SR 127 North. Look for 16th Avenue NE (SR 127) on the left (you'll see Viewmont School at the intersection). Turn left, heading north on SR 127. Drive about a half mile and look for 6th Street cutting back sharply to the right under a flashing yellow light. Turn right onto 6th Street. Go almost 1 mile and turn left into the park, making a quick right into the upper parking lot. The trailhead for the single- and double-track lies at the end of the paved greenway looping along the line of trees northeast of the lot. The paved loop goes straight at the bridge, ending at a paved, gated service road. As the pavement gives way to gravel after approximately 50 yards, look to the left for the main trail.

Source of additional information:

First Flight Bicycles
2435 North Center Street
Hickory, NC 28601
(828) 324-9350

Notes on the trail: At the trailhead, look for the three-way intersection: if you go left you'll ride along a ridge, if you go right you'll hit a small counterclockwise loop of about 1 mile, or you can go straight up the hill for the main artery, along which many single-track sections cross. Most of the single-track sections connect the two ends of what is basically an out-and-back along the same elevation. One end begins next to the subdivision boundary, and the other point dead-ends at a sign up-creek. The interconnecting single-track sections provide the most dramatic riding opportunities. Never on the level, they twist and turn to create an intricate maze, bordered on one side by a subdivision and on the other by double-track. Explore and enjoy.

RIDE 26 · Bur-Mil Runner's Trail

AT A GLANCE

Length/configuration: 3.5-mile loop on a double-track

Aerobic difficulty: Little difficulty if taken at a slow pace

Technical difficulty: This smooth, wide, unpaved trail makes it easy

Scenery: A mile of shaded woods along a small creek, mostly pine forest

Special comments: Part of this trail serves as the connector to Owl's Roost Trail (see Ride 27), a more advanced section of single-track also found within Bur-Mil Park

Greensboro, North Carolina, has established itself as the leader in mountain biking destinations within the Tarheel State's Triad: Greensboro, Winston-Salem, and High Point. Perhaps the best example of what's available can be found in the 3.5-mile loop inside the city's Bur-Mil Park. The trail circles through the forest and winds along a creek on easily ridden and well-groomed double-track.

Of course, hikers and runners are seen frequently on the trail, but the park is also a popular site for many other recreational activities. Golf heads the list at Bur-Mil. There are separate areas for volleyball and soccer. Tennis and swimming, and even horseshoes and fishing, draw folks to Bur-Mil. And, yes, you can have a picnic there, too. Or a convention. Bur-Mil is big on reunions and company outings. The park has a country club, which provides a complete line of services for the total comfort and enjoyment at these events: catered meals, a ballroom, even a piano tuner on standby.

General location: Bur-Mil is located north of Greensboro, North Carolina, just off US 220 on the shores of Lake Brandt.

Elevation change: There are no long climbs, only gently rolling hills.

Season: An all-season trail.

Services: Bur-Mil provides many services—bathroom, water, and more—if you're a registered guest. Greensboro proper has the rest, including a bike shop.

Hazards: Be alert to other trail users (runners, hikers); branches sometimes litter the trail; watch out for the occasional rock.

RIDE 26 • Bur-Mil Runner's Trail

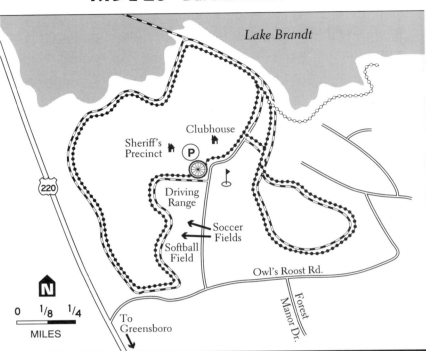

Rescue index: A rescue would be easy at Bur-Mil; a police precinct is located adjacent to the parking lot. The double-track is wide enough for park vehicles to drive. This trail has a large number of bikers, hikers, and, of course, runners using it throughout the day, making a quick rescue likely.

Land status: Owned and operated by the Greensboro city government.

Maps: A good map is located at the information rack inside the clubhouse; also, a map is posted at the trailhead.

Finding the trail: Exit Interstate 40 or I-85 onto US 220 North, which becomes Battleground Avenue. After approximately 10 miles, you'll pass Pisgah Church Road (approximately 2.5 miles north of Brassfield Shopping Center). Just past this point, look for the small sign on the right and turn onto Owl's Roost Road. Then turn left onto Bur-Mil Club Road and park in the paved lot near the driving range. The trailhead is located southwest out of the parking lot, just below the golf pavilion.

Source of additional information:

Bur-Mil Park
5834 Owl's Roost Road
Greensboro, NC 27410
(336) 545-5300

An example of the wide
double-track found on
Bur-Mil Runner's Trail.

Notes on the trail: The recommended direction of travel is clockwise, but there
is no rule against riding it the other way, and it certainly is wide enough. The
intersections leading to the soccer fields are well marked. The connector leading away from the fields turns right. Three creeks are crossed in the next 2 miles.
After that, a **T** intersection is made with a well-groomed double-track. Turn right.
The double-track continues straight for about a half mile before going around
Little Loop, an additional 1-mile loop.

RIDE 27 · Owl's Roost Trail

AT A GLANCE

NC

Length/configuration: An out-and-back (3 miles one way, 6 miles total) with a 2-mile loop at the turnaround point; the trail width alternates between single- and double-track

Aerobic difficulty: No sustained climbs, but several steep hills call for a brief, extra effort

Technical difficulty: Tough moves are required over a few deadfalls, rocks, and angled roots

Scenery: It's a pretty ride along Lake Brandt, but you won't have time to look around while riding; be sure to stop and enjoy the view

Special comments: Part of the Greensboro Waterway Trails, sponsored by the Greensboro Fat Tire Society

These eight miles of single- and double-track (a two-mile loop at the end of a three-mile, one-way out-and-back) are only for those seeking a challenge. There are no lengthy climbs, but several technical ascents—along with each corresponding descent—make this trail a worthy proving ground for the best of riders. I spent as much time off the saddle as I did on it, some by design and some by accident.

Despite the technical demands (or maybe because of it), Owl's Roost Trail has become a local favorite, which partly explains the erosion of the more difficult sections. But Greensboro has a plan. They've hired a director, Mike Simpson, for its Lakes, Trails, and Greenways Division. On the day I arrived, Mike was busy preparing to install a 240-foot-long bridge on Lake Brandt, one of a series of lakes Greensboro uses as its water supply.

"Owl's Roost Trail used to cross the lake on a long trestle," Mike told me. "One day, in 1993 I believe, someone set fire to the trestle. Have you ever seen wood soaked in creosote burn? It burned for three days. Never could get it out." Plans are for rebuilding the trestle one day, but should that happen, mountain bikers will most likely never be allowed on it, restricting the ride to Lake Brandt's western side.

General location: Owl's Roost is located within Bur-Mil Park, just north of Greensboro, North Carolina, off US 220.

Elevation change: Most of the elevation change occurs along the short, steep climbs and descents on either side of small creek ravines near the lake. Otherwise, it is basically level.

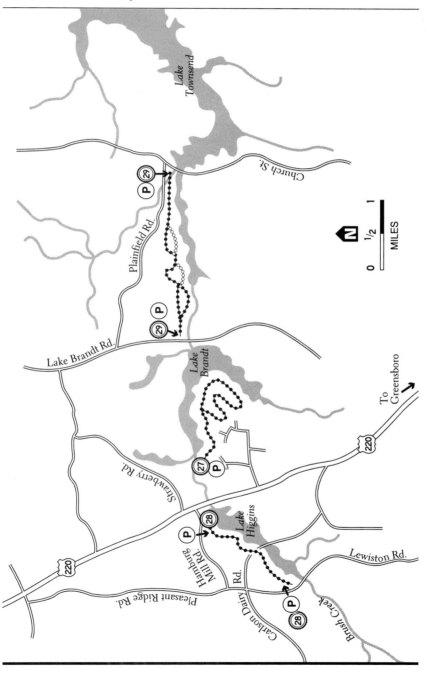

Season: This trail is open year-round.

Services: Bur-Mil Park has rest rooms and water. Nearby Greensboro has the rest, including a bike mechanic to tune your bike after the visit to Owl's Roost.

Hazards: Deadfalls provide hopping aplenty . . . and stopping. Angled, slick roots from trees lining the single-track can topple even the most agile. Watch for other bikers coming from the opposite direction.

Rescue index: The farthest reaches of Owl's Roost could provide a difficult setting for an easy rescue. Ride this trail prepared for self-rescue.

Land status: This is part of Greensboro's greenway, a buffer surrounding Higgins, Brandt, Jeanette, and Townsend Lakes, the city's water supply.

Maps: Greensboro Watershed Trails map is provided by the Parks and Recreation Department. But the map doesn't show the precise layout of the trail. Using my own notes, I drew the map here, which shows some (but not all) of the many of the intersections.

Finding the trail: Exit Interstate 40 or I-85 onto US 220 North, which becomes Battleground Avenue. After approximately 10 miles, you'll pass Pisgah Church Road (2.5 miles north of Brassfield Shopping Center). Look for the small road sign on the right for Owl's Roost Road. Turn right here. Then turn left shortly onto Bur-Mil Club Road and park in the paved lot near the driving range. The trailhead for the Bur-Mil Trail is located southwest out of the parking lot, just below the golf pavilion. Take this trail until it comes into Owl's Roost Trail, near the fishing pier, or ride directly to the clubhouse on the gravel road, which also leads to the fishing pier.

Source of additional information:

Mike Simpson
Lakes, Trails, and Greenways Director
Parks and Recreation Department
City of Greensboro
5834 Owl's Roost Road
Greensboro, NC 27410
(336) 545-5300 or 545-0172

Notes on the trail: Beginning at the fishing pier, start down the double-track for approximately 10 yards and turn left onto the single-track. A "Hail Mary" downhill occurs soon and is marked at the top by a juniper bearing scars from many a bike collision. Soon after, a portage through a quagmire has to be completed. Signs point the way through the various intersections, and the well-worn trail should be easy to follow. The trail forks 2.5 miles from the fishing pier. Take the right fork and follow more blazes for a counterclockwise loop. After completing the approximate 2-mile loop, go straight past the left turn (it began the loop, remember?) and ride the route back to the fishing pier.

RIDE 28 · Bald Eagle Trail

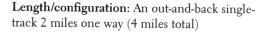

AT A GLANCE

Length/configuration: An out-and-back single-track 2 miles one way (4 miles total)

Aerobic difficulty: The general grade of this trail is level

Technical difficulty: Some sections require above average handling skills, giving inexperienced bikers a challenge

Scenery: As the name suggests, you might spot a bald eagle along this lakeside trail

Special comments: This is another trail sponsored by the Greensboro Fat Tire Society

The two miles of this out-and-back single-track (four miles total) eventually make it to the backwaters of Lake Higgins, one of a series of lakes supplying the greater Greensboro area with its municipal water. Much of the trail passes under the canopy of fairly young woods, comprised mainly of Virginia pines and sweet gum trees. The forest floor sports an assortment of viny growth: Virginia creeper, creeping cedar, and poison ivy.

The trail follows a ridge line of former farmland. What forced the farmers to move, however, gave bald eagles and humans a good fishing hole. The trail used to extend another mile one way (2 miles total), reaching Long Valley Road. City officials, however, allow hiking only past Lewiston Road.

General location: Bald Eagle Trail is located north of Greensboro, North Carolina, just west of US 220.

Elevation change: Very little change occurs on this trail.

Season: This trail is open to bikers all year.

Services: The trailhead has naught but a parking lot, but US 220 is nearby, a main Greensboro highway that leads to a full range of goods and services.

Hazards: Hikers may be present on this trail; also, oncoming bike traffic is likely. A creek crossing may be a challenge for some bikers.

Rescue index: A rescue should be easy to carry out on this trail. This area is fairly well developed, with subdivisions nearby. The trail never gets far from a paved road, should a walk out become necessary.

Land status: This route is part of the Greensboro Watershed Trails system, a network of trails designed by the Greensboro city government.

Sloshing across a small slough on Bald Eagle Trail. Photo by Joe Surkiewicz.

Maps: The basic map, Greensboro Watershed Trails, is free for the asking from the Parks and Recreation Department.

Finding the trail: Exit Interstate 40 or I-85 and head north on US 220, which becomes Battleground Avenue. After approximately 10 miles and crossing Lake Higgins, turn to the left on Hamburg Mill Road. The parking lot for the trailhead is bordered on two sides by a chain-link fence. The turn into the lot is the second possible left, just past the entrance to the Lake Higgins Marina.

Sources of additional information:

Mike Simpson
Lakes, Trails, and Greenways Director
Parks and Recreation Department
City of Greensboro
5834 Owl's Roost Road
Greensboro, NC 27410
(336) 545-5300 or 545-0172

Greensboro Fat Tire Society
P.O. Box 9524
Greensboro, NC 27429-0524
(336) 373-1029

Notes on the trail: The out-and-back route is plainly marked. Watch for cars when crossing Carlson Dairy Road. This trail is an ideal destination for those just beginning to bike off-road. Enough challenge, however, is present so that it stays interesting even for the experienced rider.

RIDE 29 · Reedy Fork Trail

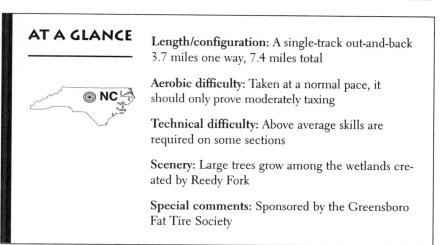

AT A GLANCE

Length/configuration: A single-track out-and-back 3.7 miles one way, 7.4 miles total

Aerobic difficulty: Taken at a normal pace, it should only prove moderately taxing

Technical difficulty: Above average skills are required on some sections

Scenery: Large trees grow among the wetlands created by Reedy Fork

Special comments: Sponsored by the Greensboro Fat Tire Society

The 3.7 miles of single-track on this lakeside out-and-back (7.4 miles total) represent the best of Greensboro off-road biking. This network of trails weaves in and out of a mature, mixed hardwoods forest, never on the level for long. Large specimens of beech and maple trees tower above the understory, looking like sentinels with their fat trunks. The trail sometimes splits narrowly between some of the trees, and the trail lacks, for the most part, any aerobic demand. But its twisting, narrow route requires above average handling skills and concentration.

When I rode it, the trail showed signs of recent construction, with several fresh-looking routes splitting off and reconnecting to the trail later on. The trail's layout diverts traffic away from the sensitive wetter areas close to the creek. The addition of trails to the basic out-and-back design caters to the way a biker—and not a hiker—travels, which comes as no surprise since the sponsoring club is Greensboro's Fat Tire Society, a hardworking group of hammerheads who know the value of a trail well laid. Their efforts have made Reedy Fork a fun place to ride.

General location: Reedy Fork Trail is located north of Greensboro, North Carolina, just east of US 220.

This view of Lake Brandt can be seen near the eastern trailhead at Plainfield Road.

Elevation change: There is only slight change. The trail is comprised mainly of rolling terrain, with an occasional short, steep hill.

Season: This trail is open to bikers all year. The dense forest cover makes for a shady ride during the hot months.

Services: Greensboro lies 10 or so miles to the south, where most services can be found. The trailhead has no water or rest rooms.

Hazards: Nothing out of the ordinary; however, riding over some exposed roots can be tricky, especially when they are wet.

Rescue index: This trail lies close to main roads, making rescue a relatively easy affair.

Land status: Part of Greensboro's Watershed Trail system.

Maps: The map of the Greensboro Watershed Trails gives trail locations and parking areas, but no specific information about the ride. The map can be obtained from area bike shops or the office for the Lakes, Trails, and Greenways Division of Greensboro's Parks and Recreation Department. The map here was drawn using notes taken and placed on a tracing taken from the DeLorme *North Carolina Atlas & Gazetteer.*

Finding the trail: Exit Interstate 40 or I-85 and head north on US 220, which becomes Battleground Avenue. Turn right on Strawberry Road and travel a short distance. Turn right again on SR 150 and go until you see the sign for Lake Brandt Road on the right. Turn here. Just before you cross the bridge, turn left into a small gravel parking lot, which marks the trailhead.

Sources of additional information:

Mike Simpson
Lakes, Trails, and Greenways Director
Parks and Recreation Department
City of Greensboro
5834 Owl's Roost Road
Greensboro, NC 27410
(336) 545-5300 or 545-0172

Greensboro Fat Tire Society
P.O. Box 9524
Greensboro, NC 27429-0524
(336) 373-1029

Notes on the trail: Most out-and-backs follow the same leg out and back. Reedy Fork basically follows this configuration, but the main route often forks, offering a route over low, wetter areas or high, drier ones. Take the higher route whenever possible, especially during periods following a rain. Paper arrows tacked to trees mark these intersections. A short, quarter-mile section of trail uses a somewhat busy gravel road just long enough to cross a bridge. Immediately after crossing the bridge, look for the right turn onto single-track leading back into the forest. Of course, if you want a shorter out-and-back, turn around at the bridge and make it a 5-mile total trip. The best section, however, lies east and across the bridge leading toward Plainfield Road.

RIDE 30 · Catawba Riverfront Mountain Bike Park

AT A GLANCE

Length/configuration: A 12-mile loop, mostly single-track

Aerobic difficulty: Some stretches that work the lungs extra hard

Technical difficulty: Be prepared to use combat moves in order to stay upright on some sections of this trail

Scenery: The sound of Interstate 85 on the southern border takes away somewhat from this county park along the Catawba River; both a gas line and power line cut their way through some of the single-track sections; there are some pretty spots along the river

Special comments: I was told this is where the serious mountain bikers come to sharpen their skills for upcoming races

RIDE 30 · Catawba Riverfront Mountain Bike Park

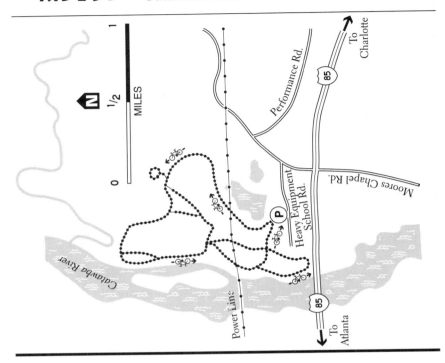

This 12-mile loop (mostly single-track, with some double-track) along the Catawba River has sections as demanding as anywhere in Charlotte. Touted as the showcase for the Tarheel Trailblazers, Charlotte's off-road biking club, Catawba Riverfront Mountain Bike Park draws riders from all over the southeast to compete in and train for races. This trail can be extremely demanding as it winds through a young forest. Some sections call for precise handling for a clean run between two tree trunks, with less than an inch of clearance on either side of the handlebars.

Catawba's best asset is its central location. Located barely off I-85, Charlotte-area bikers flock here at all times of the day, but its heaviest use occurs, naturally, in the afternoons and on weekends. Catawba is crisscrossed with signs of urban sprawl (power lines and gas lines, the hum of interstate traffic just beyond the tree-line), but what it lacks in natural beauty is balanced by its exclusivity: Mecklenburg County set aside this acreage at the end of Heavy Equipment School Road for mountain bikers only. No horses. No hikers. Hammerheads only.

General location: Located just west of Charlotte and just off I-85.

Elevation change: Due to the natural topography in the Piedmont region, there aren't any places with long, sustained climbs. Still, the trail builders used the lay of the land well and incorporated several short, steep climbs.

The typical trail seldom stays straight—or flat—for long. Photo by Pam Jones.

Season: I don't know how many riders actually adhere to the posted advisory for wet-weather riding, but the stated rule is "Wait 3 days after a rain" before taking to the single-track. Otherwise, it's an all-season trail.

Services: No services are found at the trailhead; however, Charlotte, a major metropolitan area, is just a traffic jam away.

Hazards: Rocks, roots, and drop-offs make up the bulk of obstacles. The recommended direction of travel on this trail is counterclockwise, but watch for misdirected riders coming head-on.

Rescue index: The trail's popularity makes receiving quick assistance likely. The interstate is nearby.

Land status: Managed by Mecklenburg County, North Carolina.

Maps: *The 5th Official Edition of the Charlotte Area Mountain Bike Ride Guide*, really a packet of maps that costs $2, is available at many area bike shops. It lists this trail and three others. Proceeds from the sale of this guide go to Tarheel Trailblazers, a worthy and hardworking group of mountain bikers who do regular trail maintenance on this and other area trails.

Finding the trail: Take exit 29 (Sam Wilson Road) and head west out of Charlotte on I-85. Turn right (north) and take the first left onto Performance Road. Where Performance Road comes into Moore's Chapel Road, turn left. Take the next right onto Heavy Equipment School Road. The trail begins at the end of the road.

Sources of additional information:

Tarheel Trailblazers
P.O. Box 35273
Charlotte, NC 28235
(704) 559-8076

B.I.K.E.S. of Charlotte/Mecklenburg
4825 Deanscroft Drive
Charlotte, NC 28226

Notes on the trail: Begin the counterclockwise loop by riding west past the gate and into the power-line clearing. Take a right before crossing the clearing. The trail goes into the forest on the east (trailhead) side of the right-of-way. After passing a pond on the right, parallel the opening until you get to the edge of the trees. Look for a large mound. Go over it and continue straight for about 40 yards. After a short distance, turn left. Then watch for the trail to go right. A sign is posted at the treeline. Take the right at this point and ride onto the double-track service road. Look for the single-track to go back into the woods about a half mile farther up on the left. This is where the loop begins its bend back to the trailhead. The single-track stays in between the power-line opening and the river. Cross the gas line right-of-way and turn right onto the single-track. Ride along the Catawba's banks before making a final climb toward the trailhead. About halfway up the final climb, look for the clockwise loop going off to the right. It reenters the main trail on the right, just before the power line right-of-way.

RIDE 31 · Cane Creek Park

AT A GLANCE

Length/configuration: 4 miles of double-track (with some single-track) loop combinations of various lengths (8 miles total), connected to a 3.2-mile out-and-back (6.4 miles total); if you ride the entire length, it's almost 15 miles

Aerobic difficulty: There are no long, grueling climbs

Technical difficulty: Except for a couple of rocky drop-and-climbs in and out around creeks, this is a fairly easy trail—a good one for bikers building an experience base

Scenery: The single-track generally follows the banks of Cane Creek Lake

Special comments: The camping facilities at the park make it easy to stick around and spend a couple of days exploring side trails, fishing, and swimming

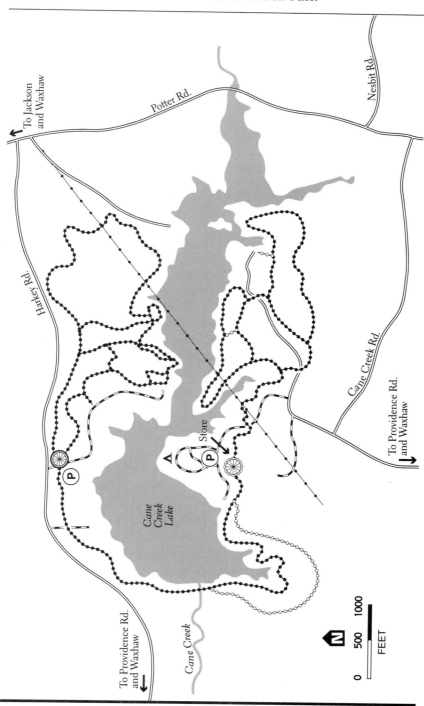

Potter Rd.

Nesbit Rd.

To Jackson
and Waxhaw

Harley Rd.

Cane Creek Rd.

Store

To Providence Rd.
and Waxhaw

Cane
Creek
Lake

Cane Creek

To Providence Rd.
and Waxhaw

N

0   500   1000
FEET

My son Jared and I showed up at this Union County (North Carolina) park, near the border of South Carolina, knowing only that there were approximately 15 miles of moderately difficult double-track (with some single-track) scattered throughout the park. After picking up a map at the entrance to the day-use area, we saw that there are basically two loop combinations: one on the southern side of Cane Creek Lake by the campground, and another on the northern (day-use) side. They are connected by an open double-track on top of the dam.

Since we wanted to set up the tents first, we headed over to the campground and its trailhead. The store where guests register was closed. We wanted to get set up, so we waved to a county deputy patrolling the area in his cruiser. He said we could go ahead and enjoy our ride and that another deputy would be at the store later to check us in.

It was getting late in the afternoon, and we weren't sure what we were getting ourselves into, so we started behind the camp store and rode north to the day-use area. The mixed hardwood forest arching over the single-track kept us shaded for the most part until we reached the dam. The lake was created back in 1976 as part of a combined project (the Cane Creek Watershed Project) completed by the Union County and federal governments. It's a popular fishing spot.

As we rode closer to the lake, we heard huge carp plopping into the water. Great blue herons and osprey took positions on lakeside branches, looking for a meal. Although the deer were bedded down for the day, we saw plenty of their hoof prints in the sand. Riding back to the campground, mushroom thunderheads began piling up over the lake, promising an evening shower.

General location: About 25 miles south of Charlotte, North Carolina, outside of Waxhaw.

Elevation change: The bulk of the elevation change occurs around the few creeks flowing into this Piedmont region lake.

Season: This is an all-season trail, with trail maintenance generally scheduled for winter's less busy days. We rode the trails in midsummer, when many trails typically suffer erosion from heavy use, but we found the trails in great shape.

Services: Cane Creek Park is a full-service facility with water, rest rooms, and showers. Jared and I stayed at the less-developed primitive campground, a 100-yard walk to the campsites down on the lake bank. A small camp store has the basics, but Charlotte—one of the southeast's major cities—is not far.

Hazards: Horseback riders and hikers use the trail system; be prepared to yield the trail. Some steep, rocky areas near the creeks can give trouble to bikers with relatively little experience. The trail crosses the park road in places; watch for traffic.

Rescue index: A rescue should be fairly easy. The trail never goes far from the paved road outside the park's boundaries. Several houses are nearby.

Land status: A Union County (North Carolina) park.

Jared warms up on the wide trail at Cane Creek Park.

Maps: A detailed map (which was used to complete the map found here) can be picked up for free at the day-use office during normal business hours.

Finding the trail: From your starting point, choose the most direct way to Waxhaw, North Carolina, and head west on NC 75. Less than a mile from downtown, a sign for the park will point to the right turn onto Old Waxhaw-Monroe Road. Drive for just under 2 miles and turn right onto Providence Road, where a sign for the park is posted. After stopping at and crossing NC 200, it's nearly another 3 miles to the left turn onto Harkey Road. The entrance to the day-use area is a mile up on the right. Turn here and look for the trail crossing the pavement before you reach the office and the parking lot.

Source of additional information:

Cane Creek Park
5213 Harkey Road
Waxhaw, NC 28173
(704) 843-3919

Notes on the trail: The trail system is divided into two parts: the northern portion, located nearest the day-use area, and the southern single-track, nearest the campground. The 3.2-mile (6.4 miles total) out-and-back connector between the two sides of the lake (purple blazes) goes over the dam, with Cane Creek flowing to the west in the valley. A variety of trail networks, each blazed a different color, can be ridden on either side of the lake. However, the yellow blazes are for foot travel only.

RIDE 32 · Beech Spring Mountain Bike Park

AT A GLANCE

Length/configuration: 4.8 miles of loop combinations, mainly single-track

Aerobic difficulty: There are no long climbs, but excitement alone can keep you breathing hard

Technical difficulty: Although many of the extremely technical sections can be avoided by taking easier routes, some have to either be ridden . . . or walked

Scenery: As suggested by its name, several large beech trees grow on the ridges above the spring forming Slippery Rock Creek

Special comments: Devil's Drop, Gravity Cavity, and Rock Dam—after riding these, the names will be branded on your brain; Beech Spring is great fun, but it's not for the faint of balance; this is a pay-per-ride single-track, and worth every penny

My son and I showed up at the trailhead of this 4.8-mile single-track (with some double-track) loop combination expecting a short but technical ride. We were not disappointed. After unloading our bikes, we signed the mandatory waiver at the bulletin board. The $2 fee per bike is collected on an honor system, with signs clearly stating that failure to pay is considered trespassing.

We headed off counterclockwise, down the hill to the right on a recently graded double-track farm road. Tractors regularly travel this road in order to reach the three nearby fields, planted in peanuts, a common cash crop in this part of Appalachia. The southern section is relatively easy if you don't ride down Devil's Drop. This hellish descent offers one of three ways down: rutty, ruttier, or ruttiest. And the choice is never clear.

RIDE 32 · Beech Spring Mountain Bike Park

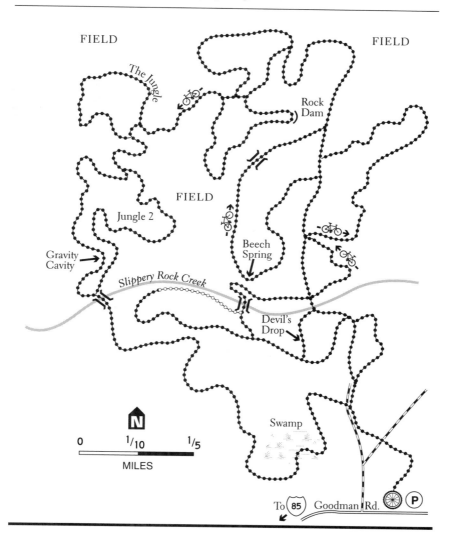

The owners of the farm, who also run the mountain bike park (and live across the street from the trailhead), have spanned Slippery Rock Creek with three different bridges. Numerous "Optional Trails" are clearly marked and lead off the main (red-blazed) trail. The next difficult challenge comes at Rock Dam. It's a good spot to ride the chute several times before going on to Gravity Cavity.

This depressed bowl is approximately 30 yards long by a little more than 10 yards wide. The radical vertical change in elevation will give the newcomer reason to pause before plunging over the lip. The short drop (a 10-yarder) makes

This young rider completes his first flight through Gravity Cavity, displaying a common symptom— the dropped jaw.

you feel like a fighter pilot in a nose dive. After reaching the bottom, the bike's momentum will nearly sling it all the way back up an equally steep ascent—but in order to clean the climb, a few strokes near the top are required, a somewhat difficult move the first time. The longer chute (30 yards across) allows time to pick up speed in the bottom of the bowl; catching air on the far side is the preferred exit move.

In addition to all the technical thrills here, Beech Spring is pretty. The large trees around the creek make for nice rest stops—or first-aid stations. While Jared and I were catching our breath, a young rider came up the hill near the last bridge. He had taken a spill in Gravity Cavity (who hasn't?) and fallen on his palm. Since he had been riding with no gloves, he had quite a gash. I put the first-aid kit to good use on him, and he was off, riding and smiling again . . . hopefully, to go buy some gloves.

General location: Approximately 15 miles north of Charlotte, North Carolina, very near Interstate 85.

Elevation change: Most sections with any significant elevation change aren't long, but if they got any steeper it would be like riding on your head.

Season: An all-season trail.

Services: The owners, who live across the street from the trailhead, would most likely allow the use of their facilities if there were an emergency; however, come to the trailhead prepared with water, etc. Charlotte is close by and has whatever other services you may require.

Hazards: Rocks, roots, steep drops, and deadfalls will present hazards. Helmets, of course, should always be worn, but they are especially recommended (and required) for legal riding on this trail.

Rescue index: This is a fairly busy trail. Jared and I rode in the middle of a week-day morning and encountered several riders on the trail and at the trailhead. Because of the large number of riders here, someone should ride by fairly soon should assistance be needed.

Land status: This is private property. Don't forget to pay and sign the waiver; otherwise, you're trespassing.

Maps: Maps were available free at the information station; they are accurate and well done. The map is also included in *The 5th Official Edition of the Charlotte Area Mountain Bike Ride Guide*, price $2, available at many area bike shops. The guide includes this trail and three others. Proceeds go to Tarheel Trailblazers, a worthy and hardworking group of mountain bikers who do regular trail maintenance on this and other area trails.

Finding the trail: This one's easy. Head north out of Charlotte on I-85. Get off at exit 52 (Poplar Tent Road) and turn left over the interstate. Take Goodman Road (the first right) and travel approximately a mile. You'll see the parking lot on the left. The trail begins heading downhill on the double-track blazed with a red arrow.

Source of additional information:

Tarheel Trailblazers
P.O. Box 35273
Charlotte, NC 28235
(704) 559-8076

Notes on the trail: Ride this one counterclockwise as the map suggests. The trail is clearly and frequently marked. Each intersection is easy to find on the map. The trail starts off with a moderate section, twisting through a rock jumble and exposed roots. The trail's expert sites—Gravity Cavity and Devil's Drop—come halfway through the ride. The nameless sections occurring in between these two challenges, however, can be just as tough. The trail crosses the creek twice: once on the way out, and once on the way back in.

PISGAH NATIONAL FOREST: PISGAH DISTRICT

O ther places in North Carolina get recommended as *the* place to ride, but if I had to choose to ride in only one Appalachian area, the Pisgah District of the Pisgah National Forest would have to be it. Containing nearly 85,000 acres of what was formerly part of the vast Vanderbilt Estate, Pisgah became the first national forest east of the Mississippi, established in 1914. Few people then would have guessed that 85 years later, off-road cyclists would be exploring its extensive network of trails.

This land, which can be rightly called North Carolina's Bicycle Belt, lies in the triangle formed by Brevard, Asheville, and Hendersonville. It is quite probable that you could spend an entire lifetime of weekends discovering all the potential rides available here. So why wait? Time to get started.

Sources of additional information:

Liberty Bicycles
1987 Hendersonville Road
Asheville, NC 28803
(828) 684-1085

Breakaway Bicycle Shop
127 Charlotte Highway
Asheville, NC 28803
(828) 299-8770

Pisgah Bicycle Center
210 East Main Street
Brevard, NC 28712
(828) 966-9606

Shining Rock exhibits the type of elevation change found in Pisgah National Forest near Brevard, North Carolina.

RIDE 33 · Bent Creek

AT A GLANCE

NC

Length/configuration: A 6.5-mile loop of single- and double-track with a 1.6-mile one-way out-and-back (3.2 miles total)

Aerobic difficulty: This is no more than a moderate workout

Technical difficulty: Most of the route is not a challenge; there are, however, short sections requiring greater than beginner's skills

Scenery: Bent Creek Experimental Forest and Lake Powhatan

Special comments: Five different trail sections can be ridden from the same trailhead

The nearly 10 miles of double-track and single-track open for biking in Bent Creek Experimental Forest are comprised of a 6.5-mile loop, with a 1.6-mile one-way out-and-back (3.2 miles total) tacked on for good measure. This

RIDE 33 · Bent Creek

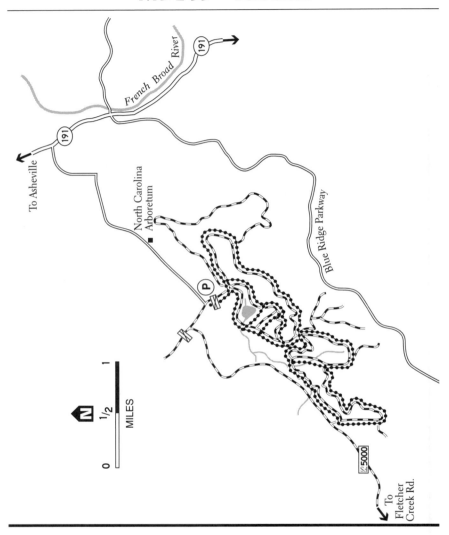

popular trailhead, actually called Hardtimes, is named for the gated road lead-ing to nearby Lake Powhatan. The road leads into a part of the original 1,100 acres George Vanderbilt purchased south of Asheville, part of which now con-tains the Biltmore House and its estates.

In 1935, 5,200 more acres were added on to the 1,100, and the Bent Creek Experimental Forest was formed. Its mission is to manage and develop natural resources, especially forests and wetlands—the perfect setting for mountain bik-ing. I showed up to ride this trail system on a bitterly cold and windy day, sure the trail would be empty, but the parking lot was overflowing. Bikers of all ages

Jared zips along under
some tall timber.

were heading out in large and small groups. Once I got out on the trail, I understood their excitement.

The loop around the lake is a good place to catch kingfishers and great blue herons stalking the shallows. And although I didn't see one, eagles hunt here as well. Otters also patrol these waters. As I made my way along the creek, I spotted a shadow darting in the small shoals. I watched it swim slowly against the current, nosing rocks and diving in shallow pools, searching for crawdads or minnows. At a small confluence, I noticed another sleek, brown body rise up from the ripples and chatter a greeting to its mate. I watched the two disappear into a curve upstream before returning to the trailhead—another ride well taken.

General location: Southwest of Asheville, North Carolina.

Elevation change: Changing some, but not much.

Season: An all-season trail.

Services: The trailhead has only parking and information. The campground at Lake Powhatan (just a hundred yards away) has water and rest rooms when it's open during the warmer months. Asheville, however, is just a short distance away and can provide all the goods and services.

Hazards: Other bikers and hikers are the biggest hazard. Some slippery spots and exposed roots require extra attention.

Rescue index: Rescue is easy on this trail. Asheville is nearby, and just down the road is the North Carolina Arboretum and a subdivision. It is unusual for this trail to be deserted.

Land status: In the Bent Creek Experimental Forest part of the Pisgah National Forest.

Maps: The trails are shown on the Pisgah District Trail Map, on sale at most local biking and hiking stores and, of course, at the Pisgah National Forest Visitor Center.

Finding the trail: Exit Interstate 26 at Highway 191 south of Asheville. Head south on Hwy. 191 for 2 miles, turning right at the light for Brevard Road. If you pass under the Blue Ridge Parkway, you've gone too far; look for a church on the left and turn around in its parking lot. Head back over the parkway and turn left at the next light (Brevard Road). The Hardtimes trailhead is 2.5 miles down Brevard Road, past the arboretum, and on the left.

Sources of additional information:

Bent Creek Experimental Forest
Southern Research Station
USDA
1577 Brevard Road
Asheville, NC 28806
(828) 667-5261

Pisgah District Ranger
USDA Forest Service
1001 Pisgah Highway
Pisgah Forest, NC 28768
(828) 877-3265

Notes on the trail: Take Hardtimes Road toward Lake Powhatan and turn right onto the orange-blazed Homestead Loop (a 1-mile loop around the lake) for about a half mile. Take the right onto the blue-blazed Pine Tree Loop and ride almost a mile, turning right onto the yellow-blazed Explorer Loop. After a little over a mile, Explorer Loop comes into a **T** intersection with 479H. Turn left and ride up Long Branch for about half a mile. Continue riding the yellow-blazed Explorer Loop by turning left again and heading northeast. Sleepy Gap Trail (an out-and-back of 1.8 miles one way, 3.6 miles total) turns off to the right a long mile farther; take it or pass it by. About a quarter mile past this intersection, turn left and cross Beaten Branch. Return to the blue blazes of Pine Tree Loop and turn right, riding a little over half a mile. A right turn onto Dew Field Trail (yellow blazes) leads into Homestead Loop Trail and along Lake Powhatan. After riding the lake's south shore for about half a mile, turn left onto Hardtimes Road, which takes you back to the trailhead.

RIDE 34 · Fletcher Creek Trail

AT A GLANCE

Length/configuration: A loop of single- and double-track, just over 9 miles

Aerobic difficulty: Not much hard breathing for this one

Technical difficulty: Moderately challenging in places, but mostly easy

Scenery: It's got a bit of everything: creek crossings, wildlife openings, and forest shade

Special comments: This ride begins at a common trailhead for several other trails

This nine-mile loop uses a wide, gated, and lightly graveled road, known as the Neverending Road for its long climb up Big Ridge, as a connector to an easy single-track coming back and following Fletcher Creek. For those with advanced or intermediate skills, other trails intersect with Fletcher Creek Road and can be added for additional mileage (see Notes on the Trail, below).

It's easy to understand why this area is so popular among mountain bikers. The mixed hardwood forest provides plenty of shade on those hot, midsummer rides. And in the winter, after leaf fall, expansive views open up to show the North Fork Mills River flowing between the twin cliffs of Forge Mountain and Bryson Mountain.

The double-track route is not only easy for beginning bikers to cruise, it is also a popular spot for wildlife of all sorts to leave their mark. On one stretch just before reaching the turnoff for the single-track, I observed buck ruts and bobcat scat. In the mud I saw the pug mark of a black bear. Oh yeah, I also identified two hammerheads and a scad of pokers.

General location: Just north of Brevard, North Carolina.

Elevation change: Very little change occurs, and most of it takes place between Spencer Branch and Fletcher Creek.

Season: An all-season trail.

Services: The North Mills River campground—at the intersection of FS 5000 and FS 1206—has bathrooms, water, and phones. Asheville and Brevard are the nearest sources of more specialized services.

Hazards: Other bikers, hikers, and horseback riders present the biggest hazards.

Rescue index: This trail poses little challenge for rescue. It has a wide forest service road nearby, but you should still ride prepared for self-rescue. The overall

RIDE 34 · Fletcher Creek Trail

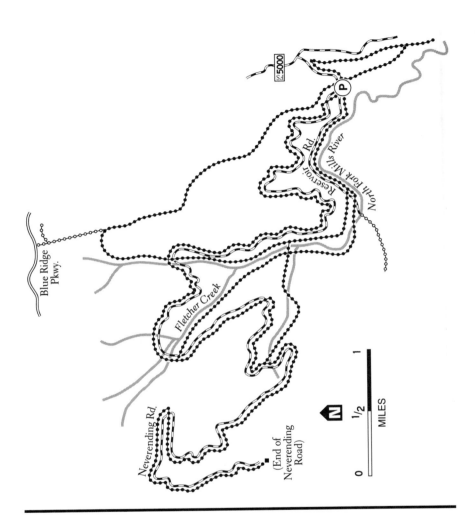

remoteness of the trail and the availability of other, adjoining trail destinations means bikers are spread out over more trails, so it's less likely you'll be discovered quickly.

Land status: In the Pisgah National Forest.

Maps: The trails are shown on the Pisgah District Trail Map, on sale at most local biking and hiking stores and, of course, at the Pisgah National Forest visitor centers.

Midwinter biking affords long, open views. Photo by Pam Jones.

Finding the trail: Leave Brevard headed north on US 64. Turn left onto US 276. Travel approximately 11 miles. Pink Beds Visitor Center is on the right. Travel another third of a mile and look for the right turn onto FS 1206. North Mills River Campground will be on the left approximately 12.5 miles east, signaled by a series of speed breakers. Look for FS 5000 and turn left. After 2 miles, look to the left for a turn across a bridge and onto FS 142. The trailhead and parking is a half mile ahead.

Source of additional information:

Pisgah District Ranger
USDA Forest Service
1001 Pisgah Highway
Pisgah Forest, NC 28768
(828) 877-3265

Notes on the trail: Fletcher Creek Road starts out behind the gated road farthest north (on the immediate right, facing the information station). A long mile later, cross Long Branch and begin a southerly track along the base of Coffee Pot Mountain. The North Fork Mills River is likely the sound heard below for the next mile on the turn back north. Fletcher Creek, then Spencer Branch, washes over the rocks, which can be seen down on the left. Spencer Branch Trail intersects 4.5 miles from the trailhead. Very little elevation is gained for the next mile. After crossing the three small creeks forming Fletcher Creek, take a left onto the blue-blazed Fletcher Creek Trail. Nearly 2 miles farther along, cross a big open-ing and continue downstream on the right (west) side of Fletcher Creek. The orange-blazed Middle Fork Trail comes in from the right after another short mile; bear left here and cross the creek. The next mile connects to Hendersonville Reservoir Road, which is the next **T** intersection. Turn left and take this gated ser-vice road another mile back to the parking lot.

Additional trails: The Fletcher Creek trailhead can be used for a combina-tion of trails, varying in length and difficulty.

Middle Fork: This orange-blazed trail is reached by following the Hender-sonville Reservoir Road west out of the parking lot. Turn right and take the Fletcher Creek Trail to the bridge. The intersection with Middle Fork occurs 25 yards past the bridge. After another 2 miles, you'll reach Fletcher Creek Road. Take a right and follow it until the intersection with Fletcher Creek Trail. Fol-low it back to the trailhead.

Big Creek: Take Hendersonville Reservoir Road west out of the parking lot. Continue straight past the intersection with Spencer Branch where the yellow blazes of Big Creek Trail begin. This trail follows an old railroad bed, but you'll get your feet wet on some of the bridgeless crossings of Big Creek. This is essen-tially a 6.5-mile one-way (13 miles total) out-and-back, with the far end occur-ring at the Blue Ridge Parkway, where, unfortunately, no parking is allowed.

Spencer Gap: This 8-mile loop begins by leaving the parking lot and heads back down FS 142, veering left at the intersection with FS 5000. The 2.5-mile climb up to Spencer Gap Trail is steep, but note the actual trail beginning (yellow blazes) on the left in a sharp right-hand switchback on FS 5000. The carsonite post is set back from FS 5000 approximately 100 feet. Take the next right fork through an opening. The gap is signaled by an intersection with Trace Ridge Trail. Turn left, followed by a quick right to continue on what begins Spencer Branch Trail. This section leads across Fletcher Creek Road, then to an intersection with Fletcher Creek Trail (blue blazes). Either turn left onto Fletcher Creek Trail or go straight toward Hendersonville Reservoir.

Trace Ridge Trail: This is the most difficult trail leaving the Fletcher Creek trailhead. Take the red-blazed upper trail (the one farther on the right, facing the information station) splitting off of Fletcher Creek Road at the gate. It's a long, 2-mile climb right out of the gate. You're Blue Ridge Parkway bound, but don't go all the way to the parkway. Turn left instead at the intersection with Spencer Branch Trail and ride a combination of Fletcher Creek Road, Fletcher Creek Trail, or Middle Fork Trail, or head up Big Creek.

North Fork Mills River–Wash Creek: These two trails make a short but diffi-cult 4-mile loop. Leave Fletcher Creek parking lot headed west on Henderson-ville Reservoir Road. Take the blue-blazed North Fork Mills River Trail to the left. Another left turn at the river leads to a series of bridgeless crossings—ideal for a summer day but not so good when it's cold or the water's up. Turn left to complete the counterclockwise route back to an intersection with Wash Creek Trail (yellow blazes), or continue on the blue blazes. If you take Wash Creek, turn left onto FS 142, a gravel road about a half mile away from the trailhead.

RIDE 35 · Slate Rock–Pilot Cove

AT A GLANCE

Length/configuration: A 7-mile, mostly single-track loop

Aerobic difficulty: Portions of this trail will require maximum aerobic exertion

Technical difficulty: Expect to dismount for pushes up, down, and across some obstacles unless your technique is magnifique

Scenery: The tall mountains on the left are Slate Rock and Pilot Rock; the two creeks are Pilot Cove Creek and Slate Rock Creek—beautiful any time of the year

Special comments: Don't expect to ride this in less than 2 hours; some sections require a slow go for both safety's and beauty's sake

The technical and aerobic challenges of this seven-mile loop (over five miles of which is single-track, the remainder on a lightly graveled road) have a large return. The scenery along the bowl formed by Laurel Ridge to the north is a mountain biker's dream. Open hardwood forests give shady relief on the hottest day, and with the sights and sounds of several creeks splashing down the mountainside, it's easy to take "just one more break."

The steep climb up to Slate Rock Ridge will require a dismount and push, but the view is more than worth it. A series of rollers follows Slate Rock Creek, which quickly grows larger from the small streams pouring into it, down the wet side of Laurel Ridge. In places, ferns blanket the ground with large swatches of green. The sound of Slate Rock Creek builds to a roar after the trail turns south. Large rocks and boulders form the streambed under a nearly uninterrupted cascade of white water, punctuated by two tall, prominent waterfalls.

General location: Just north of Brevard, North Carolina.

Elevation change: Nearly a thousand feet is gained, much of it in the first couple of miles.

Season: This is an all-season trail, with the best times for riding coming in the warmer times of spring and fall.

Services: The Pink Beds Visitor Center has rest rooms, water, and a phone. Nearby Brevard provides a full range of goods and services.

Hazards: This trail is also open to hikers and, naturally, other bikers. There is

N

0   1/2   1
MILES

Bradley Creek

Slate Rock Creek

Pilot Cove

P

P

S. 5014

S. 1206

Slate Rock, as seen from
FS 476.

no established direction of travel, so watch for oncoming bikers and hikers on
the narrow stretches.

Rescue index: Chances are good that someone else will be riding this trail and
can lend a helping hand on a weekend, but the overall remote setting makes it
a good idea to ride prepared for self-rescue at other times.

Land status: In the Pisgah National Forest.

Maps: The trails are shown on the Pisgah District Trail Map, on sale at most
local biking and hiking stores, and, of course, at the Pisgah National Forest visitor centers.

Finding the trail: Leave Brevard headed north on US 64. Turn left onto US
276. Travel approximately 11 miles. Pink Beds Visitor Center is on the right.
Look for the right turn onto FS 1206 about a third of a mile farther down. Go
about 3.5 miles farther. FS 476 will be on the right. The westernmost trailhead
for Slate Rock and Pilot Cove will be on the left, 2 miles from the intersection
of FS 1206 and FS 476. It's another 1.6 miles to the easternmost trailhead, also
on the left, just after crossing the bridge. Choosing when you want to climb the
gravel road (first or last) will determine where your ride begins. I like to climb

the gravel road first; therefore, the directions I've given begin from the eastern-most trailhead and follow a clockwise direction.

Source of additional information:

Pisgah District Ranger
USDA Forest Service
1001 Pisgah Highway
Pisgah Forest, NC 28768
(828) 877-3265

Notes on the trail: By the time the approach is completed from the eastern trailhead to the western trailhead on FS 1206 all muscle groups will be sufficiently warmed and ready for the aerobic onslaught on the climb to Slate Rock Ridge. Take the right turn off the road onto the blue-blazed Slate Rock–Pilot Cove Trail and reach an intersection with a road coming in from the left. From here to Slate Rock Ridge is a steep climb, with a gain of 400 feet in approximately a half mile. Continue straight at the second creek crossing, after which a loss of nearly a thousand feet occurs down to the bridge at FS 1206. Note the waterfalls at the top and yet another falls shortly before the trailhead at the bridge. Take care not to disturb the troll under the bridge.

Additional Routes Nearby: From the western trailhead for Slate Rock–Pilot Cove, ride past FS 5055 a third of a mile. Laurel Mountain Trail (blue blazed) begins here on the left and goes approximately 7 miles before joining the Laurel Connector (yellow blazed) and turning south (to the left) for a third of a mile. It intersects with the difficult and steep Pilot Rock Trail (orange blazed), which intersects with FS 1206 2 miles away. Turn left after reaching FS 1206 to complete the loop back to the Laurel Mountain trailhead, 4.6 miles east.

And if that isn't enough for one area, continue east from Laurel Mountain trailhead a quarter of a mile and start out on the gated road to the right, FS 5015. It takes a little over 2 miles to reach the orange-blazed Bradley Creek Trail. Taking a right at this point leads back to FS 1206 about 2 miles north; however, a left turn at the intersection of FS 5015 and Bradley Creek Trail will make a clockwise loop of approximately 5 miles, achieved by first passing the yellow-blazed Laurel Creek Trail on the right and then taking right turns at the next four intersections, ending at the intersection of Laurel Creek Trail and Bradley Creek Trail.

RIDE 36 · The Pink Beds

AT A GLANCE

Length/configuration: An approximate 7.75-mile loop, mostly single-track

Aerobic difficulty: This is not a demanding ride aerobically

Technical difficulty: Relatively easy

Scenery: Creek crossings amid lush growth of rhododendron

Special comments: This ride is open to mountain bikes from October 15 to April 15 only

This loop of approximately 7.75 miles has a bit of every surface: single-track, double-track, gravel road—even a tiny piece of pavement. The grade stays relatively flat, which makes the Pink Beds a good destination for bikers just beginning to discover the joys of off-road riding. Call it a "Cradle of Cycling."

But the real cradle in the region is the Cradle of Forestry, where Carl Schenck and Gifford Pinchot first established a school just down the road to study the production of timber as a renewable resource. Of course, modern forestry's founders had no way of knowing that the network of logging roads they used would one day be developed as mountain bike trails.

The area was named for the abundance of pink flowers that bloom in the boggy bottoms. But since the majority of the blooming takes place after mid-April (the time when bikes must leave the trail to hikers only), this spectacular display must be explored on foot. But when the hike is over, head back to the car and hop on the bike. A great ride is just five minutes away in Pilot Cove (see Ride 35).

General location: Just north of Brevard, North Carolina.

Elevation change: Expect only nominal changes in elevation on this route—what little elevation is gained and lost is done so gradually.

Season: This trail is open for bikes October 15 through April 15.

Services: Pink Beds Visitor Center has rest rooms, water, and a phone. Nearby Brevard can provide a wide range of services.

Hazards: Be alert for hikers on this popular trail. Some slippery, rooty, rutty sections can be a problem for the inattentive. Also, the third of a mile that is on US 276 deserves caution since it is a busy highway with cars, trucks, and long-bodied RV campers.

RIDE 36 · The Pink Beds
RIDE 37 · Buckwheat Knob

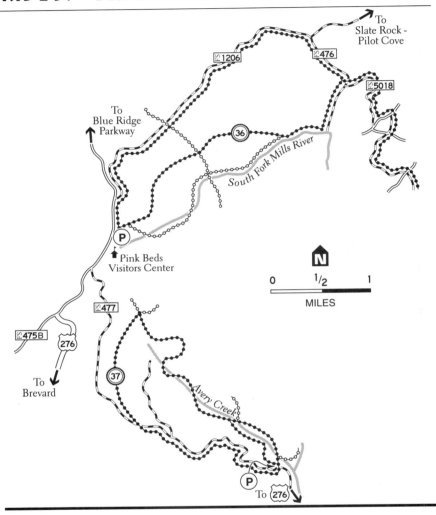

Rescue index: The Pink Beds Trail provides one of the more convenient places for a rescue, with a major paved highway and a visitor center nearby.

Land status: In the Pisgah National Forest, Pisgah District.

Maps: The trails are shown on the Pisgah District Trail Map, on sale at most local biking and hiking stores and, of course, at the Pisgah National Forest visitor centers.

Finding the trail: Leave Brevard headed north on US 64. Turn left onto US

Sharp turns and a tight track: two good reasons to visit the trails at Pisgah National Forest. Photo by Pam Jones.

276. Travel approximately 11 miles. After passing the Cradle of Forestry on the right, look for the sign for Pink Beds. Turn right and park in the lot.

Source of additional information:

Pisgah District Ranger
USDA Forest Service
1001 Pisgah Highway
Pisgah Forest, NC 28768
(828) 877-3265

Notes on the trail: Leave the parking lot headed east on the orange-blazed trail. After a short distance, take the left fork at the intersection, where a sign for the right fork indicates no bikes are allowed regardless of the season. It's approximately 2.5 miles from this intersection (and three creek crossings) to the intersection with the eastbound (white-blazed) Pink Beds Extension Loop. Slightly less than a mile from here, cross over the creek (actually the beginning of the South Fork Mills River) and intersect with FS 476 where a left turn begins the nearly 1.5-mile section to FS 1206. Along FS 476, look on the right for the gated gravel road about halfway to FS 1206. This gravel road can be ridden for an additional 2 miles one way, 4 miles total. Turn left onto FS 1206 for the 3.5 miles back to the intersection with the paved US 276. It is a third of a mile back to the Pink Beds Visitor Center along the paved busy highway.

RIDE 37 · Buckwheat Knob

AT A GLANCE

NC

Length/configuration: A 7.25-mile loop of mostly single-track

Aerobic difficulty: Many rides in the Pisgah National Forest will tax your heart and lungs, and Buckwheat Knob is no exception

Technical difficulty: This is not an easy trail in places; rocks, roots, and stream crossings all contribute to Buckwheat's moderately demanding technical challenge

Scenery: Rhododendron and hardwoods cling to the steep sides of Buckwheat Knob in the Avery Creek watershed

Special comments: Frequent primitive camping spots near the trailhead can make a day on the trail as easy as riding out of camp

This seven-mile-plus loop uses nearly five miles of single-track and a little over two miles of forest service road for what is a technical journey deep into Pisgah's woods. Plan for a couple of hour's worth of riding, part of which will be on the steep uphill (probably off-bike) climb to Buckwheat Knob. But don't let that scare you off. A biker once told me, "If you aren't hiking, you aren't biking." Also, what goes up will come back down—and in a shirt-flapping hurry on this ride.

The climb along the rolling ridge leading to Buckwheat Knob takes place among a mature hardwood forest, where the year-round users of this region are frequently seen: deer, turkeys, squirrels, and hawks, to name a few. The sounds of the southern Appalachians are a special dimension of mountain biking at Pisgah. I was surrounded by an orchestra of songbirds twittering and chittering when I rode this trail—that is, when the wind wasn't whistling through my helmet.

General location: Just north of Brevard, North Carolina.

Elevation change: An overall gain of about 1,500 feet.

The only thing better than a day in the woods is a day in the woods on a bike. Photo by Pam Jones

Season: An all-season trail; in late fall and winter, the trail has fewer users, making for a more intimate setting.

Services: The Pisgah Ranger Station has rest rooms, water, and a phone. Nearby Brevard provides a complete list of services.

Hazards: Along with the typical trail hazards found in steep terrain (rocks, roots, and stream crossings), add hikers and other bikers to the list. The portion of the loop that is on FS 477 is narrow and is traveled by cars and horses.

Rescue index: Even though Pisgah National Forest is a popular destination for hikers and bikers, trail traffic can be infrequent at certain times of the year, making a rescue at those times less likely. So ride prepared for self-rescue.

Land status: In the Pisgah National Forest.

Maps: The trails are shown on the Pisgah District Trail Map, on sale at most local biking and hiking stores and, of course, at the Pisgah National Forest visitor centers.

Finding the trail: Leave Brevard headed north on US 64. Turn left onto US 276. Just past the ranger station on the right (less than a mile), look for a gravel road (FS 477), also on the right. A sign for the horse stables is posted at the turn. The hitching post for horses (on the right at Clawhammer Road) is the next landmark. Avery Creek trailhead is approximately three-quarters of a mile from Clawhammer Road on the right. Park here and begin with the double-track FS 477 portion of the clockwise loop. Or drive farther up on FS 477 to the trailhead of Trail 24, start with the single-track, and end with the section on FS 477.

Source of additional information:

> Pisgah District Ranger
> USDA Forest Service
> 1001 Pisgah Highway
> Pisgah Forest, NC 28768
> (828) 877-3265

Notes on the trail: If you park at the Avery Creek trailhead, you'll climb the forest road first (this is the route I prefer). No matter which section you choose to ride first, I recommend riding in a clockwise direction. About 2.5 miles after beginning at the intersection of Avery Creek trailhead with FS 477, the yellow-blazed Buckwheat Knob single-track trail begins on the right. Ride the single-track for about 1.5 miles to an intersection with (and at) Club Gap. Turn right onto Avery Creek Trail. The next intersection occurs a couple of miles up. Twin Falls begins on the left (foot travel only), Upper Avery Creek Trail is the right fork, and Avery Creek Trail continues straight. Go straight, bearing right at the next intersection with Clawhammer Cove (foot travel only). FS 477 is rejoined a couple hundred yards farther up.

RIDE 38 · Thrift Cove

AT A GLANCE

Length/configuration: 4-mile double-track loop

Aerobic difficulty: Moderate to strenuous

Technical difficulty: Easy to moderate

Scenery: The ride follows the curve inside a mountain cove; creeks and springs are prominent, as are expansive views through a mixed hardwood forest

Special comments: Riding this trail in both directions is legal, but the counterclockwise direction allows the wettest, steepest, and rockiest section to be ridden downhill

RIDE 38 · Thrift Cove

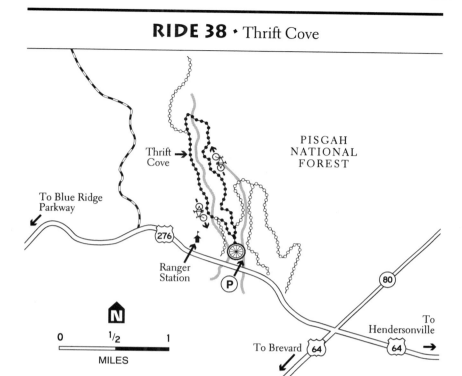

Thrift Cove

To Blue Ridge Parkway

PISGAH NATIONAL FOREST

276

Ranger Station

P

80

To Hendersonville

To Brevard 64

64

N

0   ¹/₂   1

MILES

This four-mile classic climb-and-drop (two miles up, two miles down) double-track loop can be used as the starting point for at least 12 more single-track miles adjoining it. Thrift Cove has been described in some guides as easy (even the official Pisgah National Forest map describes it that way), but it's misleading to reach this trailhead expecting an easy ride. The technical requirements on the wet and rocky western downhill demand skill, strength, and agility. The opening climb lasts long enough to make most bikers work moderately hard.

The shady cover provided by the thick forest of mixed hardwoods and evergreens stays unbroken nearly to the source of Thrift Cove Creek, located at approximately the halfway point. Once on top, the trail seldom strays far from this rocky, rushing mountain stream. At times, the trail slides over into the shallow creek bed, making the descent on the western portion of the loop a potentially slippery affair.

The generally low-key skills needed for most of this ride make it a perfect setting for an easy pace, one that may allow you to see some of the natural drama playing out around you. While stopped for a water break, I saw a king snake crawling toward a hole in the crook of a sourwood. Two frantic chickadees flew around the six-foot-long snake, trying to draw its attention elsewhere, but to no avail. As the two birds watched, the snake slowly entered the nest.

The narrow remnants of old logging trails, called skid roads, are abundant in southern Appalachian forests and are sometimes easily cleared to make new bike trails. Photo by Pam Jones

General location: Just north of Brevard, North Carolina.

Elevation change: Approximately 500 feet gained and lost per lap.

Season: An all-season trail.

Services: The Pisgah Ranger Station has rest rooms, water, and a phone. Nearby Brevard supplies all services.

Hazards: Oncoming bikers and hikers may be in your way or headed your way. The rocky, wet, and steep western section has plenty of places where a bike could come out from under you.

Rescue index: US 276 leads to Brevard, which is only a few miles away. The trail follows a wide road bed for most of the way, which can easily be traveled by vehicle.

Land status: In Pisgah National Forest.

Maps: The trails are shown on the Pisgah District Trail Map, on sale at most local biking and hiking stores and, of course, at the Pisgah National Forest visitor centers.

Finding the trail: Leave Brevard headed north on US 64. Turn left onto US 276. A little over a mile up, look for the small gravel lot on the right—before reaching the Pisgah Ranger Station. A chain-link fence along the west side of the lot serves as an easy landmark. The trail begins on the double-track gravel road at the north end (away from the highway) of the lot.

Source of additional information:

Pisgah District Ranger
USDA Forest Service
1001 Pisgah Highway
Pisgah Forest, NC 28768
(828) 877-3265

Notes on the trail: Officially, only a little over 2 miles of this route is classified as Thrift Cove Trail, with the remainder officially classified as part of Sycamore Cove Trail and Black Mountain Trail, both of which are part of the Mountains-to-the-Sea Trail. Ride up the approach trail. The first intersection is where Black Mountain Trail comes down on the left in a sharp right curve; this is Thrift Cove's return to the approach trail. Continue riding up a steady, steep grade. Near the top, a trail enters from the left and leads back to Black Mountain Trail. Just a few yards past this intersection, a trail turns to the right for a shortcut to Sycamore Cove Trail. Shortly after these two intersections, Grassy Road is the orange-blazed trail splitting to the right. Thrift Cove Trail officially begins at this intersection, bearing to the left. The next intersection is with Black Mountain Trail; take a right to explore this trail. The left leads back to the approach trail. After reaching it, turn right to go back to the parking lot.

TSALI TRAILS

Located on the southern shore of Fontana Lake, the nearly 40 miles of single- and double-track in the Tsali Recreation Area have been ridden by mountain bikers from all over the world. The trails are divided into four loops (Right, Left, Mouse Branch, and Thompson), so bikers of all abilities will find trails to meet their individual experience levels. In addition to the developed trail sections, bikers can also ride any gated or open national forest service road that hasn't been posted closed to bikes.

Created in the late 1980s, the Tsali trails have achieved recognition as a mecca for mountain bikers. Although mountain bikers are prone to exaggeration, few words of praise surpass the reality of Tsali. Groomed single-track (and some say too groomed) narrows down to less than a foot wide in some places. Double-track, the leftovers of old logging roads, connects the tighter sections. Bikers can choose rides ranging from a short afternoon outing to a day-long pedal of over 20 miles. However, the trail is split in half and its use alternates daily—one 20-mile section is open to horseback riders only and the other 20-mile section is open to bikers only. On alternating days, bikes and horses swap trails. So the entire 40-mile length cannot be ridden all in one day (except on race days and during other special events).

Sources of additional information:

Cheoah Ranger District
Nantahala National Forest
Route 1, Box 16-A
Robbinsville, NC 28721
(828) 479-6431

Nantahala Outdoor Center Bike Shop
13077 Highway 19W
Bryson City, NC 28713
(800) 232-7238
(828) 488-2175, extension 158

Motion Makers
17 East Main Street
Sylva, NC 28779
(828) 586-6925

Freeman's Motel and Cabins
P.O. Box 100
Almond, NC 28702
(828) 488-2737

RIDE 39 · Right Loop

Length/configuration: 11 miles of looping single-track and double-track

Aerobic difficulty: Few stretches require much more than moderate exertion, unless you're shooting for a sub-hour lap

Technical difficulty: A moderately experienced biker should be able to maneuver easily on all sections

Scenery: Tsali's incredible scenery encourages a slower pace; Right Loop's overlook of the Great Smoky Mountains and Fontana Lake is a nice stop

Special comments: This is a good trail to take an advanced beginning biker on; take some extra time to explore the side routes

This 11-mile loop is made up of both single-track and double-track winding around the eastern half of the high ground between Mouse Branch and Battles Branch, small feeder creeks for Fontana Lake. Technically, this loop has little challenge for a moderately experienced biker. Its aerobic demands, likewise, also border on the ho-hum. But the scenery! Whoa! Every corner has its own pristine view of either the expanse of Fontana Lake or the narrow mountain gorges this region is known for.

Take plenty of time to enjoy this route and pack a lunch and several snacks. There is an overlook at the end of a 1.5-mile out-and-back (3 miles total) that starts on the north section of the loop. A rich variety of songbirds twitter overhead in the limbs, while across the water, eagles and vultures sail in thermals rising off the green, jagged peaks. Perhaps due to the heavy use this small area receives nearly year-round, relatively little evidence of wildlife can be seen on the ground. Most of the fauna you'll observe will be astride a mountain bike, yelping and hooting with the excitement of having found the off-road cyclist's Shangri-La.

General location: Tsali Recreation Area is located off State Road 28, approximately 40 miles northeast of Murphy, North Carolina, just across Fontana Lake from the Great Smoky Mountains National Park.

Elevation change: Despite the presence of surrounding mountains, the trails themselves have relatively little elevation change. There is a change of about 260 feet per lap, with only a small portion of it coming in steep sections.

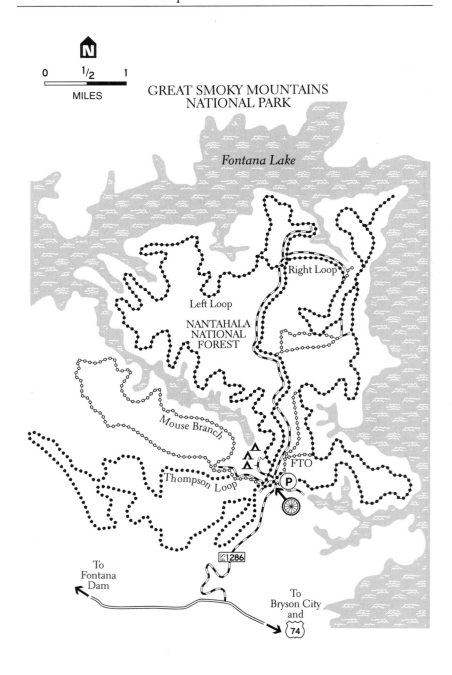

Sandy cycles a section of
Tsali.

Season: This part of North Carolina can turn bitterly cold in winter, but some years it remains clement enough to ride whenever the mood hits. Few other places receive more rainfall in a year than western North Carolina. Fortunately, the track holds up well when wet. Hunting season—late fall through early winter—means hunters will be nearby. Hunting is not allowed on the trails at Tsali, but it is a good idea to arrive at the trailhead donning plenty of fluorescent orange during those times when hunters are nearby. Call to find out the season start dates.

Services: The Tsali campground has 41 campsites, complete with showers and porcelain thrones. The surrounding area has been developed in order to serve the needs of visitors. The Nantahala Outdoor Center, in nearby Wesser, offers a complete line of goods and services for biking. Also, the Nantahala National Forest allows primitive camping anywhere except where signs are posted specifically forbidding it. Water bottles can be topped off at the spigot to the right of the fee pipe and rest rooms at the bikers' parking lot (unless it's during the freeze months, when the water's turned off). The water main at the bike wash station is turned off during winter months, too.

Hazards: Taken as a whole, the Tsali trails offer few hazards; however, some sections may pose significant problems. Ride anticipating oncoming traffic from other bikers, hikers, and horseback riders (along with their skittish steeds). Stay alert for loose gravel, slick clay, exposed roots, and ruts; they are uncommon but may be encountered.

Rescue index: This area receives many visitors, but that doesn't automatically mean it's easy to get rescued. Yes, you most likely will be found and helped quickly if you need minor assistance; however, the roads leading to Tsali are narrow and winding, requiring significant time to travel the distance to the nearest facilities, so rescues requiring professional medical assistance can take longer. It's a good idea to ride these trails prepared for self-rescue—and prepared to render aid.

Land status: In the Nantahala National Forest.

Maps: Look for the very good topo map posted at the 5-mile mark on Left Loop. The "official" map (Tsali Recreation Area: Mecca for Mountain Bikers, Horseback Riders), which you can pick up at the trailhead, may well be the same outdated and incomplete one that's been used for several years. It leaves several critical intersections out and has caused more than one group of bikers to become temporarily disoriented—but it's better than nothing. The map included with this ride description will keep the turns straight, so to speak.

Finding the trail: Travel north out of Andrews, North Carolina, staying on US 19 until you pass Nantahala Outdoor Center on the left in Wesser. A climb over Grassy Gap comes before the drop to the intersection with NC 28 North. Turn left toward Almond. Travel about 3 miles and then, just after the Tsali Grocery, look on the right for the Tsali Recreation Area sign. Turn right. Travel another 1.5 miles to the bikers' parking lot on the left. The trailhead for both Right Loop and Left Loop is found just beyond the fee station, rest rooms, and bike wash station in the bikers' parking lot. The turn onto Left Loop is 20 yards from the trailhead.

Source of additional information:

Cheoah Ranger District
Nantahala National Forest
Route 1, Box 16-A
Robbinsville, NC 28721
(828) 479-6431

Notes on the trail: Take the trail east away from the parking lot, bearing right and passing the sharp left used as an alternate connector to Left Loop. The next intersection occurs with a double-track to the left, approximately 3 miles from the trailhead. Orange surveyor's tape was strung across the left path when I biked this trail. Continue straight. The next intersection is a fork. Take the right turn indicated by a simple arrow on a wooden post. If you're a first-timer to Tsali, this next intersection may be confusing. A wooden post is propped against a tree, and the sign indicates Right Loop, suggesting that the sharp turn back (to the left onto an obviously infrequently used double-track) is part of Right Loop. This route does connect to the orange-blazed Meadow Branch Road, but don't take it. Continue straight in order to complete the big loop via Windy Gap Overlook.

The out-and-back follows a horseshoe section of single-track leading to Windy Gap Overlook. It begins at the next intersection straight up the hill (turn left here if you do not want to reach the overlook). At the top of the half-mile climb, one leg of the horseshoe splits off to the left, reconnecting to the out-and-back approximately a half mile later. The continued climb uphill leads to the overlook. Bypass the entire overlook out-and-back by taking a sharp left at the bottom of the steep climb. A double-track soon enters from the left; ignore it. There are two more possible left turns you can take onto double-track; bypass these as well. In order to ride what is considered the entire Right Loop, follow the blue-blazed single-track until reaching the **T** intersection, where prominent signs indicate a left turn onto County Line Road, or a right turn onto Left Loop. Yes, it can get confusing. The left leads back to the trailhead via County Line Road.

RIDE 40 · Left Loop

AT A GLANCE

Length/configuration: 12 miles of looping single- and double-track

Aerobic difficulty: There are just a few short, steep climbs, but not many

Technical difficulty: At least one section calls for excellent bike handling skills; on the whole, the demands are not tough, but beginners should be ready for a challenge

Scenery: Great Smoky Mountains, Fontana Lake, and an old homesite

Special comments: Many advanced riders looking for a high-mileage workout combine Right Loop and Left Loop for a total lap of over 20 miles

The nearly 12 miles of single-track and double-track making up Left Loop contain the same groomed trail surface found elsewhere at Tsali, but the difficulty is turned up a notch from that found on the easier Right Loop. The mixed hardwood forest of this section rarely opens up enough to allow the expansive views found on Right Loop, the exception being the spectacular "designated overlook" to the west of Meadow Branch. But the lack of views doesn't mean boredom has any chance of setting in. In fact, the increased difficulty of this route demands the beginning biker's full attention.

In the days when Mouse Branch trickled into the Tuckasegee River, settlers lived an isolated existence. Evidence of one such home can still be seen where a rock chimney stands nearly 20 feet tall. Not too much farther from this point, as the trail twists around like a snake climbing a tree, a modern version of a mountain home floats on pontoons in the middle of a small bay.

General location: Tsali Recreation Area is located off State Road 28, approximately 40 miles northeast of Murphy, North Carolina, just across Fontana Lake from the Great Smoky Mountains National Park.

Elevation change: A few sections have short, steep climbs, but the overall change is approximately 260 feet per lap.

Season: An all-season trail.

Services: The Tsali campground has 41 campsites (fee required), complete with showers and porcelain thrones. The surrounding area has been developed in order to serve the needs of visitors. The Nantahala Outdoor Center, in nearby Wesser, offers a complete line of goods and services for biking. Also, the Nantahala National Forest allows primitive camping anywhere except where signs are posted specifically forbidding it. Water bottles can be topped off at the spigot to the right of the fee pipe and rest rooms at the bikers' parking lot (unless it's during the freeze months, when the water's turned off). The water main at the bike wash station is turned off during winter months, too.

Hazards: A particularly technical section, where the trail swings northeastward, will call for all but the most advanced riders to take a hike. In addition, several stream crossings call for impeccable balance and agility in order to negotiate them without a dismount. Ride anticipating oncoming traffic from other bikers, hikers, and horseback riders (along with their skittish steeds).

Rescue index: This area receives many visitors, but that doesn't automatically mean it's easy to get rescued. Yes, you most likely will be found and helped quickly if you need minor assistance; however, the roads leading to Tsali are narrow and winding, requiring significant time to travel the distance to the nearest facilities, so rescues requiring professional medical assistance can take longer. It's a good idea to ride these trails prepared for self-rescue — and prepared to render aid.

Land status: In the Nantahala National Forest.

Maps: Look for the very good topo map posted at the 5-mile mark on Left Loop. The "official" map (Tsali Recreation Area: Mecca for Mountain Bikers, Horseback Riders), which you can pick up at the trailhead, may well be the same outdated and incomplete one that's been used for several years. But if all you're going to ride at Tsali is Left Loop (yeah, right), the official map will work fine.

Finding the trail: Travel north out of Andrews, North Carolina, staying on US 19 until you pass Nantahala Outdoor Center on the left in Wesser. A climb over Grassy Gap comes before the drop to the intersection with NC 28 North. Turn left toward Almond. Travel about 3 miles and then, just after the Tsali Grocery, look on the right for the sign for Tsali Recreation Area. Turn right. Travel another mile and a half to the bikers' parking lot on the left. The trailhead for both Right Loop and Left Loop is found just beyond the fee station, bathrooms, and bike wash in the bikers' parking lot. The turn onto Left Loop occurs 20 yards from the trailhead.

Source of additional information:

Cheoah Ranger District
Nantahala National Forest
Route 1, Box 16-A
Robbinsville, NC 28721
(828) 479-6431

Notes on the trail: Out of the parking lot, look to the left for the turn leading above the parking lot and to the main trail. Right Loop and Left Loop share about 20 yards of trail from the trailhead to where Left Loop branches off. Left Loop, generally traveled in a clockwise direction, is blazed green. Compared to Right Loop, Left Loop has few intersections and more signs along the way. The first intersection comes at about the 5-mile mark, where a map has been posted. The trail turns to the right; the left spur leads to a rest spot and an overlook. A right shortly afterward leads to a small loop at the end of an out-and-back, but this trail is for foot travel only. Continue straight until you get to the intersection at the top of a climb. A short connector for County Line Road leads up and to the right. Overlook Loop goes to the left at the intersection and adds about a mile and a half to the total ride distance, providing another spectacular view of Fontana Lake and the mountains. The junction of three trails—the connector, the overlook loop, and Right Loop—is well marked with a wooden sign pointing the way to the trailhead and the parking lot. On the way back, watch for two orange-blazed connectors coming in from the left, which, if used, make possible a variety of lengths and configurations (see Notes on the Trail for Right Loop).

RIDE 41 · Mouse Branch

AT A GLANCE

Length/configuration: A little over 7 miles (with more planned) on a single-track loop

Aerobic difficulty: A few short climbs will make you work, but otherwise the route has naught but small rollers

Technical difficulty: This is an easy trail to ride; the single-track is groomed and packed

Scenery: If you ride here during the winter—during the drawdown period for Fontana Lake—you'll get to see the steep, barren slopes usually covered by the lake's full pool

Special comments: The contiguous trail, Thompson Loop, is easily added to a day's ride, giving a total mileage of over 14 miles—nearly all single-track

I rode this seven-mile loop (mostly single-track, a little double-track) the day after a good rain. Although puddles were numerous, the track was amazingly free of big, long, nasty mudholes. I was able to zip along with impunity, taking advantage of the trail's smooth, banked curves.

The mixed hardwoods and pine forest above Mouse Branch have an extra added feature in the winter "drawdown" months. Below the full-pool line on Fontana Lake's bank, the mountain slopes have been scoured clean. Only the scree-covered contour remains, producing an eerie effect. Receding waves leave scalloped, parallel lines on the strand. And at the bottom of the draw, a tiny creek trickles its way to the distant lake waters—in some places, a quarter of a mile or more away. You're likely to spot fresh deer tracks leading to and from the creek's edge. The hawk I spooked flew into the trees and perched on a pine snag, piercing the air with its shrill whistle. As I watched it, I noticed a persimmon tree below me, where summer's waters usually lap. Its branches were loaded with its roundish fruit, a little smaller than a Ping-Pong ball. The persimmon's overall squashed-looking exterior and sooty skin don't do justice to the exquisite taste within. But eat only those fully ripened. If its ripeness is misjudged, it can put puckers on your puckers. It's good to let a friend taste first.

General location: Tsali Recreation Area is located off State Road 28, approximately 40 miles northeast of Murphy, North Carolina, just across Fontana Lake from the Great Smoky Mountains National Park.

RIDE 41 ・ Mouse Branch
RIDE 42 ・ Thompson Loop
RIDE 43 ・ Lemmons Branch

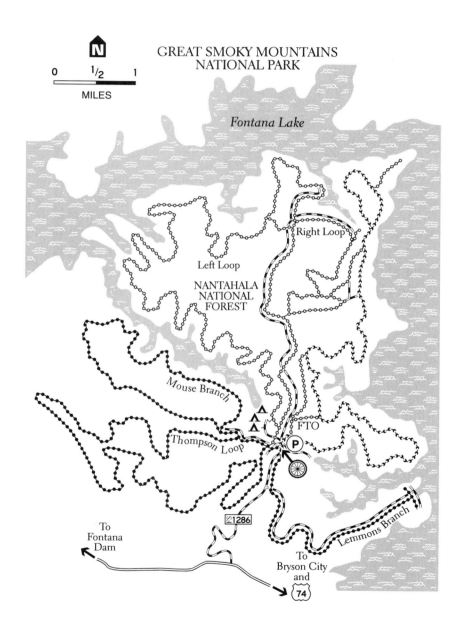

The persimmon tree was loaded with a helmet full of sweet, orange fruit.

Elevation change: Part of Tsali's popularity comes from the relative lack of elevation change on its trails, and this trail is a good example. Expect only 200 feet of change per lap, with little of it coming on steep climbs.

Season: Ride Tsali anytime. The winter has a dramatic effect on the scenery. After the leaves and the lake's water level have fallen, it is like riding a different trail.

Services: The Tsali campground has 41 campsites (fee required), complete with showers and porcelain thrones. The surrounding area has been developed in order to serve the needs of visitors. The Nantahala Outdoor Center, in nearby Wesser, offers a complete line of goods and services for biking. Also, the Nantahala National Forest allows primitive camping anywhere except where signs are posted specifically forbidding it. Water bottles can be topped off at the spigot to the right of the fee pipe and rest rooms at the bikers' parking lot (unless it's during the freeze months, when the water's turned off). The water main at the bike wash station is turned off during winter months, too.

Hazards: Taken as a whole, the Tsali trails offer few hazards; however, sections may pose problems. Other bikers, hikers, and horseback riders (along with their skittish steeds) should be anticipated. Watch for outcrops of loose gravel and slick clay.

Rescue index: This area receives many visitors, but that doesn't automatically mean it's easy to get rescued. Yes, you most likely will be found and helped quickly if you need minor assistance; however, the roads leading to Tsali are narrow and winding, requiring significant time to travel the distance to the nearest facilities, so rescues requiring professional medical assistance can take longer. It's a good idea to ride these trails prepared for self-rescue—and prepared to render aid.

Land status: In the Nantahala National Forest.

Maps: Look for the very good topo map usually posted at least once on each of the trails. The "official" map (Tsali Recreation Area: Mecca for Mountain Bikers, Horseback Riders), which you can pick up at the trailhead, may well be the same outdated and incomplete one that's been used for several years. But using it for Mouse Branch will give you no problems.

Finding the trail: Travel north out of Andrews, North Carolina, staying on US 19 until you pass Nantahala Outdoor Center on the left in Wesser. A climb over Grassy Gap comes before the drop to the intersection with NC 28 North. Turn left toward Almond. Drive about 3 miles and then, just after the Tsali Grocery, look for the sign for Tsali Recreation Area on the right. Turn there. Travel another 1.5 miles to the bikers' parking lot on the left. The trailhead for Mouse Branch and Thompson Loops is across the gravel road that leads to the campground, west of the parking lot. The trailhead is behind the gated double-track and marked by a sign. Mouse Branch shares a short stretch of trail with Thompson Loop.

Source of additional information:

Cheoah Ranger District
Nantahala National Forest
Route 1, Box 16-A
Robbinsville, NC 28721
(828) 479-6431

Notes on the trail: Leave the parking lot and head west, away from the boat ramp. Cross the gravel road leading to the campground and ride around the gate onto the double-track approach trail. Mouse Branch begins as the first trail turning to the right. The first 4 miles or so wind around many of the lake's inlets. It isn't until the ride is nearly two-thirds complete that you encounter a somewhat steep climb.

Soon after the climb, look for an intersection at a wildlife opening. Double-track, which I have been told is part of a planned extension, goes to the right. It rejoins Mouse Branch about a half mile farther down on the right. The current route requires a left turn at this intersection, which is marked by a sign. The double-track turning to the left about a mile later is not the main route, although it appears to rejoin the main trail on the right a few yards in. The final descent ends at the double-track intersection, where a left leads back to the trailhead.

RIDE 42 · Thompson Loop

AT A GLANCE

Length/configuration: 7.5 miles in a loop of mostly wide single-track

Aerobic difficulty: You won't remember this trail for its aerobic challenge

Technical difficulty: Few technical challenges exist, even for bikers with limited experience

Scenery: Creek crossings among a mixed hardwood and pine forest

Special comments: This is the wettest Tsali trail, with 6 creek crossings; none of them, however, require more than beginning skills for a safe pedal through

This 7.5-mile single-track loop (named for David Thompson, a National Forest Service ranger memorialized with a sign posted on the trail at a gorgeous overlook) is generally thought to be an inseparable companion to Mouse Branch. It makes sense—they are open for bikes on the same day, use a common approach trail, and are short and wet. Thompson alone has six stream crossings. The trail's setting, like the rest of Tsali, stays near Fontana Lake, twisting and turning its way along the banks above several small inlets.

One of the great things about mountain biking is its constantly changing—and surprising—events taking place on common and familiar ground. Consider the case of Mr. Hunter, as in .30–30 vision Mr. Hunter. Now I know, and you know, that biking and horse trails are not areas where hunting is allowed. Plus, it's in bad taste to carry a locked and loaded firearm on a recreational trail when so many nearby fire roads can be hunted. Still, on that morning, Mr. Hunter was stalking Bambi on *my* mountain bike trail. The situation could've turned ugly soon. A good old boy, Bocephus, we'll call him, meets Macho Biker storming down the trail; he comes to a skidding halt that ends nose-to-barrel with Bo's cold steel. With the wrong words said, there's a good chance somebody loses something that day—if nothing else, a lost chance to do a good turn.

As it turned out, Bo was lost—don't ask me how; Tsali's trails are, for the most part, extremely well marked. He needed reassurance that he was trudging in the right direction. So I stopped and we chatted about where the trailhead was. "Say," he asked pointing at my bike, "do you do that for fun, or just to stay in shape?" A little of both, I told him. Now I doubt Bo will ever swap his four-wheeler for a real man's bike, but I'm hoping the next time he meets a biker on

This high ground on Thompson Loop offers a quiet place for a break.

his trail, on *his* hunt, on *his* morning off, he will give the sucker a break. And, who knows, it just might be you.

General location: Tsali Recreation Area is off State Road 28, approximately 40 miles northeast of Murphy, North Carolina, just across Fontana Lake from the Great Smoky Mountains National Park.

Elevation change: Unless you're on foot and lugging along a loaded rifle, you won't remember Thompson Loop as a trail where much significant elevation change takes place. The overall change is slightly more than 200 feet per lap.

Season: The most popular season to ride this trail is summer, with the shade from large trees and a cool breeze coming off the surface of Fontana Lake. It is, however, an all-season trail.

Services: The Tsali campground has 41 campsites (fee required), complete with showers and porcelain thrones. The surrounding area has been developed in order to serve the needs of visitors. The Nantahala Outdoor Center, in nearby Wesser, offers a complete line of goods and services for biking. Also, the Nantahala National Forest allows primitive camping anywhere except where signs are posted specifically forbidding it. Water bottles can be topped off at the spigot to the right of the fee pipe and rest rooms at the bikers' parking lot (unless it's during the freeze months, when the water's turned off). The water main at the bike wash station is turned off during winter months, too.

Hazards: Taken as a whole, the Tsali trails offer few hazards; however, certain sections may pose problems. Other bikers, hikers, and horseback riders (along with their skittish steeds) should be anticipated. Watch for outcrops of loose gravel and slick clay.

Rescue index: This area receives many visitors, but that doesn't automatically mean it's easy to get rescued. Yes, you most likely will be found and helped quickly if you need minor assistance; however, the roads leading to Tsali are narrow and winding, requiring significant time to travel the distance to the nearest facilities, so rescues requiring professional medical assistance can take longer. It's a good idea to ride these trails prepared for self-rescue—and prepared to render aid.

Land status: In the Nantahala National Forest.

Maps: Look for the very good topo map posted at the 5-mile mark on Left Loop. The "official" map (Tsali Recreation Area: Mecca for Mountain Bikers, Horseback Riders), which you can pick up at the trailhead, may well be the same outdated and incomplete one that's been used for several years. It works fine for this particular loop, however.

Finding the trail: Travel north out of Andrews, North Carolina, staying on US 19 until you pass Nantahala Outdoor Center on the left in Wesser. A climb over Grassy Gap comes before the drop to the intersection with NC 28 North. Turn left toward Almond. Drive about 3 miles and then, just after the Tsali Grocery, look for the sign for Tsali Recreation Area on the right. Turn there. Travel another mile and a half to the bikers' parking lot on the left. The trailhead for both Right Loop and Left Loop is found just beyond the fee station, rest rooms, and bike wash. The turn onto Left Loop occurs 20 yards from this point. The trailhead for Mouse Branch and Thompson Loops is across the gravel road that leads to the campground, west of the parking lot. The trailhead is behind the gated double-track and marked by a sign. Mouse Branch shares a short stretch of trail with Thompson Loop.

Source of additional information:

Cheoah Ranger District
Nantahala National Forest
Route 1, Box 16-A
Robbinsville, NC 28721
(828) 479-6431

Notes on the trail: Begin by taking the double-track approach and riding the red-blazed Thompson Loop counterclockwise. Pass the first leg of Mouse Branch on the right, and then another leg, also on the right. The next trail straight ahead leads to the water of a small, shallow inlet. Instead of riding straight, take the obviously worn single-track curving to the left. A small creek crossing occurs at about the one-mile mark, with five more crossings in the next 2 miles. A turn to the right, approximately 5 miles from the parking lot, leads to a wide opening with views of the Great Smoky Mountains. Another turn to the left, just a few pedal turns later, is clearly marked by both sign and track. In a few minutes, the descent to the double-track approach trail is complete. Turn right to ride back to the parking lot and trailhead.

RIDE 43 · Lemmons Branch

AT A GLANCE

 NC

Length/configuration: A 2.5-mile (5 miles total) out-and-back on a lightly graveled service road

Aerobic difficulty: It's not flat, but close to it; however, one climb will likely require a shift into granny gear

Technical difficulty: Its surface is wide, smooth, and easily ridden

Scenery: Fontana Lake, mixed hardwood forest, view of Round Top

Special comments: A special summer treat: take a picnic to eat at the shores of Fontana Lake and cool off with a swim

With all the other great riding in Tsali Recreation Area, it would be easy to forego this 2.5-mile out-and-back (5 miles total) lightly graveled service road. Don't. If nothing else, it's a wonderful warm-up ride. But there's plenty more. The short, rolling hills of the route mostly take place under a thick shade of evergreen and mixed hardwoods. Laurel thickets crowd the banks. Despite its service road status, the ride feels remote and intimate. On one remarkable curve, the dense canopy disappears. As if in a slide show, the impressive shape of Round Top pops into view.

General location: Tsali Recreation Area is located off State Road 28, approximately 40 miles northeast of Murphy, North Carolina, just across Fontana Lake from the Great Smoky Mountains National Park.

Elevation change: Lemmons Branch has only two climb-and-drops, neither of which is long nor steep.

Season: This is an all-season trail. Hunting does occur on this gated road during late fall to early winter. It pays to show up trailside clad in bright orange, 500 square inches minimum. In addition, I avoid any closed service roads (like Lemmons Branch, FS 2553) when a tell-tale vehicle (pickup with an empty gun rack) is parked nearby.

Services: The Tsali campground has 41 campsites (fee required), complete with showers and porcelain thrones. The surrounding area has been developed in order to serve the needs of visitors. The Nantahala Outdoor Center, in nearby Wesser, offers a complete line of goods and services for biking. Lemmons Branch allows primitive camping (primitive camping is allowed anywhere in the Nantahala National Forest except where signs are posted specifically forbidding

This scene explodes into view after rounding a curve on Lemmons Branch.

it). Water bottles can be topped off at the spigot to the right of the fee pipe and rest rooms at the bikers' parking lot (unless it's during the freeze months, when the water's turned off). The water main at the bike wash station is turned off during winter months, too.

Hazards: Expect no hazards on this gravel road; however, when I rode, some curves had been recently regraveled with rocks the size of Ping-Pong balls.

Rescue index: Lemmons Branch is not used as frequently as the other Tsali trails; therefore, it could be an uncomfortable period before someone arrived. Ride prepared for self-rescue but with the somewhat comforting knowledge that a wide, graveled road leads the short distance to NC 28, a paved highway. It's only somewhat comforting because, should you need medical assistance, it would take at least 15 minutes more to get to Robbinsville or Bryson City.

Land status: In the Nantahala National Forest.

Maps: Lemmons Branch can be found on the official Nantahala National Forest map, sold at the Ranger District offices and area bike stores.

Finding the trail: Travel north out of Andrews, North Carolina, staying on US 19 until passing Nantahala Outdoor Center on the left in Wesser. A climb over Grassy Gap comes before the drop to the intersection with NC 28 North. Turn left toward Almond. Drive about 3 miles and then, just after the Tsali Grocery, look for the sign for Tsali Recreation Area on the right. Turn there. Travel another mile. Look to the right for a closed gate across a double-track. This is the trailhead for FS 2553, Lemmons Branch. Park at the designated camping area (primitive) just past the trailhead on the right, or at the regular Tsali parking area.

Source of additional information:

Cheoah Ranger District
Nantahala National Forest
Route 1, Box 16-A
Robbinsville, NC 28721
(828) 479-6431

Notes on the trail: This route is about as uncomplicated as it gets. Begin with a slight climb, followed by a corresponding small drop. Climb again. Drop again. Ride the ridge to a **T** intersection. Each leg of the **T** dead-ends at the lake. Return the way you came.

NANTAHALA NATIONAL FOREST

The name for this huge national forest (517,579 acres) comes from the melodic Cherokee word for "land of the noonday sun," an obvious connection to the steep mountains and narrow gorges found here. This rugged landscape has attracted a scad of folks who just want to be outside. The Appalachian Trail winds its way through the Nantahala, from Courthouse Bald in the south to Fontana Dam, crossing into Tennessee inside the Great Smoky Mountains. The Nantahala River floats tons and tons of kayaks, canoes, and rafts each year. And the nationally famous Tsali trail network is perhaps the most popular destination for mountain bikers in the southeast.

Each of the ranger districts within the Nantahala National Forest— Highlands, Tusquitee, Cheoah, and Wayah—has plenty of places where mountain biking is allowed. In the case of the Cheoah Ranger District, home of the Tsali Recreational Trails, mountain biking is even encouraged. The Highlands Ranger District contains the spot where Georgia, South Carolina, and North Carolina meet, Ellicott Rock. Although the rock itself lies in a wilderness area open only to foot travel, the national forest adjoining the wilderness area can be explored on bike at Blue Valley and Round Mountain.

Sources of additional information:

Highlands Ranger District
2010 Flat Mountain Road
Highlands, NC 28741
(828) 526-3765

Cheoah Ranger District
Route 1, Box 16-A
Robbinsville, NC 28771
(828) 479-6431

Tusquitee Ranger District
201 Woodland Drive
Murphy, NC 28906
(828) 837-5152

Wayah Ranger District
90 Sloan Road
Franklin, NC 28734
(828) 524-6441

Nantahala Outdoor Center Bike Shop
13077 Highway 19 West
Bryson City, NC 28713
(800) 232-7238
(828) 488-2175, extension 158

A lone chimney marks
the passage of an earlier
explorer.

RIDE 44 · Calfpen Gap

AT A GLANCE

Length/configuration: An out-and-back total of approximately 13 miles (6.5 miles one way) on a double-track service road, lightly graveled with a dirt base

Aerobic difficulty: A moderate, steady, 1,000-foot climb makes for a good workout

Technical difficulty: The road is smooth and wide, with little loose gravel

Scenery: This route heads south on the west side of Round Top, nearly reaching the Appalachian Trail at Grassy Gap

Special comments: A single-track cuts off from the road and connects to Panther Creek Road; ride this gravel road back to NC 28, turn right, and ride 2 paved miles back to the trailhead for Calfpen Gap

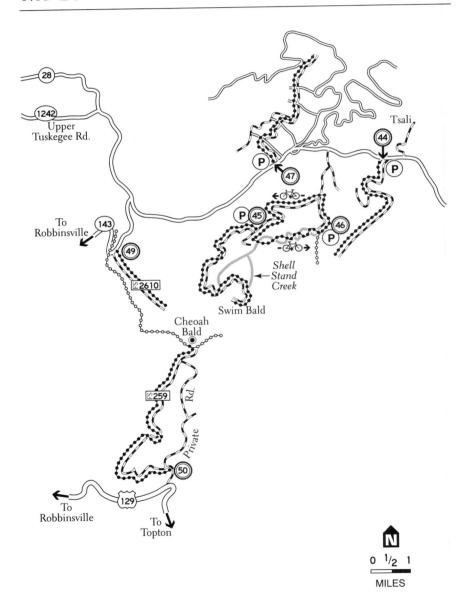

Riding fire roads often leads to overlooks.

When is a Calfpen Gap a Horse Branch Road? When directions are being given to this 6.5-mile (13 miles total) out-and-back double-track, of course. The Department of Transportation apparently spurned local tradition by giving this gravel road, located a quarter mile north of Tsali Recreation Area, a name different than the gap where it begins. So instead of being named Calfpen Gap, it is called Horse Branch Road for the small creek beginning about a third of the way through the ride on the right.

The road climbs steadily with a nearly unchanged, steep grade. The high canopy overhead keeps the trail shaded during the summer, except when the road turns a curve in the middle of a recent clear-cut. At this point, the road follows the Graham-Swain county line. The valley below is home to Stecoah and, if you can find it, Hidetown.

General location: Between Bryson City and Andrews, North Carolina.

Elevation change: About 1,000 feet—very little rolling on the way up. It basically climbs the entire way.

Season: This is an all-season trail; however, I recommend riding another place if it looks as though a hunter's truck is parked at the gate (look for the conspicuously empty gun rack).

Services: Tsali Recreation Area is on the other side of the highway, a little over a quarter of a mile east. The Nantahala Outdoor Center, in Wesser, has all the goods and services that are likely needed. The surrounding area is a popular vacation spot, and it has the amenities to provide amply for guests.

Hazards: Hunters provide the most significant hazard on this nontechnical trail. On the descent, it's easy to pick up a great deal of speed, making it tricky to turn in some of the gravel sections.

Rescue index: The road is wide and easily traveled, thereby enabling an easy rescue. But a 6-mile walk out would still be a chore. There are many nearby trails available for biking, which reduces overall traffic on any given trail, making it likely you would have a long wait before someone came along. Ride prepared for self-rescue.

Land status: Part of the Nantahala National Forest.

Maps: A good investment for bikers wanting to explore the Nantahala National Forest would be the map by the same name, sold at the Ranger District office and at local bike stores.

Finding the trail: Travel north out of Andrews, North Carolina, staying on US 19 until you pass Nantahala Outdoor Center on the left in Wesser. A climb over Grassy Gap comes before the drop to the intersection with NC 28 North. Turn left toward Almond. Drive about 3 miles and then, just after the Tsali Grocery, look for the sign for Tsali Recreation Area on the right. The parking for Calfpen is slightly over a quarter mile past the recreation area entrance on the left, marked by a green sign for Horse Branch Road.

Source of additional information:

Cheoah Ranger District
Nantahala National Forest
Route 1, Box 16-A
Robbinsville, NC 28721
(828) 479-6431

Notes on the trail: This simple out-and-back gains over 1,000 vertical feet in approximately 6.5 miles—a stout, steady climb. Ride past the (normally closed) gate. About 2 miles out, look for FS 2630A turning to the right; it goes another mile or so before ending. The only other intersection you'll see before you reach the end, where you turn around, is with the steeply dropping single-track connector to Panther Creek Road (on the right about to the end of the gravel road). A loop can be made using the single-track with Panther Creek Road (it's the gravel road where the single-track ends). Turn right on Panther Creek Road and keep straight until you reach paved NC 28. It's a 2-mile paved ride to the right up to Calfpen Gap and the trailhead.

RIDE 45 · Shell Stand Road–Swim Bald

AT A GLANCE

Length/configuration: An out-and-back service road of 8 miles (16 miles total)

Aerobic difficulty: Occasional stretches will bring on bouts of deep, rapid breathing

Technical difficulty: Its wide double-track is easy to navigate, but some sections have been heavily graveled; the rest of the surface is light gravel on top of a dirt base

Scenery: A slow climb on the inside of the mountain cove north of Cheoah Bald

Special comments: The single-track trail, Shell Stand Creek, is located nearby and can be added for an extra 6-mile loop

Cheoah Bald has three different routes up its flanks. Shell Stand Road's 8 miles (one way) on a 16-mile (total) out-and-back is one of them. The majority is a gravel road (more grass than gravel the farther up you go). A little over a mile of single-track lies at the end of the road. You may need to use snips to clear a path on this tight section; either that or be prepared to lose some hide tearing through the blackberry canes. But the double-track is a pleasure anytime of year. During a late fall ride, as a strong cold front pushed through, I pedaled my way through a gathering dusk. The mountain tips were trimmed in white. A howl came from the ridge tops where the wind was blowing off a veil of snow. As I turned the first of many curves on the long climb, I raised my head just as an owl was spooked from its roost.

I enjoy climbing at least as much as I enjoy communing with nature. And this ride ranks with the best: nearly a nonstop climb with spectacular scenery. But this is North Carolina, and it's supposed to be pretty, right? What sets this route apart from some other very pretty rides is the presence of long views across deep, wooded ravines. In more than one place, the road ahead can be spotted rising in the distance, a curved line drawn on the side of Swim Bald. Huge chunks of rock lie broken off from cliffs in smooth-sided slabs, some big enough for a pool table. This is what local biker, Jim Freeman, had in mind when he told me, "I like riding fire roads. They're really nice." Yeah, buddy.

General location: In between Bryson City and Andrews, North Carolina.

Elevation change: Expect nearly 2,000 feet of change over the course of 8-plus miles. It's almost one big climb, with one notable descent on the way out.

These peaks, frosted with an early winter's snow, rise above Shell Stand Road.

Season: Any time of year is good, but hunting season (usually late fall to early winter) may be a good time to ride elsewhere, especially if it looks like a hunter's truck is parked at the gate.

Services: Tsali Recreation Area is nearby. Water is available there except during winter months, when the water mains are shut off. The Nantahala Outdoor Center, in Wesser, has all the goods and services any biker will ever need, year-round, seven days a week.

Hazards: Hunters provide the most significant hazard on this nontechnical trail. Prepare to avoid fallen rock, some of which may be large yet hidden in tufts of grass.

Rescue index: The road is wide and easily traveled, thereby enabling an easy self-rescue. But an 8-mile walk out would not be fun. Also, should you require medical assistance, it may be a long time before you're discovered. Under the best of circumstances, it is a long, slow ride to civilization. You will note some houses at—and near—the intersection with Panther Creek Road.

Land status: Part of the Nantahala National Forest.

Maps: A good investment for bikers wanting to explore the Nantahala National Forest would be the map by the same name, sold at the Ranger District office and at local bike stores. See page 166 for our map of this ride.

Finding the trail: Travel north out of Andrews, North Carolina, staying on US 19 until you pass Nantahala Outdoor Center on the left in Wesser. Climb over

Grassy Gap and drop to the intersection with NC 28 North, turning left toward Almond. Go approximately 7 miles, turning left onto Panther Creek Road. A sign for Tumbling Waters Campground is also found at this turn. At the intersection of Shell Stand Road and Panther Creek Road, turn right and cross the bridge. Drive another 2.25 miles. The gates across both FS 418 (to the right) and FS 419 (to the left) will most likely be closed. Park here along the shoulder.

Source of additional information:

Cheoah Ranger District
Nantahala National Forest
Route 1, Box 16-A
Robbinsville, NC 28721
(828) 479-6431

Notes on the trail: The beauty of this ride may be its simplicity—straight out and straight back. But what's in between is certainly worthy of exploration on bike or on foot. For example, after you reach the gate at the beginning of FS 418, about 4 miles in, look for an overgrown-looking single-track going up to the right. A little farther in, a creek goes under the road. Just beyond, at about the 5-mile mark, two man-made promontories would make good spots for a couple of tents or a whole bunch of sleeping bags. After a slight widening in the road, about 7 miles in, the double-track gets noticeably narrower, becoming a single-track overgrown by brambles and grasses. It remains mostly open for an additional mile or more, hooking to the south and then east before coming to a stop facing Cheoah Bald.

RIDE 46 · Shell Stand Creek

AT A GLANCE	
 **NC**	**Length/configuration:** A 6.3-mile loop with a creekside single-track and a lightly graveled service road
	Aerobic difficulty: 800 feet gained over 2.5 miles, making for a moderate workout
	Technical difficulty: The single-track creek crossings and rocky descents are demanding
	Scenery: How many ways can you say "gorgeous"? You'll say it on the way down, along, and through Shell Stand Creek
	Special comments: Fourteen creek crossings

Allow plenty of time to enjoy the technical demands of this 6.3-mile loop. The single-track section has creek crossings galore, some of them foot-soakers. A real pain in the cooler months, but definitely a summertime treat. The rest of the route uses a gated (normally closed) service road, plus a dirt road section open to vehicles. Expect to surprise wildlife on its way to and from the creek. Deer, turkey, and squirrels are common. The mixed hardwoods and abundant rhododendron are home to a wide range of chortling, trilling songbirds. Signs of bobcats and bears and the occasional whiff of a skunk are reminders of the connections made out in the woods on a bike.

General location: In between Bryson City and Andrews, North Carolina, on NC 28.

Elevation change: From the bridge at the intersection of Paint Creek and Shell Stand Road to the gate, about 1,000 feet is gained, a pretty demanding stint.

Season: Periods immediately following a lot of rain could make this trail more work than fun, especially if it is cold. You may want to pick a different trail to ride that day if a pickup with an empty gun rack is parked at the gate. A hunter is probably down the road and would become irritated at the sight of some Lycra-clad cyclist ruining his hunt. Can't say that I blame him.

Services: Tsali Recreation Area is nearby. The Nantahala Outdoor Center, in Wesser, has a complete list of the goods and services bikers need. This general area has been developed with the needs of the vacationer in mind, so most services are easily available.

Hazards: The steep and technical descents along, through, and beyond the numerous creek crossings demand a high level of skill for safe passage. In fact, they may require waiting until the creek level is down. The final creek crossing occurs not too far upstream from the bridge at the intersection with Paint Creek Road and Shell Stand Road. If the water looks too high to cross here, it may be best to ride another time, when water levels are lower. Hunters (generally in the late fall and early winter), bikers, and wild animals may be present on the trail.

Rescue index: It is remote territory despite the gravel road nearby. Travel prepared for self-rescue. There are several houses close by and at the intersection of Paint Creek and Shell Stand Roads.

Land status: In the Nantahala National Forest.

Maps: A good investment for bikers wanting to explore the Nantahala National Forest is the map by the same name, sold at the District Ranger office and at area bike stores. See page 166 for our map of this ride.

Finding the trail: Travel north out of Andrews, North Carolina, staying on US 19 until you pass Nantahala Outdoor Center on the left in Wesser. Climb over Grassy Gap and turn left at the intersection with NC 28 North, toward Almond. Go approximately 7 miles, turning left onto Panther Creek Road. A sign for Tumbling Waters Campground also marks the left turn. At the intersection of Shell Stand Road and Panther Creek Road, turn right and cross the bridge.

Drive another 2.25 miles. The gates across both FS 418 (to the right) and FS 419 (to the left) will most likely be closed. Park here along the shoulder. The alternate trailhead is found on Panther Creek Road—go back to the bridge and cross it, but turn right onto Panther Creek Road. Go about a quarter mile to where you should see a pullout on the left. This is near where the single-track crosses the creek for the final time, and near where Shell Creek enters Panther Creek.

Source of additional information:

Cheoah Ranger District
Nantahala National Forest
Route 1, Box 16-A
Robbinsville, NC 28721
(828) 479-6431

Notes on the trail: Take this trail counterclockwise, riding down FS 419, the gated road on the left. It drops to a creek crossing a mile and a half from the gate. The single-track begins on the left just after the crossing. Less than a mile later, the trail seems to end at an opening. But on the far side, near the creek, it picks back up. Be prepared to shift sides of the creek another sopping-wet 12 times before you reach the fork leading to Panther Creek Road; bear left. Turn left at Panther Creek Road (alternate trailhead). The intersection with Shell Stand Road comes on the left about a quarter mile up. Turn left to end with a climb up the final 2.5 miles.

RIDE 47 · Meetinghouse

AT A GLANCE	**Length/configuration:** An 8-mile one-way (16 miles total) out-and-back on a lightly graveled (dirt base) service road

Aerobic difficulty: Small rollers make up most of this easily climbed route

Technical difficulty: The wide gravel surface is easily ridden

Scenery: If it looks a lot like Tsali, that's because the famous trail system is just east, on the other side of Fontana Lake's Wolf Inlet

Special comments: The mileage can be increased by riding the adjoining abandoned logging roads

The moderate grade of Meetinghouse Mountain's 8-mile, one-way (16 miles total), lightly graveled service road is a good alternative to nearby Tsali's trails, especially for those times when single-track isn't as important as solitude. I was told once that every ridge in the national forest has had a logging road built on it at one time or another. After riding Meetinghouse Road (FS 2540), you'll have no doubt about this. This forest of tree-covered rock was harvested long ago, with logging companies building roads to haul out the fallen logs. Some roads have become too tangled with recent blowdown to ride easily; others, however, are just perfect for the tread of a mountain bike. On these side trips you'll discover many tiny creek branches, which feed Wolf Creek.

Pileated woodpeckers patrol this forest, clinging to dead oak trunks, hammering out their territory, and attracting mates. As it also chisels and pries out Sawyer grubs, the giant bird's red head moves so fast it blurs, nearly lost in a shower of wood chips. Its flight—signaled by a flash of red, black, and white—is generally accompanied by its raucous call, a sound straight out of a Tarzan movie.

General location: In between Bryson City and Andrews, North Carolina, off NC 28 and near Tsali.

Elevation change: There aren't big changes along the roadbed; however, exploration of the adjoining spurs will occasionally lead to very steep slopes.

Season: This is an all-season trail; however, the late fall and early winter are times when hunters are likely nearby, letting lead fly. My rule of thumb during hunting season is this: if I see a truck parked at the trailhead, gun rack empty, I go to another trail.

Services: Tsali Recreation Area is nearby. The Nantahala Outdoor Center has complete goods and services for the off-road biker. The surrounding area is a popular vacation spot, thereby assuring that most of your immediate needs can be met.

Hazards: Hunters provide the most significant hazard on this normally gated service road.

Rescue index: The road is wide and easily traveled, thereby enabling easy access by vehicles. But an 8-mile walk out would still be a chore. Also, this route is not heavily used, which means it could be an uncomfortably long time before someone discovers you. I recommend riding prepared for self-rescue.

Land status: Part of the Nantahala National Forest.

Maps: A good investment for bikers wanting to explore the Nantahala National Forest is the map by the same name, sold at Ranger District offices and at area bike stores. See page 166 for our map of this ride.

Finding the trail: Travel north out of Andrews, North Carolina, staying on US 19 until you pass Nantahala Outdoor Center on the left in Wesser. Climb over Grassy Gap and drop to the intersection with NC 28 North, taking the left toward Almond. Go approximately 7 miles, passing the turn to Tsali on the right. After you cross the third bridge west of Tsali (approximately 3.5 miles from its entrance), look for the prominent green road sign on the right—Meetinghouse Road, FS 2540. Park here without blocking the gate.

Source of additional information:

Cheoah Ranger District
Nantahala National Forest
Route 1, Box 16-A
Robbinsville, NC 28721
(828) 479-6431

Notes on the trail: It's a straightforward out-and-back on FS 2540. Four creeks flow under the road before you reach the portion overlooking Fontana Lake. Approximately halfway out, FS 2541 turns off to the left, southwest. It has the potential for connecting with FS 2537, but a difficult climb over the mountain would be required. The mountains across Fontana Lake are Welch Ridge, Big Fork Ridge, and Pilot Ridge—left to right respectively.

RIDE 48 · Wauchecha Bald

AT A GLANCE

Length/configuration: A 7.5-mile (total) out-and-back lightly graveled service road—3.8 miles one way

Aerobic difficulty: Some intense aerobic work is necessary on this climb

Technical difficulty: It starts easy and gets progressively harder as the elevation increases

Scenery: Part of the Cheoah Mountains, and, of course, Wauchecha Bald

Special comments: The Appalachian Trail is connected to the road via a foot trail that intersects with the road near the end of its climb

This out-and-back starts out easily enough behind the normally closed gate for FS 438, a lightly graveled dirt base. It's almost a full four-mile climb to the top, making an eight-mile total ride. The moderate grade starting at the trailhead switches dramatically after crossing the creek, just after passing 438A on the right. Before you reach the top, it will become a difficult ride both physically and technically. The steep slopes have rhododendron thickets where I spooked

RIDE 48 • Wauchecha Bald
RIDE 52 • Fontana Village

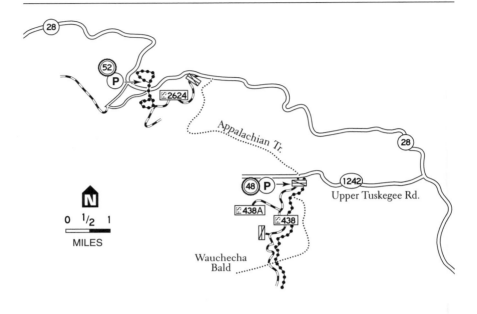

grouse in two different spots. A flock of five turkeys had already roosted for the evening, but when I chugged by they took off. It was cold the day I rode here, so cold that the many rhododendrons lining the road had dropped their leaves parallel to the trunk in the "flaps down" position, giving them a shriveled, burned appearance.

A private road on the right—gated—leads to a high mountain meadow. The route up to Wauchecha switches back just beyond this road. The steepness of the grade from this point on will make most riders grunt. Not only that, a spring splits the roadbed and large rocks lie hidden among the grass. The last section up to Wauchecha Bald is covered by a high, dense network of interlocked boughs high overhead. But, as is often the case, the hard work to gain the summit is worth it. The view from Wauchecha Bald is incredible. And the ride back down is a thrill at any speed.

General location: Just a few miles north of Robbinsville, North Carolina.

Elevation change: About 1,000 feet in just under 4 miles, with much of it coming the last mile and a half.

Season: This is an all-season ride. Late fall and early winter, when hunting season is open, are times when it is good to ride somewhere else if a pickup is parked at the gate, and wear lots of antihunter (fluorescent) orange even when

The more the trail curves on its way up to Wauchecha Bald, the steeper it gets.

the road appears unoccupied by hunters. A hunter could park at the gate after you leave and be stalking a deer as you make the descent.

Services: Tsali Recreation Area is nearby. The Nantahala Outdoor Center has a complete list of goods and services required by bikers. The surrounding area is a popular vacation spot, with all the amenities.

Hazards: Losing your breath and encountering hunters on the trail are the main hazards; however, some tricky washouts occur closer to the top, caused by a spring washing down the middle of the road.

Rescue index: Despite the wide and open service road, this is remote country. Plan for self-rescue.

Land status: In the Nantahala National Forest.

Maps: A good investment for bikers wanting to explore the Nantahala National Forest is the map by the same name, sold at the Ranger District office and at local bike stores.

Finding the trail: Travel north out of Andrews, North Carolina, staying on US 19 until you pass Nantahala Outdoor Center on the left in Wesser. Climb over

Grassy Gap and drop to the intersection with NC 28 North, taking the left toward Almond. Go approximately 7 miles, passing the sign for Tsali on the right and pedaling through the community of Stecoah. Turn left onto Upper Tuskegee Road, NC 1242 (on a slight uphill grade, in the middle of a right-hand curve in the highway), and continue to Cable Gap and Wauchacha [sic] Road, FS 438, on the left. The ride begins behind the closed gate.

Source of additional information:

> Cheoah Ranger District
> Nantahala National Forest
> Route 1, Box 16-A
> Robbinsville, NC 28721
> (828) 479-6431

Notes on the trail: This out-and-back contains few choices, other than turning around. The first mile or so on FS 438 parallels the creek forming the uppermost leg of Yellow Creek. The intersection with 438A on the right, an additional ride, signals the beginning of a series of progressively steeper switchbacks leading to Wauchecha Bald. A sign in the curve of the first switchback gives the mileage to the Appalachian Trail via the lookout tower: 2.5 miles. After a steady, hard climb of at least 10 minutes, you'll see a private road and a field on the right. Continue straight—and up—on an even more steeply pitched roadbed, until you finally gain the summit. Return the way you came.

RIDE 49 · Stecoah Gap

AT A GLANCE

Length/configuration: An 8-mile total (4 miles one way) out-and-back lightly graveled (dirt base) service road

Aerobic difficulty: Very little, even taken at a quick clip

Technical difficulty: The wide, graveled roadbed poses no problems

Scenery: The northwest ridge of Cheoah Bald, with views of the Snow Bird Mountains and the Great Smoky Mountains National Park

Special comments: The Appalachian Trail stays to the right of the road and out of sight, all the way to Locust Cove Gap

The slight four-mile climb begins at Stecoah Gap, using the lightly graveled service road for an eight-mile (total) out-and-back. This route is one of the three different trails exploring the flanks of Cheoah Bald, which remains pretty much straight ahead of the rider the entire trip out. Of the three bike rides near Cheoah Bald—Shell Stand Road and Cheoah Bald being the others—the road up from Stecoah Gap has the most moderate elevation gain: less than 100 feet per mile. When I rode this trail, it was a snowy morning. A half inch covered the ground, making it easy to see I was the first one to make tire tracks. But not the first to lay tracks. I followed a bobcat's path made only a few hours (or was it minutes?) earlier, no doubt in its hunt for breakfast. Although a bobcat is likely to feed on anything about its size or smaller, my guess was that this morning the preferred prey was bird—juncos, to be exact. A small pile of gray and white feathers lay on the shoulder of the trail. When I rounded a curve, I saw a flock of dark-eyed juncos, or snowbirds as they are sometimes called locally, thick as gnats. They were feeding on the many dried flower heads, pecking out the seeds, and when I startled them, we all flew off together in a cloud of bike and feathers.

General location: In between Bryson City and Andrews, North Carolina, on SR 143 near NC 28.

Elevation change: Only about 600 feet over 4 miles.

Season: All seasons, but use discretion (or at least a liberal amount of orange) during hunting season—late fall to early winter.

Services: Tsali Recreation Area is nearby. The Nantahala Outdoor Center has all the goods and services a mountain biker is ever likely to need. The area near Stecoah on NC 28 has cabins, campgrounds, small diners, and convenience stores.

Hazards: Hunters provide the most significant hazard on this nontechnical trail.

Rescue index: The road is wide and easily traveled, thereby enabling an easy rescue. But a 4-mile walk out would still be a challenge. And, unless it's hunting season, it could be quite some time before anyone discovered you.

Land status: Part of the Nantahala National Forest.

Maps: A good investment for bikers wanting to explore the Nantahala National Forest is the map by the same name, sold at the District Ranger office and local bike stores. See page 166 for our map of this ride.

Finding the trail: Travel north out of Andrews, North Carolina, staying on US 19 until you pass Nantahala Outdoor Center on the left in Wesser. Climb over Grassy Gap and drop to the intersection with NC 28 North, taking the left toward Almond. Go approximately 8 miles, just past the tiny community of Stecoah. NC 143 turns left toward Robbinsville. Travel just under 2 miles and look for a sign posted at Stecoah Gap, elevation 3,165 feet. The gated road lies in between the parking lot and the entrance to the Appalachian Trail, marked to the right of the parking lot by a white diamond inside a green rectangle.

Source of additional information:

Cheoah Ranger District
Nantahala National Forest
Route 1, Box 16-A
Robbinsville, NC 28721
(828) 479-6431

Notes on the trail: Not much to ponder on this one. Ride past the gate and enjoy the sights. Reach the end and turn around. A foot trail connects this road (FS 2610) to the Appalachian Trail, about three-fourths of the way out to the turnaround.

RIDE 50 · Cheoah Bald

AT A GLANCE

———————

NC

Length/configuration: A 6.5-mile (one way) out-and-back (13 miles total), mostly on a lightly graveled (dirt base) service road

Aerobic difficulty: A strenuous workout, portions of which will require you to dismount

Technical difficulty: The wide, open service road gives little challenge; closer to the top, however, prepare for more technical riding

Scenery: Cheoah Bald and the climb up to over 5,000 feet above sea level

Special comments: A hike of at least a half mile one way (1 mile total) is necessary in order to gain Cheoah's summit

The ultimate route along Cheoah Bald's flanks is the Cheoah Bald Trail, a 6.5-mile one way (13 miles total) lightly graveled service road. Saddle up in the knowledge that the total gain will be over 2,000 feet in 6 miles. *Ooh-ee!* My legs ache just thinking about it. It may take several stages to complete the climb, but the work is worth it.

It is probably no coincidence that outdoor recreation is centered along Cheoah Bald. With the Appalachian Trail intersecting on top with the bike trail, and the famous Nantahala River in the gorge immediately to the east, three popular sports come together near this towering rock face.

The rocky cliffs and steep forests surrounding the road are home to tough and adaptable creatures. Deer and turkey fatten on the abundant mast from oaks.

A fire road winds its way toward a gap on the other side of a wide, steep cove.

The biker with an observant eye may be able to pick out owls roosting on hemlock boughs, and spotting a ruffed grouse is likely. They're normally seen only after they've been spooked, wings whistling, flying off like a missile.

General location: About 20 minutes north of Andrews, North Carolina, near US 129.

Elevation change: If the summit is reached, plan on gaining about 2,300 feet. The last half mile is especially steep.

Season: This is an all-season trail. As always, when in the National Forest during the late fall and early winter, wear lots of bright orange.

Services: The Nantahala Outdoor Center, in nearby Wesser, North Carolina, has all the goods and services required by bikers.

Hazards: The steeper sections require some caution, especially on the descent. Other than that, hunters are the only significant hazards, usually limited to the late fall and early winter, and never on Sundays in North Carolina.

Rescue index: The road is wide and easily traveled, enabling a fairly easy rescue by vehicle and by foot. But a 6.5-mile walk out would be difficult. This is a remote setting getting only sporadic use, so it could be an uncomfortably long time before anyone accidentally discovers you.

Land status: Part of the Nantahala National Forest.

Maps: A good investment for bikers wanting to explore the Nantahala National Forest would be the map by the same name, sold by the District Ranger office and at local bike stores. See page 166 for our map of this ride.

Finding the trail: From Murphy, North Carolina, head north on US 129/19. In Topton, turn left on US 129 and go approximately 2.5 miles. Look for the first paved road to the right and turn. It turns into a private road shortly, where FS 259 starts on the left. Park on the side of the road here.

Source of additional information:

Cheoah Ranger District
Nantahala National Forest
Route 1, Box 16-A
Robbinsville, NC 28721
(828) 479-6431

Notes on the trail: The route remains simple for the first leg—up to a gate at the 6.5-mile mark. At this point it gets too steep to ride, so hop off and enjoy the walk. A private road comes in on the right, just before a **T** intersection. Turn left at the **T**. Stow the bike, if you haven't done so already, before you reach the Appalachian Trail. Take a left on the AT for the final walk up to Cheoah Bald for a spectacular view. On the return, don't forget to turn right at the first intersection, bear right again at the next fork, where a private road goes left.

RIDE 51 · Knobscorcher

AT A GLANCE
─────────────

NC

Length/configuration: A 4-mile loop, mostly single-track

Aerobic difficulty: Some short, steeper sections will require an intense performance by the heart and lungs

Technical difficulty: Large rocks, roots, and especially gullies made from horses make the route technically demanding in places

Scenery: Views across a narrow finger of Fontana Lake, and of the surrounding mountains; shaded, protected coves

Special comments: A popular venue for a spring and fall race series called Knobscorcher

I pulled into the parking lot of Nantahala Village looking for the four-mile (mainly single-track) loop bearing the alluring name Knobscorcher. I saw a young man repairing the office for Nantahala Village, a network of small vaca-

RIDE 51 · Knobscorcher

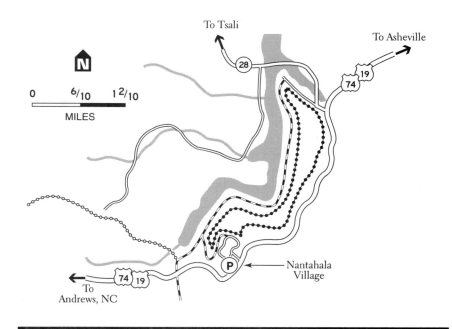

tion homes built on the slopes near the Nantahala Outdoor Center. His cropped, bleach-blond hair, dark roots, and ears bejangled with green earrings suggested to me that he would know something about nearby mountain biking opportunities. I was sure of it when I saw he also had his upper eyebrow pierced with a chain link.

"Just start it here, dude," he said.

"Okay," I said, "but where do I go from here?"

He pointed behind the building. "Go down this road until you come to a brown house. Look for the trail on the right, just past the house." The trail's use as a race site in the spring and fall contributes largely to its popularity. Radical bikers will like its demanding passages through horse-made ruts, crank deep. It is a fast course with steep drops and sharp curves. Due to heavy horse use, though, it stays muddy longer after a rain than do some of the other area trails. Several alternate connections and routes allow for creativity in direction and length. Part of the trail follows the boundary line for a farm located below Nantahala Village.

General location: In between Bryson City and Andrews, North Carolina.

Elevation change: About 300 feet gained per lap, with most of it occurring in one section.

A section of Knobscorcher overlooks the lake, with the Great Smoky Mountains in the background.

Season: The summer traffic of horses from nearby stables renting to vacationers makes either early or late riding advisable in the tourist months of summer; there are large portions of Knobscorcher open for horseback riding. Winter riding requires a wait of several days after a rain before resuming responsible use. Watch for hunters in the fall.

Services: A restaurant is located at the Nantahala Village trailhead. Nantahala Outdoor Center is just a few miles south on US 129 and can meet most bikers' total needs.

Hazards: Hikers, horses, and other bikers, along with deep ruts and mudholes, can make things tough.

Rescue index: Since the trail is squeezed in between two paved roads, a rescue here is about as easy as it gets, at least in this neck of the woods. The sound of the highway is close for at least a quarter of the ride. And, of course, being close to the resort community makes it easier to get help.

Land status: A portion of the trail is on land connected to the resort community of Nantahala Village, and the rest passes through Nantahala National Forest.

Maps: I used my own notes, along with the Nantahala National Forest map and local sources, to draw the map appearing here. The USGS 7.5 minute series topographical map covering this ride is called Wesser.

Finding the trail: There are two trailheads from which to start this ride. To reach the Nantahala Village trailhead, head north on US 19 past Nantahala Outdoor Center at Wesser, North Carolina. At the top of the hill, about a mile past the center, the sign for Nantahala Village will be on the left. Turn in and park. Ride behind the buildings on the paved road to Observation Point (a small playground is on the right). At the bottom of the hill, take a right and an immediate right again onto the single-track, which is posted with a white "No Riding Past Dark" sign.

To reach the NC 28 trailhead, go past Nantahala Village and turn left onto NC 28, going north toward Almond. Turn left onto the first paved road after crossing the first bridge. Stop and park on the side of the road. The gated double-track service road, 30 yards north (away from the bridge), begins the trail.

Source of additional information:

Nantahala Village
4900 Highway 19W
Bryson City, NC 28713
(828) 488-2826
(800) 438-1507 outside North Carolina

Notes on the trail: Beginning at the NC 28 trailhead and traveling in a counterclockwise direction, ride around the normally closed gate on the FS 28 road, heading south along the slow-moving waters of the Nantahala River, which is more lake than anything at this point. A left turn onto single-track occurs shortly after you pass through the gate. Or continue straight on the double-track. The single-track rejoins the double-track approximately 1.5 miles later on a steep downhill. Another single-track connection to the left is made a hundred yards farther up. Take this to make a really short loop back to Nantahala Village. For the full loop, continue past this turn and descend on the double-track, getting into the ruttiest portion of the loop. About halfway through, at the first **T**, turn left up into some more washed-out ruts. A little farther on, at the next **T** intersection, turn left again. Do not cross the creek on the right; the road leads to a barn and livestock pen. Turn left and bypass the horse trail coming down on the right. A climb of slightly over a quarter of a mile leads to an intersection with a paved ridge road, part of Nantahala Village. Turn left (although it's more like continuing straight), passing the right turn up the hill to Observation Point and the highway. The single-track turns off to the right just past the house on the corner; it may still be marked by a white sign posted to a tree. At the next intersection, you'll see single-track go off to the right. Take it and the next right as well. It is blazed red. This section of trail drops steeply, ending where it intersects with the paved road. Turn left back to the highway, a scant quarter mile away. The narrow finger of a Fontana Lake inlet will be on the right.

RIDE 52 · Fontana Village

AT A GLANCE

NC

Length/configuration: Two different rides—the 3.2-mile Lewellyn Cove Loop (single-track and lightly graveled service road) and a 2-mile loop (mostly wide single-track) on the other side of the NC 28, across from Lewellyn Cove Loop's trailhead

Aerobic difficulty: Places are extremely steep, capable of generating great oxygen debt

Technical difficulty: It can be difficult for a beginner, but not overwhelming

Scenery: Fontana Dam as seen from the Yellow Creek Mountains

Special comments: One loop is located on the south side of NC 28 (Lewellyn Cove Loop); the other is located on the north side of NC 28

Traveling northwest from Tsali Recreation Area and just across Fontana Lake from the Great Smoky Mountains National Park, a mostly single-track loop (a 3.2-miler) and a double-track loop (a 2-miler) begin near Fontana Dam, which at 480 feet, is the tallest dam east of the Rockies. It is nearly a half mile across and serves as the Appalachian Trail's southern entry into the Great Smoky Mountains National Park, which begins immediately on the other side.

I began my ride here in late fall, the off-season. I turned up the hill where a sign on the highway indicated I might find information on Fontana Village and the surrounding area. I set out on the red-blazed trail at the end of the road (about 50 yards from the highway) unprepared for what I would find. After reaching an intersection where I could see some of the resort homes below, I made a steep climb. There was fresh-turned dirt on the newly constructed trail, and loose, flat rocks covered the surface, all of which made the going tough.

Off the backside of a small unnamed peak, I rolled through a rhododendron thicket. While I was setting up the camera for a picture, my heart flew into my throat. The cold afternoon's stillness was broken by the wingbeats of three ruffed grouse exploding off their roost and firing off across the meadow below.

General location: On NC 28, 2 miles (as the car drives) south of Fontana Dam.

Elevation change: Over 1,000 feet, with some drastic and extreme changes along the way.

Season: I would recommend riding here during the off-season: late fall, winter, and early spring. During the peak season, hikers may crowd the trail too much.

These rhododendron
near Fontana Village
have their leaves in the
flaps down position to
counter the extreme cold.

Services: Fontana Village has a good restaurant and places to stay, but the Nantahala Outdoor Center is the closest destination if you need special biking services. The economy around here is based on catering to the needs of the traveler, so most basic services—food, lodging, and gas—can be found in nearby towns.

Hazards: Some steep sections (with radical washouts) make portions of this trail system inadvisable for the biker with little experience.

Rescue index: Getting a rescue carried out should be no trouble here. The highway is nearby, and the forest service road can be easily accessed by vehicles. But the overall remoteness of the area makes it a good idea to ride prepared for self-rescue, especially during the off-season of late fall and winter.

Land status: Much of the trail lies on land inside the Nantahala National Forest.

Maps: A good investment for bikers wanting to explore the Nantahala National Forest is the map by the same name, sold at the District Ranger office and at local bike stores. See page 176 for our map of this ride.

Finding the trail: Drive north from Murphy, North Carolina, on US 74/19 to the intersection with NC 28 and turn left toward Almond. The Tsali Recreation Area entrance will be seen on the right about 3 miles north of the intersection. Continue heading northwest on NC 28 for 30 minutes or so, until you reach a stop sign where a right turn leads to Fontana Dam and a left turn goes to Fontana Village. Turn left and drive less than 2 miles. Pass a gated forest service road on the left (FS 2624, another possible ride), or continue a short distance to the parking area on the left for Lewellyn Cove Loop. Lewellyn Cove trailhead is obvious—marked with a sign. The smaller loop, which is not so obvious, begins across the highway from the Lewellyn Cove trailhead, up the hill, and at the end of the road, which has a sign advertising information on Fontana Village.

Source of additional information:

> Cheoah Ranger District
> Nantahala National Forest
> Route 1, Box 16-A
> Robbinsville, NC 28721
> (828) 479-6431

Notes on the trail: The 2-mile loop begins at the top of the hill on the road across the highway from the parking lot for Lewellyn Cove. Pick up the red-blazed trail around an open garage piled with odds and ends. A short piece of single-track leads to the intersection with a paved road; a gate is on the right, and the highway can be seen to the left. Continue straight until coming to another fork, reached in about 5 minutes, where the highway should again be obvious to the left. Bear right, and climb steeply. Head to the top of a ridge and quickly begin a descent through the rhododendron, a technical section hugging the hillside. Thirty yards later, note the intersection with a paved road, the same gated road found at the first intersection. Go through the gate at the top of the climb and turn left onto the single-track. Lewellyn Cove: Note two trails at the trailhead. Take the one closest to the parking lot and begin a counterclockwise loop. At the first intersection, go straight. At about the 1.5-mile mark, it is possible to turn right onto FS 2624, which dead-ends after another 2.5 miles, for a 5-mile total out-and-almost-back to the intersection with Lewellyn Cove Loop. Instead of coming back all the way to the intersection of FS 2624, take the right turn off the gravel road (FS 2624) for the single-track onto Lewellyn Cove Loop. Be prepared for a steep descent. Turn left at the next intersection and bear left at the bridge, which leads back to the trailhead.

RIDE 53 · Hanging Dog Trail

AT A GLANCE

Length/configuration: 4 miles total on a 2-mile (one way) out-and-back service road, combined with to-be-determined single-track loops off the main out-and-back

Aerobic difficulty: Two fairly long climbs, both of which are steep

Technical difficulty: The road has a thick layer of gravel in most places

Scenery: Hiwassee Lake

Special comments: Construction plans call for single-track loops to complete the total mileage available on this route

My visit to this steep, two-mile out-and-back gravel service road (four miles total) at Hanging Dog Recreation Area had been predicted by a neighbor's prescient dog, who barked constantly until 2:30 the night before my ride. Sleepy and tired, I arrived at the Tusquitee Ranger District office in Murphy not expecting to find any other places to ride in the Nantahala National Forest but the famous Tsali off-road network. I perked up when I heard of plans to add single-track coming off the existing gravel road leading to the Ramsey Bluff boat ramp by converting a section of "an old skid road." A skidder, of course, is a large tractor used to haul logs out of the forest to the site where the loader puts them on the truck. The proposed entrance for the single-track can be seen through the middle of a lush patch of North Carolina poison ivy. In the deeper shade of the white oaks, hemlocks, and pines, the former logging road runs along the ridge before falling steeply into the cove below. The rangers at the district office were quick to point out that Hanging Dog is slated for even more single-track, to be determined by availability of funds, which is coincidentally in direct proportion to interest shown by users—i.e., mountain bikers. Who knows? Maybe one day bikers will speak of Hanging Dog with as much awe as they do Tsali.

General location: Hanging Dog Recreation Area is located in between the Hanging Dog and Grape Creek communities, about 5 minutes northwest of Murphy on State Road 1326.

Elevation change: It's a three-quarter-mile, 15-degree climb right at the start. For more details, consult the Murphy topo map of the 7.5 minute series put out by the USGS.

RIDE 53 · Hanging Dog Trail

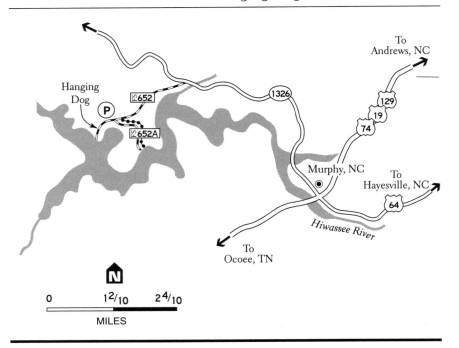

Season: The gravel on the double-track ensures a ride here all year long, except for those snowy, icy times.

Services: A small store in Hanging Rock, 1.5 miles outside the recreation area's entrance (toward Murphy), can provide the basics. The camping area has water and showers, but it is seasonal, open from April 15 through November 15. Most food, lodging, and supplies can be acquired in Murphy, except for biking supplies; those are most closely and reliably obtained at Nantahala Outdoor Center, 35 miles away in Wesser.

Hazards: Loose, thick gravel on the service can create an unexpected skid. Also, vehicles pulling boats may be encountered since the road leads to the Ramsey Bluff Boat Ramp; this hazard is not present, however, when the gate is closed.

Rescue index: The service road is nearby, as is Murphy. This is a frequently used recreation area. All of which suggests it would be an easier rescue here.

Land status: In the Nantahala National Forest.

Maps: Since the trail is in the planning stages, no official map has been drawn; however, the Nantahala National Forest Map shows the recreation area, while the Murphy quadrangle in the 7.5 minute topo series shows detailed information on the surrounding area. The service road appears on the Nantahala National Forest map, available at the Ranger District offices and area bike shops.

Finding the trail: Leave Murphy, North Carolina, on NC 1326, Murphy's main downtown drag and head northwest. Approximately 2 miles past the store in Hanging Dog and almost immediately after crossing a narrow one-lane (!) bridge, turn at the sign on the left. Travel another mile, pay the user fee, and continue 1 mile to the parking lot above a swimming area. The gate across FS 652E to Ramsey Bluff Boat Ramp is back toward the entrance a little over a quarter mile on the right.

Sources of additional information:

Tusquitee Ranger District
Nantahala National Forest
201 Woodland Drive
Murphy, NC 28906
(828) 837-5152

Nantahala Outdoor Center
13077 Highway 19W
Bryson City, NC 28713-9165
(828) 488-2175

Notes on the trail: The existing double-track may be short on distance, but it is long on potential. Used as an out-and-back, the gravel road is planned to be the dividing line between single-track loops on both sides. As it is, the out-and-back consists of a simple yet steep climb-and-drop to a peninsula sticking into Hiwassee Lake's narrow backwater just west of Murphy. When completed, the single-track portion will be bordered on the east by water and on the west by FS 652.

RIDE 54 · Panthertown Valley

AT A GLANCE

Length/configuration: 4.6-mile combination (2.8-mile loop with out-and-back spur; spur is .9 mile one way)

Aerobic difficulty: Overall fairly easy; the climb back to the trailhead is short but steep

Technical difficulty: Minimal but gets your attention; sand bogs, rocky sections, and two small creek crossings keep you on your toes

Scenery: Often called the "Yosemite of the East;" bring a camera

Special comments: A great trail network, campsites, a shelter, waterfalls, and incredible scenery combine to make this a great weekend getaway

*This profile was contributed by Steve Thompson; source material for this profile's map was created by John Derry.

This 4.6-mile combination trail (a 2.8-mile loop with an out-and-back spur; the spur is .9 mile each way) is a great introduction to the interior of Panthertown Valley. Mostly level, moderately technical, and a lot of fun to ride, this trail follows a jeep road, double-track, single-track, and a grassy logging road as it rolls through rare southern Appalachian bog and swamp forest-bog complexes. A couple of small creek crossings, sand bogs, and rocky terrain make this a great ride for beginners to practice technical skills.

Often referred to as the "Yosemite of the East," Panthertown Valley is an ancient place. Geologists estimate that the mountains used to be about a mile higher than they are today. The granite domes visible from Salt Rock Overlook are called plutons. These were formed about 390 million years ago when mountain-sized pieces of metamorphic rock melted deep beneath the ground and then cooled. Eons of erosion have uncovered these plutons, and today they are called Big Green, Little Green, and Cold Mountain.

This area is fairly new to the Nantahala National Forest system. As of this writing, there is no "official trail system" in place. The Forest Service manages Panthertown Valley as a Management Area 5. This means that nonmotorized semiprimitive recreation (hiking, biking, fishing, and camping) is allowed. The Panthertown Valley ecosystem is very fragile. In order to assure that biking in this special area continues, please stay off the footpaths shown in the accompanying map.

General location: About 2 miles east of Cashiers, North Carolina.

Elevation change: The majority of the trail is gently rolling high mountain valley. The beginning of the trail is steep downhill that must be climbed on the way out.

Season: This trail is best ridden in the summer and fall. The fall foliage is spectacular, but traffic on US 64 during the leaf season can be terrible. Parts of the trail could be under water during times of high rainfall.

Services: All services are available in Cashiers, NC.

Hazards: During the winter months, ice and cold weather can make the waterfalls and granite overlooks treacherous.

Rescue index: Help can be summoned in nearby Cashiers. This area is fairly popular with hikers during the summer months. During the winter, however, Panthertown Valley can be deserted.

Land status: Nantahala National Forest.

Maps: Nantahala National Forest Map. Call or write the Highlands Ranger District office for detailed trail maps of the entire valley. A commercially available map called *A Guide's Guide to Panthertown Valley* can be obtained from Burt Kornegay (a professional guide with Slickrock Expeditions), P.O. Box 1213, Cullowhee, NC 28723. If you're planning on exploring the valley on trails that aren't in this book, then a detailed map is essential.

RIDE 54 · Panthertown Valley

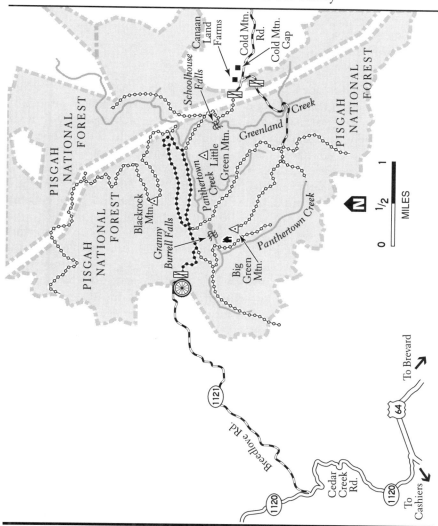

Finding the trail: From Cashiers, NC: Head east on US 64 for 2 miles. Turn left onto Cedar Creek Road (NC 1120). Continue on NC 1120 for 2.2 miles and take a right onto Breedlove Road (NC 1121). Stay on NC 1121 for 3.5 miles as it makes its way through Christmas Tree farms and new development. The road will end at a gate with a small parking area to the right. Park here, being careful not to block the gate. The trail begins at the gate and heads down the gravel road beyond.

Source of additional information:

Highlands Ranger District
2010 Flat Mountain Road
Highlands, NC 28741
(828) 526-3765
The ranger station is located 4 miles east of Highlands, NC, on US 64.

Notes on the trail: Ride around the gate at the parking area and down the hill on the gravel jeep road. This hill is steep and fun, but keep an eye out for hikers and llama trekkers. About .3 mile down the hill, you'll come to Salt Rock Overlook on the left; this makes a great rest stop as you climb the hill on your way out. Continue down the hill for now. At approximately .5 mile into the ride, a trail comes in on the right. This trail will take you to the shelter (1.2 miles from the intersection). Continue straight on the jeep road. After another one-third mile, you will come to an intersection of trails; this is the end of the out-and-back section of the trail. The trail to the right will take you to a campsite (about .1 mile from the intersection). Take the middle trail. The trail becomes single-track and will eventually begin to follow Panthertown Creek. You'll pass a small wooden shelter on the right. There is a beach here and a great swimming hole. About .5 mile from the shelter, there will be a grassy logging road that comes in on the left; make a sharp left turn onto this road. You'll ride along the base of Black Rock Mountain before coming to an old wooden bridge. Cross the bridge and continue on the trail for a couple hundred yards until you come to an intersection of trails. This completes the loop section of the trail. Take a right on the jeep road and climb back to the trailhead and parking lot, resting at Salt Rock Overlook if you like.

RIDE 55 · Canaan Land Loop

AT A GLANCE

Length/configuration: 7.5-mile combination (5.7-mile loop with out-and-back spur; spur is .9 mile one way)

Aerobic difficulty: There are several long, gradual climbs; the climb back to the trailhead is steep but short

Technical difficulty: Several sections of the trail are very technical, though not extremely so; expect rocky downhills, creek crossings, and sandbogs as well as scenic, flat double-track

Scenery: The scenery in Panthertown Valley is spectacular; granite domes, lush vegetation, and white pine stands make this a special place

Special comments: There are several side trails to waterfalls on Panthertown and Greenland Creeks; these two creeks are the headwaters for the Tuckasegee River

The Canaan Land Loop is a 7.5-mile combination trail (5.7-mile loop with an out-and-back spur; the spur is .9 mile one way) that gives the rider a glimpse into the past of Panthertown Valley. The rider will travel on gravel roads, old logging roads, and great single-track as the trail explores the eastern end of Panthertown Valley. The trail is not that tough physically, but there is some significant climbing involved. This is a fairly technical trail, though not overly so. You will encounter areas of loose rock, sand bogs, fast "rooty" downhills, and a couple of slippery creek crossings. But for the most part, the trail conditions make for easy riding.

This trail gets its name because it passes historic Canaan Land Farms, a Christian retreat, which in the 1920s was known as Camp Toxaway. Before that, it was called Baccus Lodge, a retreat and hunting lodge for people such as Thomas Edison and Henry Ford. Just after passing Canaan Land Farms, the trail passes the home of Carlton McNeill. McNeill built and still maintains most of the trails in the valley, and he knows the area like the back of his hand. Both Canaan Land Farms and McNeill's house are private property and should be respected as such.

The trail follows remnants of skid trails and logging roads built in the 1920s, when extensive logging started here. The switchback section of this trail follows

*This profile was contributed by Steve Thompson; source material for this profile's map was created by John Derry.

RIDE 55 · Canaan Land Loop

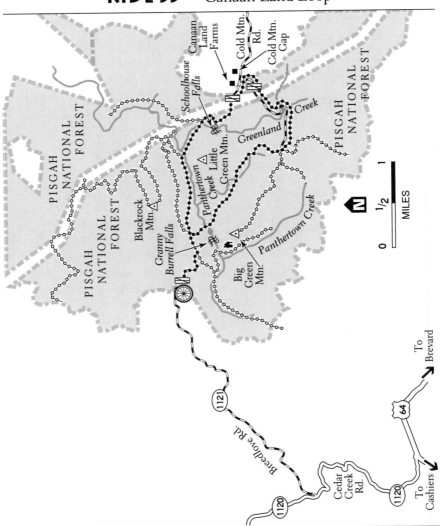

what used to be a railroad bed built to move lumber over Cold Mountain Gap. This area was almost completely denuded by logging operations and the ensuing erosion. In the 1960s, Liberty Properties purchased the valley. The white pine stands that the trail winds through were planted by Liberty, which planned to dam the Tuckaseegee River and sell resort and golf properties in the valley. Fortunately for outdoor enthusiasts, these plans never materialized.

In 1987, Duke Power Company bought the property with plans to build a power line through the valley. Although opposed by environmental groups,

Duke Power built the lines. You pass beneath these lines on a great single-track downhill section of trail. After completing construction, Duke Power sold the land to the Nature Conservancy, which in turn turned the property over to the Forest Service in 1989. Part of the charm of this ride is seeing how Panthertown Valley has started to recover its natural beauty.

General location: About 2 miles east of Cashiers, North Carolina.

Elevation change: The trail starts with a rather steep downhill to the valley floor. From there, you'll gradually climb for a couple of miles, crossing a ridge before heading back to the valley. A short but steep climb takes you back to the trailhead.

Season: The fall colors are spectacular. You may wish to avoid this ride during extremely cold weather because there is no way to stay dry on the creek crossings.

Services: All services are available in nearby Cashiers.

Hazards: During the winter months, the granite overlooks and waterfalls can be treacherous due to ice. The Greenland Creek crossing is deep and should be avoided during cold weather and after heavy spring rains.

Rescue index: Help can be summoned in nearby Cashiers. This area is fairly popular with hikers during the summer months. During the winter, however, Panthertown Valley can be deserted.

Land status: Nantahala National Forest.

Maps: Nantahala National Forest Map. Call or write the Highlands Ranger District office for detailed trail maps of the entire valley. A commercially available map called *A Guide's Guide to Panthertown Valley* can be obtained from Burt Kornegay (a professional guide with Slickrock Expeditions), P.O. Box 1213, Cullowhee, NC 28723. If you're planning on exploring the valley on trails that aren't in this book, then a detailed map is essential.

Finding the trail: From Cashiers, NC: Head east on US 64 for 2 miles. Turn left onto Cedar Creek Road (NC 1120). Continue on NC 1120 for 2.2 miles and turn right onto Breedlove Road (NC 1121). Stay on NC 1121 for 3.5 miles as it makes its way through Christmas Tree farms and new development. The road will end at a gate with a small parking area to the right. Park here, being careful not to block the gate. The trail begins at the gate and heads down the gravel road beyond.

Source of additional information:

Highlands Ranger District
2010 Flat Mountain Road
Highlands, NC 28741
(828) 526-3765
The ranger station is located 4 miles east of Highlands, NC, on US 64.

Notes on the trail: Ride around the gate at the parking area and down the hill on the gravel jeep road. This hill is steep and fun, but keep an eye out for hikers and llama trekkers. About .3 mile down the hill, you'll come to Salt Rock Overlook on the left; this makes a great rest stop as you climb the hill on your way out. Continue down the hill for now. At approximately .5 mile into the ride, a trail comes in on the right. This trail will take you to the shelter (1.2 miles from the intersection). Continue straight on the jeep road. After another one-third mile, you will come to an intersection of trails. The trail to the right will take you to a campsite (about .1 mile from the intersection). Take the middle trail. You will start following Panther Creek and will pass a wooden structure next to a sandbar. This is a fairly popular swimming hole in the summer. Just beyond the sandbar (a couple hundred yards) you will bear right and cross a wooden bridge. At about 2.3 miles you will come to another wooden bridge. Just before this wooden bridge will be a small sandy trail on the right. This path is for foot traffic only; it leads to Schoolhouse Falls.

Moving on, cross the wooden bridge over Greenland Creek. Just past the wooden bridge, a logging road comes in on the left; continue straight. You will begin to climb a gradual grade as the road ascends toward Cold Mountain Gap. You will go through a couple of switchbacks before coming to a gate (3 miles). Continue straight to another gate. Pass the gate and cross a metal bridge. Just beyond the bridge, a wooden fence begins. This is the beginning of Canaan Land Farms property. After passing the main entrance to Canaan Land Farms, turn right onto the first gravel road (3.3 miles). Head up the hill for a couple hundred yards, and you will come to a gated road on the right. Turn right onto the single-track trail, which begins on the far side of the gate. This section of trail is a really fun downhill. At about 3.7 miles, you will pass beneath power lines. The trail will come to an opening next to a creek. Turn right and cross Greenland Creek. The trail continues to another creek at about 4.3 miles. Cross this creek and travel about .1 mile before coming to yet another creek. Take care crossing this creek; it's much more technical than it looks. At about 4.8 miles, a trail comes in on the left; continue straight to an intersection of trails. Take the trail on the right (north). Stay on this trail to another intersection of trails. This is the end of the loop section. Take a left and head up the hill back to the trailhead.

RIDE 56 · Blue Valley

AT A GLANCE

Length/configuration: 14-mile out-and-back (7 miles one way)

Aerobic difficulty: Moderately difficult; there are some long climbs that will test your aerobic fitness

Technical difficulty: The trail is on hard-packed gravel road and is easy to ride

Scenery: Lush rhododendron, hardwood forest, waterfalls, and granite domes give this ride its charm

Special comments: There are many roadside campsites and picnic areas along the trail, and it's located only 5 miles from beautiful Highlands, NC

Until 1981, Highlands was the highest town east of the Mississippi. Located in one of the most scenic areas of western North Carolina, Highlands is popular for its quaint shops, fine inns, and good restaurants. The Highlands area is extremely popular during the fall foliage season. The two-lane US 64 can be unbelievably crowded during this time.

This 14-mile out-and-back trail (7 miles one way) is located about 5 miles south of Highlands. As you descend the hard-packed gravel surface to the turn-around at Abes Creek, you will pass several wildlife openings, newly logged areas, and views of Blue Valley. The trail is fairly tough physically as you climb back from Abes Creek to the trailhead. The only technical challenge is loose gravel in places. If you ride mostly flat trails, this is a great introduction to riding mountainous terrain.

General location: 5 miles south of Highlands, North Carolina.

Elevation change: The trail is mostly downhill to the turnaround. The climb back to the trailhead will test your aerobic capacity.

Season: Fall and winter are the best times for this ride. In the fall, the leaves are spectacular. In the winter, the bare trees allow better views of the surrounding ridges.

Services: All services are available in Highlands, North Carolina.

Hazards: The trail is open to vehicular traffic.

Rescue index: Help can be summoned in nearby Highlands.

---

*This profile was contributed by Steve Thompson; source material for this profile's map was created by John Derry.

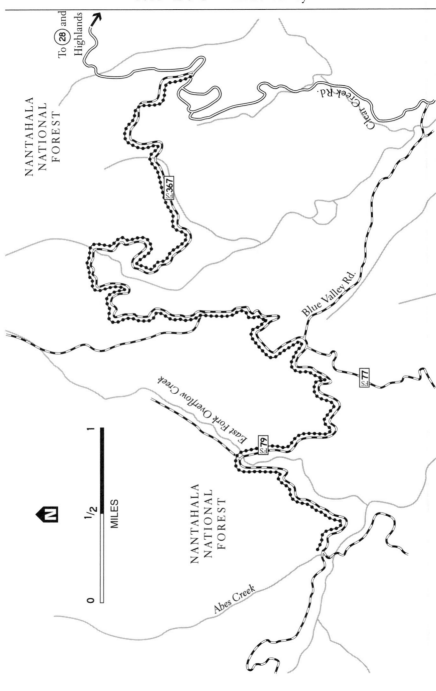

Land status: Nantahala National Forest.

Maps: USGS 7.5 minute quads: Highlands and Scaly. Nantahala National Forest Map. *Tennessee Atlas and Gazetteer* available from Delorme, P.O. Box 298, Yarmouth, Maine 04096.

Finding the trail: From the intersection of US 64 and NC 28 in Highlands, drive south on NC 28 for 2 miles to Clear Creek Road. Turn left onto Clear Creek Road and travel 1.3 miles to FS 367, which is on the right after a sharp hairpin turn. Turn right onto FS 367 and park on the left shoulder, where there are 4 to 6 parking spaces. You can shorten this trail a bit by parking farther in on FS 367.

Sources of additional information:

Highlands Ranger District
2010 Flat Mountain Road
Highlands, NC 28741
(828) 526-3765
The ranger station is located 4 miles east of Highlands, NC, on US 64.

There is some great information about the area in Kevin Adam's *North Carolina Waterfalls—Where to Find Them, How to Photograph Them*, available from John F. Blair, Publisher, Winston-Salem, North Carolina.

Notes on the trail: From the parking area, go west for about 5 miles until you reach a **T** intersection at FS 367 and FS 79. Turn right (west) onto FS 79. After a hundred yards or so, you will pass FS 77 on the left. Bear right here to stay on FS 79. Continue another 1.5 miles until you come to another **T** intersection. There will be an information kiosk here. Turn left to stay on FS 79. About .5 mile from the kiosk, there will be a picnic area on the left. A couple of hundred yards from the picnic area will be a small parking area on the right, next to a small creek (Abes Creek). Turn around here and head back to the trailhead the same way you came in.

NORTH GEORGIA

Mountain biking in north Georgia means mountain biking in the Chattahoochee National Forest. Over 760,000 acres of forest, stream, and dale stretch from Ellicott Rock in the northeast to the Cohutta Mountains in the west. And prettier country you've never seen. Lush, green, and wet. It's not a rain forest, exactly. But with an average of over 60 inches of rain a year in some places, the Chattahoochee comes close.

All that rain has to go somewhere. And that somewhere is the seemingly endless number of rivers, creeks, and springs. Expect to get wet feet on many rides in north Georgia. Numerous fords across deep creeks and shallow rivers will sometimes be crank deep and more. Most of the mountain biking trails in the Chattahoochee National Forest are under solid shade. Majestic trees—oaks, maples, hickories—interlock their leaves and boughs 70 to 100 feet above the saddle. After the leaves fall, the forest views open up, revealing a rich and dark green growth of pines, laurel, hemlock, and rhododendron.

Sources of additional information:

Brasstown Ranger District
Chattahoochee National Forest
Highway 715 West
Blairsville, GA 30512
(706) 745-6928

Chestatee Ranger District
U.S. Forest Service Business Center
102 Memorial Drive
Dahlonega, GA 30533
(706) 864-6173

Cohutta Ranger District
National Forest Service
401 Old Ellijay Highway
Chatsworth, GA 30705
(706) 695-6737 or 695-6736

RIDE 57 · Lady Slipper at Lake Russell

AT A GLANCE

GA

Length/configuration: 6.2 miles (mostly single-track) total, made up of a loop on the end of an approach trail

Aerobic difficulty: Moderately difficult; the steep sections are short, and the initial mile-long climb is a good workout

Technical difficulty: Only an extraordinary biker can ride the entire length without having to dismount at least once—that is, until bridges go up at all stream crossings; the overall difficulty of this trail falls somewhere in the middle

Scenery: Lake Russell and the northeastern section of the Chattahoochee National Forest

Special comments: This ride is located inside a USDA Fee Area and is open to horseback riding

I was introduced to this moderately strenuous 6.2-mile loop of combination single- and double-track by the owner of Woody's Bike Store in Helen, Georgia, who was kind enough to act as guide-for-the-morning. "The first time I rode this trail," Woody said, "I missed a turn. I wound up making a 30-mile loop around Currahee Mountain." There's little chance of that happening now, though. In addition to dispensing invaluable advice and service to the local biking community in northeast Georgia, Woody also arranges regular work days here and at other area trails. One project included signing turns and blazing trails. Lady Slipper's important intersections are well marked, with blue blazes appearing at frequent intervals. Other markings can also be found here. Woody pointed out fresh bear sign in the middle of the trail, which answered an often asked question. Later, as we crossed a creek, we saw another pile, but this one was made of feathers, freshly strewn either by a fox or a bobcat. No doubt, the songbird meal was finished off with a long drink from the creek, whose banks—despite it being late fall—sported half a dozen gentian blooming fresh and blue.

After gaining the northeast flanks of Red Root Mountain, Woody and I made a counterclockwise loop around its summit. With a final climb up to an overlook, Lady Slipper uses part of a lightly graveled road (normally closed) to finish the loop before rejoining the single-track approach trail. After a walk along Lake Russell Trail (reserved for foot travel only) and a snack, you can take another lap before heading home. Chances are, you'll agree Lady Slipper is a perfect fit.

RIDE 57 • Lady Slipper at Lake Russell

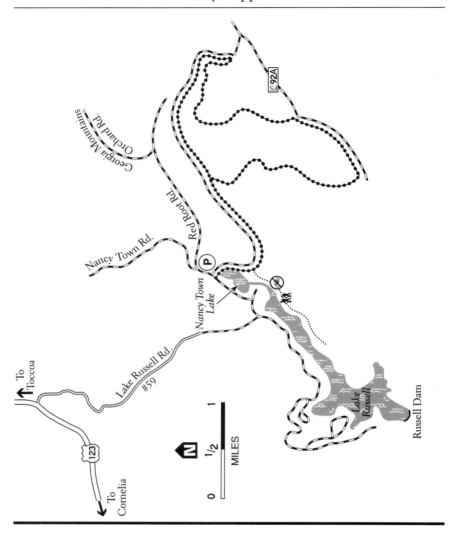

General location: Just east of Cornelia, Georgia, in the Chattahoochee National Forest, where Habersham, Banks, and Stephens Counties join.

Elevation change: Overall, the gain approaches approximately 500 feet of climbing per lap, with most of it occurring on fairly moderate sections.

Season: This is an all-season trail, making it an especially suitable destination during hunting season (late fall and early winter) since hunting is not allowed here.

The older a forest is, the better the mountain biking. Photo by Pam Jones.

Services: The Lake Russell Recreation Area has a fully developed campground, complete with showers and designated swimming area. The medium-sized cities of Cornelia (pronounced Kor-KNEE-yur by locals) and Clarkesville have all the basics, plus a good deal more. For the biker in need of some work done on the steel steed, a 30-mile drive to Helen (and Woody's) is the closest and best place for friendly service.

Hazards: A few ditches will challenge even experienced bikers. Bridges, built with hikers in mind, also give a technical challenge. Muddy areas, where springs ooze out of Red Root's side, are best traveled on foot. One notable downhill stretch will have you nearly sitting on the back tire: beware the switchback at the bottom and a big drop over a deadfall at the beginning. The waterbars on the initial climb were described by Woody as "hospital bills" for their ability to launch speeding, downhill bikers into uncontrolled flights and landings. Also, horses may be present.

Rescue index: Most areas are easily accessed by vehicle should the need arise.

Land status: Chattahoochee National Forest (fee area).

Maps: The Lake Russell Recreation Complex map is available at the pay station, and it shows Lady Slipper Trail, as well as two other trails: Lake Russell and Sourwood (foot travel only).

Finding the trail: Take US 123 north out of Cornelia, approximately 3 miles. On the right, across from Lake Russell Convenience Store, turn onto Forest Service Road 59. Just a little over a mile, look on the left for a gravel road (gated but normally open) where a self-pay station is found on the other side of Nancy Town Creek. After paying the required fee, continue uphill and park in the second lot on the right. The trail begins at the south end of the lot.

Source of additional information:

Chattooga Ranger District
P.O. Box 196
Burton Road
Clarkesville, GA 30523
(706) 754-6221

Notes on the trail: After leaving the parking lot, continue south past Nancy Town Lake. Notice Lake Russell Trail forking to the right, but take the left and pedal up nearly a mile, grunting and groaning over the waterbars. At the top, hang a left on a gravel road for less than a mile before turning right onto the single-track, which is marked by a wooden sign. The first section rolls up and down a couple of creek ridges, crossing the creeks in between. The trail joins FS 92A and follows it to the right (northeast) for about three-quarters of a mile. Be looking for the sign indicating the left turn back onto single-track; if a gravel road comes in on the left, you missed the turn. Turn around and take the right onto the single-track. It winds its way across some more rollers and creek crossings before making a climb up to Red Root Road. Just before reaching the road, turn sharply to the left. The single-track makes a short but steep climb to the best overlook on the trail. A daring downhill follows, ending on some double-track that goes along a ridge. Look for the right turn that leads back to the trailhead via the approach trail.

RIDE 58 · Unicoi

AT A GLANCE
————————

Length/configuration: A 7-mile loop on narrow double-track

Aerobic difficulty: You'll be wishing you had an extra lung on a couple of climbs

Technical difficulty: It's tough, but not so tough a dedicated novice can't enjoy it

Scenery: Unicoi State Park, creek crossings, and a mature hardwood and pine forest

Special comments: The park has a good restaurant, plus it's a good place to camp or rent a cottage

When NORBA's competition director, Brian Stickel, began searching for a Deep South venue for the 1994 National Championship Series, he wound up talking to Don Hoche at Unicoi State Park. At the time, Unicoi had no trail for mountain bikes in place, but Stickel was impressed with Hoche's proposal to install a trail where the best of the best can compete in cross-country cycling.

A deal was struck, and plans went ahead for incorporating the existing double-track with some new single-track into a loop of approximately seven miles. Although NORBA has since dropped Helen as a scheduled race site, the trail is still home to several local races and events. But no matter. What NORBA lost mountain bikers from all over the country gained.

Unicoi (pronounced oo-NEE-ko-WEH in its native Cherokee tongue, meaning "where the white man goes") was first established in 1954 as a small 250-acre park lying mainly north of present-day Smith Lake and centered on what is still the area's chief attraction, Anna Ruby Falls.

In the late 1960s, 750 acres were added. Logging inside the park was stopped over 40 years ago, so the forest has matured with mixed hardwoods rising seventy feet tall, shading steep slopes of rhododendron and laurel.

No visit to Unicoi is complete without a visit to the small town of Helen, where lederhosen-clad locals march in oompah bands. During Oktoberfest, the town hosts what can only be called a Teutonic extravaganza. It is a time when the language most often heard on the streets is German, but with a definite southern drawl. For those who want a more traditional experience, visit the Goofy Rooster (home of the monthly meetings of the Helen chapter of the Southern Off-Road Bicycle Association, or SORBA) or Fred's Famous Peanuts. And while you're grabbing a paper poke of boiled goobers from Fred, stop by and see Woody next door.

General location: Helen, Georgia, is nestled in the mountains 70 miles northeast of Atlanta.

Elevation change: Although a change was made from the first course layout, which called for a back-breaking climb right out of the gate, long ascents will still have to be made by pedal or push.

Season: No seasonal restrictions apply here. In fact, when hunters are squeezing off rounds at anything that moves inside the nearby national forests, this state park, where hunting is prohibited, is a good place to ride.

Services: Helen has made its living since the late 1960s by catering to the needs of tourists, so all services, including a great bike shop, can be found here.

Hazards: Sections steep enough to wrap your cheeks around your ears. One area has a spring coming out of the bank, right above a falls. It can be particularly hazardous, even though regular trail maintenance is performed by the Helen bike club. Also be alert for hikers.

Rescue index: Most portions of the path can be reached by a four-wheeler fairly easily . . . once you're discovered. A walk out of no more than 2 miles would be

RIDE 58 · Unicoi

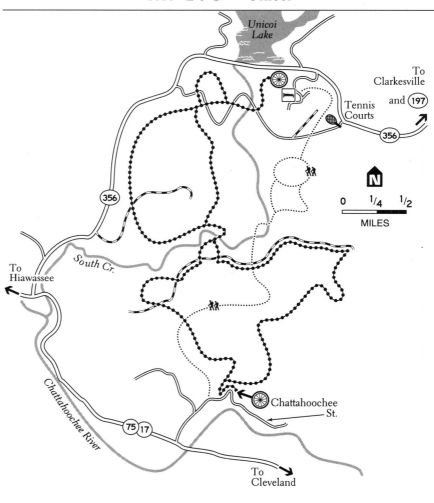

required should an irreparable flat occur. By toting a cell phone, you could call Woody and see if he's able to do a trail call.

Land status: The Department of Natural Resources manages this land as a state park.

Maps: Maps are available at the Unicoi State Park office. Ask for the Unicoi Mountain Bike Trail Map.

Finding the trail: To reach the Lodge trailhead, leave Helen headed north on GA 75. Turn right onto GA 356 toward Unicoi State Park. Cross the dam.

Woody wheels under a winter canopy at Unicoi State Park.

Approximately a half mile farther down, turn right toward the lodge and register. (Don't forget the pass includes the day-use fee for the entire park.) Return to GA 356 and turn right toward the tennis courts. About a quarter mile farther down on the highway, turn at the sign for the tennis courts. Go about a quarter mile, and park in the lot for the tennis courts on the right. The trail begins down the paved road on the left, past the maintenance building on the right where a water hose is hooked up for bikers to use.

To reach the Helen trailhead, first find the Welcome Center and register (registration is required for all bikers, regardless of which trailhead is used). Come into Helen from Cleveland on GA 75. Pass the water treatment ponds on the right and look for the putt-putt course just past them on the right. Take the next paved street (Brucken Strasse) to the right and go past the post office. The welcome center is on the left; park here.

Note: Registration is required in order for bikers to use the trail legally, and it's a good idea anyway for a number of reasons, perhaps the best one being that registration keeps tabs on the number of bikers using the trail. The more users, the more funding for trail maintenance and construction.

Sources of additional information:

Georgia Department of Natural Resources
Highway 356
Helen, GA 30545
(706) 878-1590 or 878-3982

Woody's
P.O. Box 774
Highway 356 (next to Fred's Famous Peanuts)
Helen, GA 30545
(706) 878-3715

Unicoi State Park and Lodge
Highway 356
Helen, GA 30545
(706) 878-2201
For reservations, call (706) 878-2824

Notes on the trail: From the Lodge trailhead, cross an opening where an abundance of autumn olives have been planted (if you ride in late spring here, you'll always remember the wonderfully sweet smell and the sound of thousands of bees buzzing among the blooms). Cross the creek by using the bridge and turn left past the gate. Turn for a climb uphill and begin following the red blazes. As sure as each hill leads up, a descent follows. Prepare for at least three significant climbs, crossing the creek twice before completing the loop on the downstream side of Smith Lake, on the service road just below the dam. Cross the creek and return to the tennis courts a short climb away.

From the Helen trailhead, leave the welcome center, riding toward the river. Do not cross the bridge; instead, turn left and ride past Fest Hall. The singletrack begins across the paved road at the **T** intersection a quarter-mile past Fest Hall.

RIDE 59 · Davenport Mountain

AT A GLANCE

Length/configuration: A 5-mile loop of narrow double-track

Aerobic difficulty: You will have to work hard in places

Technical difficulty: Washouts and rock outcrops can make climbing or descending more difficult than a dedicated novice can easily handle

Scenery: Davenport Mountain overlooks Nottely Lake

Special comments: This trail was built with motorcycles and four-wheelers in mind, but those infernal combustion machines seldom use this trail

This narrow double-track 5-mile loop is bisected by a gravel forest service road (FS 143). True to its origins as a site for motorcycles and four-wheelers, steep climbs will present a challenge for most mountain bikers. Despite the possibility of having to share the treadway with an occasional motorized vehicle, it isn't likely because—you guessed it—it isn't steep enough for most motorcycles.

The mountain circumscribed on the route is named for the area's earliest white settler, John Davenport, whose 1832 log cabin still stands—although in a different location from its original site. Nottely Lake, which can be seen from the trail, was formed by the backed up waters of the Nottely River in 1942, which prompted the relocation of Davenport's historic home, reached via FS 143.

General location: Just outside of Blairsville, Georgia.

Elevation change: Maximum elevation is 2,280 feet above sea level, and the minimum is 1,900 feet. Some changes are dramatic—at least by mountain biking standards.

Season: Wait a few days after a soaking rain before getting on the trail. Other than that, this trail is an all-season destination.

Services: Nearby Blairsville has the basics with some specialized goods and services. For bicycle repairs, it's almost as quick to head north to the Nantahala Outdoor Center as it is to go south to Dahlonega, southwest to Ellijay, or southeast to Helen. The trailhead has only a trail marker and parking.

Hazards: Motorcycles and four-wheelers on the trail are the bane of mountain biking, and, since the trail remains an officially designated ATV trail, one or two

RIDE 59 · Davenport Mountain

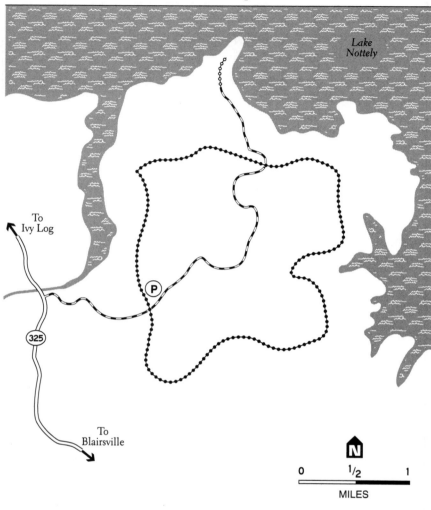

might show up at any time. That likelihood increases on weekends. Some severe washouts may require hiking either up or down.

Rescue index: A rescue can be carried out here with little difficulty. The forest service road gets no farther away than 1.5 miles. Blairsville is close by, as are several houses.

Land status: In the Chattahoochee National Forest.

Maps: The Blairsville Ranger Station on GA 715, west of Blairsville, provided copies of the Davenport Mountain ATV trail map.

Finding the trail: Leave Blairsville, Georgia, headed west on GA 715. Approximately 7 miles from the intersection with US 19/129, turn right onto GA 325. After about 3 miles, look on the right (before crossing the bridge over Hitchcock Branch) for a gravel road heading downhill (Davenport Mountain Road). After another right turn at the bottom of the hill (before crossing the one-lane bridge), go another mile to the parking spot on the left in the middle of an **S** curve. The single-track comes down the mountain on the right, follows the service road about 10 yards, and goes back up on the left.

Source of additional information:

Brasstown Ranger District
Chattahoochee National Forest
Highway 715 West
Blairsville, GA 30512
(706) 745-6928

Notes on the trail: Begin by taking the trail up the hill in a counterclockwise direction. A roller down to a small creek is followed by a climb up the steepest portion of double-domed Davenport Mountain. Straight up. The first 2 miles are complete at the intersection with FS 143. Don't forget to look for the cabin. An added trip can be made by taking the left turn down the gravel road to Nottely Lake. Go straight across the intersection to another creek crossing, a roller, and another creek crossing. A final climb-and-drop over to the west side of the mountain makes the loop to the parking lot. Put in a couple of laps for good measure.

RIDE 60 · Turner Creek Loop, No-Tell Trail

AT A GLANCE

Length/configuration: 5.5-mile loop of single-track and gated service road

Aerobic difficulty: At least 3 climbs will keep your pulse rate high for periods lasting from 10 to 15 minutes each

Technical difficulty: It's easy to handle under normal conditions

Scenery: This upper Etowah River watershed inside the Chattahoochee National Forest is as pretty a forest ride as anywhere

Special comments: This trail is one of four individual trails in the immediate area: all 5-mile or longer loops, on mostly single-track

After the March 13, 1993, blizzard leveled huge tracts of white and yellow pines in the north Georgia mountains, it took nearly two days to open back up primary highways. The forest service roads in the Chattahoochee National Forest remained closed for months. The scale of devastation made it difficult to find any sort of off-road trail open. Yet out of the destruction came one of the finest trails anywhere in the woods.

The leadership of the Southern Off-Road Bicycle Association (SORBA) met with the rangers at the national forest district office in Dahlonega and agreed on plans to construct a mountain bike trail in the upper Etowah River watershed. By February 1994, single-track had been built, connecting gated logging roads and current forest service roads and making a 5.5-mile loop.

It was on this trail late one spring afternoon that a friend and I detoured to a wildlife opening. As soon as we arrived, we were greeted by the sight of an obviously agitated turkey hen flying in an erratic, mock-broken-wing circle around the perimeter of the clearing. Before we could get off our bikes, a chirping broke out at our feet. Two turkey chicks scooted away through the shin-high grass. But as we looked closer, another chick stood still—and unharmed—less than three inches from the back tire of my friend's bike.

We backtracked while the hen flew ahead of us in awkward circles as she tried to draw us away from her newly hatched family. After we had ridden a couple of hundred yards, the turkey finally peeled off and returned to the clearing in an iridescent glide of brown.

General location: This spectacular trail is located 20 minutes northwest of Dahlonega, Georgia.

Elevation change: There are at least three significant climbs lasting from a half mile to a mile, with 200 feet or more gained in each climb.

Season: This trail holds up well during wet weather, but it is best left alone a day or so following a soaking rain. Riding on this surface after a thaw from a hard freeze will leave big ruts. Although hunters are not supposed to hunt near trails and roads, it happens; be forewarned that hunting season (late fall through early winter) inside the Chattahoochee National Forest could possibly have lead flying uncomfortably, if not dangerously, close.

Services: Most services can be found in nearby Dahlonega or Dawsonville. Atlanta, however, will be able to provide it all.

Hazards: Oncoming bikes on the single-track, automobiles on the forest service road, some rocks, limbs, and roots present hazards. During hunting season—especially the first few weekends—try a different trail. Wear an orange vest and make frequent noise when traveling out in the remoter sections of national forests during any hunting season.

Rescue index: This is a fairly remote setting. Ride prepared for self-rescue.

Land status: In the Chattahoochee National Forest, Blue Ridge Wildlife Management Area.

RIDE 60 · Turner Creek Loop, No-Tell Trail

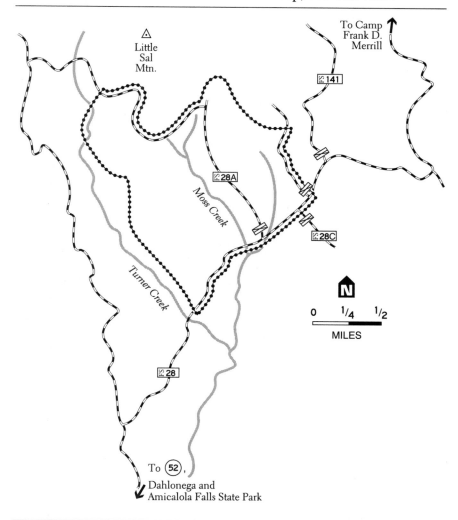

To Camp
Frank D.
Merrill

⚠
Little
Sal
Mtn.

🖭 141

🖭 28A

Moss Creek

Turner Creek

🖭 28C

N

0   ¼   ½

MILES

🖭 28

To ㊿,
Dahlonega and
Amicalola Falls State Park

Maps: If you want to do some exploring of the area, topo quads in the 7.5 minute series Campbell Mountain, Nimblewill, Noontootla, and Suches give info on nearby trails. The map of the Chattahoochee National Forest is a wise investment.

Finding the trail: From Amicalola Falls State Park, continue east on GA 52, entering Lumpkin County. After passing the second Wesley Chapel Road sign on the left, take the left in the curve at the bottom of the hill (approximately a half mile later) at the sign for Nimblewill Church. Continue toward the church,

Jared rides under the arched boughs of a giant beech.

passing it on the left and then taking FS 28, the gravel road, to the left. Approximately 2 miles from there, bear right where FS 28-1 (Winding Stair Gap Road) forks to the left. About three quarters of a mile farther down, a culvert for Turner Creek goes under the road; 10 yards before crossing it, note the gated road on the left. It is a spur leading to Turner Creek Trail. Just after crossing over the creek culvert, the end of Turner Creek single-track comes out from the left onto FS 28. Just past this, after climbing and descending a short hill, gated FS 28A goes off to the left; park here and start, or go on to the alternate trailhead at the next gated forest service road (unnumbered, and approximately three-quarters of a mile farther, after a longer climb) on the left.

From Dahlonega, leave town on GA 52/9 toward Dawsonville. Follow the signs to Amicalola State Park, but before getting to the park and after crossing the Etowah River (a large ostrich farm is on the left), look for the white building on the right where a sign for Nimblewill Church has been placed. Turn there. Just before reaching the church (it will be in sight), turn right onto FS 28. Follow directions from here as stated in previous paragraph.

Source of additional information:

Chestatee Ranger District
U.S. Forest Service Business Center
102 Memorial Drive
Dahlonega, GA 30533
(706) 864-6173

Notes on the trail: There is no rule prohibiting travel in either direction on this trail, but I recommend taking the trailhead at the unnumbered forest service road and riding counterclockwise, finishing with the gravel road climb. Ride past the gate and climb to where an old roadbed comes in from the left; continue straight for a short piece on top of the ridge. Look for the well-worn single-track turning left down the mountain. Take the right turn onto what is called No-Tell Trail, which intersects with FS 28A. Turn right and begin another climb. Look for the carsonite post indicating the trail's left turn off 28A and onto more single-track. If you ride past this left turn, you'll come to the gate on the other end of 28A; Winding Stair Gap Road is the gravel road on the other side.

The single-track section from FS 28A to where it dead-ends at FS 28 can get tight in a few places. Turn right when the single-track intersects with a level, double-track section, which leads back to FS 28. But before reaching FS 28, look for and take the sharp left turn down to the creek (marked by a carsonite post prohibiting horse travel), crossing over on a well-built bridge. A short piece of single-track dead-ends at FS 28. Take a left to complete the loop, finishing with a demanding climb up False Hope Hill.

RIDE 61 · Black Branch Loop

AT A GLANCE

Length/configuration: A 5.5-mile loop of mostly single-track

Aerobic difficulty: There are some steep hills to climb, but they're not long—they just feel that way

Technical difficulty: A few tricky moves are required, but overall, it's a low-key ride

Scenery: Few rides are more beautiful than this one deep in the forest surrounding the upper Etowah River

Special comments: This trail is one of four individual trails in the immediate area: all 5-or-more-mile-long loops on mostly single-track

There are few, if any, rides prettier than this five-and-a-half-mile loop. Over four miles of rolling single-track are connected by a short piece of lightly graveled forest service road. For those wishing to get an extremely taxing aerobic workout, take this trail clockwise. But I ride it counterclockwise and still get all the workout I need and then some.

The mixed hardwood forest used to be the site of what my friend Brian and I formerly called "the Best Trail." It became impassable after the blizzard of 1993. In addition, logging closed some of the adjoining roads, which had previously allowed us to make a long loop through Hoot Owl Holler. For those who possess enough of the Lewis and Clark mentality (and the Campbell Mountain quadrangle of the 7.5 minute topo series), the loop can still be found and ridden, but not without some degree of bushwhacking.

Wildlife sightings are among the biggest thrills you'll experience in this section of the Chattahoochee National Forest. Along with frequent observations of deer and turkeys moving through the thick summer eruptions of ferns and wildflowers, other less common animals may be seen. As Brian and I rode on the first section of single-track, we came to a halt a few feet in front of a long "black snake" stretched across the trail. When it spotted us, it showed obvious agitation by coiling and rapidly rattling its tail, à la rattlesnake. Brian thought it was eating something. But it wasn't until the four-foot-long king snake moved into the thick brush that we saw what it, indeed, had been preparing to eat: a freshly chewed skull attached to a two-foot-long body of a copperhead, whose tail made its last twitch as we watched.

General location: This splendid trail is located 20 minutes northwest of Dahlonega, Georgia.

Elevation change: There's approximately 700 feet of climbing per lap, some of it occurring in radical proportions.

Season: Although this trail holds up well during wet weather, it is best left alone a day or so following rain. Riding on this surface after a hard freeze thaws will leave big ruts. Although hunters are not supposed to hunt near trails and roads, it happens.

Services: Most services can be found nearby in either Dahlonega or Dawsonville. Atlanta, however, provides it all.

Hazards: Oncoming bikes on the either-direction single-track, automobiles on the forest service road, some rocks, limbs, and roots all present manageable hazards. During hunting season (call for specific dates, but generally fall and early winter) try a different trail.

Rescue index: This is a fairly remote area. Ride prepared for self-rescue.

Land status: In the Chattahoochee National Forest, Blue Ridge Wildlife Management Area.

Maps: I used a copy of the Campbell Mountain quadrangle in the 7.5 minute series topographic map to take notes on trail length and direction. After field checking it for accuracy, I produced a tracing.

RIDE 61 · Black Branch Loop

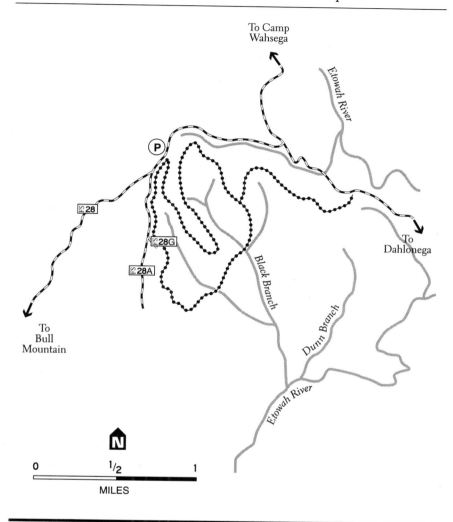

Finding the trail: From Amicalola Falls State Park, continue east on Highway 52, entering Lumpkin County. After Wesley Chapel Road reenters on the left, take the left in the curve at the bottom of the hill (approximately a half mile later) at the sign for Nimblewill Baptist Church. Continue toward the church, passing it on the left and then taking FS 28 (the gravel road) to the left. Approximately 2 miles from there, bear right where FS 28-1 (Winding Stair Gap Road) forks to the left. About three-quarters of a mile farther down, a culvert for Turner Creek goes under the road; just before you cross it, note the gated road

Chris starts carefully
across the bridge.

on the left. It is a spur leading to Turner Creek Trail. Just after crossing over the creek, the end of Turner Creek single-track comes out from the left onto FS 28. Just past this, gated FS 28A goes off to the left. Continue up the hill, passing FS 28B on the right. Park at the top of the hill off the road, where the berm on the right has a single-track.

From Dahlonega, leave town on GA 52/9 toward Dawsonville. Stay on GA 52 (GA 9 bears left) and turn right to Amicalola State Park, but before you get to the park and after you cross the Etowah River (a large ostrich farm is on the left), look for the white building on the right and a sign for Nimblewill Baptist Church. Turn here. Just before you reach the church (it will be in sight), turn right onto FS 28. Follow directions from here as stated above.

Source of additional information:

Chestatee Ranger District
U.S. Forest Service Business Center
102 Memorial Drive
Dahlonega, GA 30533
(706) 864-6173

Notes on the trail: Begin this route by riding west (back toward Nimblewill Baptist Church) on FS 28 to FS 28B, a sometimes gated gravel road on the left that heads south. Approximately a quarter mile farther on the left, FS 28G (the sign may be missing) leads to where the single-track begins at the dead end of FS 28G. After a short climb, it descends and goes into a series of rollers before crossing an unnamed creek that feeds Black Branch. Unless a bridge has been erected, expect to dismount for the crossover. After a climb out of this bottom, a descent heads into the valley holding Black Branch, and once again you must dismount to get across the creek, unless a 10-foot-long ride across an 8-inch-wide board can be completed. Heading north on the climb out of the valley, take the left fork at the intersection about halfway up the climb. (The straight shot up will lead to an intersection with a wildlife opening, at which point the double-track goes to the right, staying on the ridge before descending to an intersection with a gravel road: approximate one-way distance to the road is 1 mile.) After the next creek (unnamed), begin a swing to the south. The climb to the ridge reverses direction, heading north once again. A series of rollers ends with a climb to FS 28 on a double-track. You'll reach the trailhead after you pass over the berm.

RIDE 62 · Little Sal Mountain Loop

AT A GLANCE

GA

Length/configuration: A 9-mile loop on gated and open service roads (lightly graveled)

Aerobic difficulty: Not aerobically demanding

Technical difficulty: The basic loop is not demanding; however, abandoned logging roads (providing numerous out-and-backs) connected to the trail are very technical in places.

Scenery: Montgomery Creek watershed, the Etowah River

Special comments: Two creek crossings will water-log feet during all but the droughtiest of times

The Little Sal Mountain Loop Trail follows nine miles of forest service roads, making a loop in a remote part of the Chattahoochee National Forest. It could just as easily be called the Etowah Headwaters Trail as it winds its way up and down the ridges surrounding the major mountain tributaries of the Etowah River, but it is a good thing to remember that an army base (Camp Frank D. Merrill) trains special forces nearby. On more than one occasion I've heard the

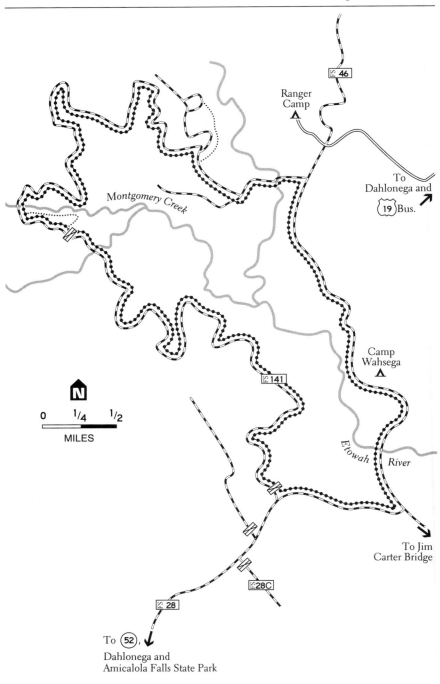

Beaver ponds—a natural spot to stop. If you're lucky, you might ride up on one of the architects.

rapid popping of arms fire, exploding grenades, and choppers flying exercises, causing me to check the cinch on my helmet. For the most part, though, it's easy to enjoy the woods of the upper Etowah River as the truly beautiful and isolated place it is.

The route rolls along the Etowah's main tributary, Montgomery Creek, one of north Georgia's spectacular mountain trout streams. And, if you're like a friend of mine who packs his fly rod with him occasionally, you may even wind up catching one of the native fish that breed in these waters. Mountain biking isn't just about catching air, you know. Despite having about half of this route open to vehicles year-round, traffic is light, except near the entrance to the ranger camp and Camp Wahsega (a 4-H camp). The exception being, of course, during hunting season, when FS 28 has pickups zooming around like downhill racers out of control. During those times (generally mid-fall to early winter), it is best to ride one of the trails nearby where hunting is not allowed.

General location: This trail winds through the Chattahoochee National Forest north of Dahlonega, Georgia.

Elevation change: Little Sal has a few places where the small chain ring will be required, but not many, as the trail only gains about 1,000 feet per 9-mile lap.

Season: Fording the Etowah River at Camp Merrill, small though it is at this point, and crossing the Montgomery Creek at levels other than mid-summer's drought will be chain-ring deep or greater. At especially high water, attempting to ford either of these by bike (or car, for that matter) is not advised.

Services: Many services can be obtained in nearby Dahlonega.

Hazards: A few motorized vehicles may be on the stretch from the ranger camp to Camp Wahsega, with even fewer on the road to Montgomery Creek. Hunters—in season (mid-fall to early winter)—will have vehicles parked at junctions where they have most likely walked down to bag a buck. It is wise to avoid this trail at those times.

Rescue index: By being in the backyard of Camp Frank D. Merrill, where army rangers train in mountain maneuvers, chances for a quick rescue are good. However, it is remote and difficult to conduct any rescue, no matter how good or close the help may be.

Land status: Though it skirts the perimeter of Camp Merrill, the ride stays inside the Chattahoochee National Forest.

Maps: Acquire the four topo maps in the 7.5 minute series—Campbell Mountain, Nimblewill, Noontootla, and Suches—for total coverage. The map of the Chattahoochee National Forest should be sufficient in most cases, however. The map in this book was traced using these two maps.

Finding the trail: From Atlanta, follow signs to Amicalola Falls State Park. After crossing into Lumpkin County and traveling about 3 miles, look for the left turn toward Nimblewill Baptist Church. Turn onto FS 28 just beyond the church. Take the right-hand fork of FS 28 and drive past a gated road on the left where a creek passes underneath the road. Make a long climb, level out for a short distance, then descend and pass another gated road on the left. The next (normally gated) road, FS 141, on the left is one of the trailheads; park without blocking the gate. For the other trailhead, continue straight for approximately 3.5 miles, turning left onto the gravel road that passes by the gym on the right. If you miss it, you will soon come to pavement and the entrance to the base. Turn around and take the second gravel road on the right. The Etowah River will have to be forded at the bottom of the first hill by vehicle, foot, or bike.

From Dahlonega, head north from downtown on GA 60 (Business) toward Suches. Turn left at the sign for Camp Merrill approximately 3 miles north of town. Camp Merrill is nearly 10 miles down the road. At the three-way stop, turn left. Take the second right on the gravel road, which passes by the gym. Either park across from the gym on the left, or ford the Etowah River by vehicle (or foot), parking on the right side of the road next to Mossy Landing Strip.

Sources of additional information:

Chestatee District Ranger's Office
U.S. Forest Service Business Center
102 Memorial Drive
Dahlonega, GA 30533
(706) 864-6173

Camp Frank D. Merrill
Camp Wahsega Road
Dahlonega, GA 30533
(706) 864-3367

Notes on the trail: If you park across from the gym and ford the Etowah by bike, bring a change of socks. Big river stones can be hit on this ford, bringing momentum to a soggy halt. I favor the upstream path, but rocks move after big rains, so scout it first. The cheat chute can be taken by walking across the footbridge (upstream) behind the swimming pool. (You're on the army base at this point— legally—so respect whatever activities may be going on nearby.) The first fork in the road offers what makes this loop exciting to ride: choices. The left fork leads down to an area above Black Falls. The main road curves right and climbs for about a half mile until another fork: a road heading off and up to the right splits with a gated road (sometimes locked) leading down and to the left. The road up and right requires a steep one-third-mile climb with a convenient spot to take a breather about halfway. At the top, stop and turn around and look to the south.

Campbell Mountain, with its twin peaks, is almost completely encircled by the Etowah River. Continue downhill another third of a mile to the dead end, where evidence of the wilderness exercises can be seen. Watch out for the barbed wire on the eastern side of the gap, off the trail. Return to the main road and take a right past the normally open gate. It's about a 3.5-mile ride to the ford at Montgomery Creek, which can be used as the "out" on an out-and-back. After crossing the creek, look immediately to the left and pick out the single-track running along the creek. It will lead back to the gravel road. Or stay straight on the gravel road. Ride past the gate and begin a climb up to the shoulder of Little Sal Mountain. Two clearings will be seen—the first one on the right, and the second on the left—before the dead end at FS 28 (the alternate trailhead). Turn left and pedal up toward Camp Wahsega. It is approximately 2 miles more from the 4-H camp to the gym (on the left).

RIDE 63 · Bull Mountain

AT A GLANCE

GA

Length/configuration: A 14.5-mile loop, much of it on single-track and the rest on lightly graveled service roads

Aerobic difficulty: Plenty of places where you'll breath heavy on this ride

Technical difficulty: The overall demands of this ride are not technical

Scenery: Jones Creek, Springer Mountain, Lance Creek, and, of course, Bull Mountain—all in a setting that you'll swear is as pretty as you've ever seen

Special comments: This ride is a popular destination among Atlanta-area mountain bikers, and as a result, the trail is crowded during much of most weekends

This 14.5-mile loop around Bull Mountain nearly reaches this mountain's summit of 2,340 feet above sea level in one fell swoop, or maybe it just feels that way. Following a combination of double- and single-track, and gravel forest service roads, the high point of the trip actually comes on an unnamed peak west of Bull at an altitude of 2,480 feet. The lowest elevation occurs more than 700 feet below on a bank somewhere along Jones Creek, the Chattahoochee National Forest's premier trout stream.

Jones Creek originates from one of the large springs gushing out of the south-western flank of, naturally, Springer Mountain. This mountain serves as the official lower trailhead of the Appalachian Trail, and the point from which many through hikers begin their "spring up the trail into Maine," ending officially at Mount Katahdin over 2,000 miles away.

Lance Creek, the other major tributary of the Amicalola watershed and whose source pours from Springer's side as well, provides sights and sounds to accompany the trip up as the trail hugs its banks for a portion of the ride. This section of trail was originally an old logging road.

The trail's length and difficulty make it an all-day affair for many bikers, although you will find those on the trail who spend only a couple of hours to make the trip. At any rate, covering the entire course with only two water bottles, especially during the summer, may require an unhealthy rationing of the H_2O. Try to pack at least another bottle or two, or consider investing in a back bottle. Don't be fooled into thinking that the fresh-running stream coming into Lance Creek can be immediately put into your bottle. There are some springs in the Chattahoochee National Forest I would bury my face in and drink from without hesitation; however, I've seen too many signs of unsanitary habits up on Springer to use this water without first bringing it to an extended boil. I have a riding buddy, however, who uses a filter system attached to his water bottle that seems to work. He fills it up at any creek he happens to be near.

This trail gets a lot of use, especially on weekends when 80 to 90 bikers zoom around it in one day. You get all kinds. This is a popular destination for Atlanta-area mountain bikers, and you can do a fairly reliable survey of current biking fashions watching the traffic pass.

General location: The mountainous region where Lumpkin, Fannin, Gilmer, and Dawson Counties come together just east of Amicalola Falls State Park.

Elevation change: The difference between the highest and lowest points on the trail is about 700 feet, but don't let that fool you. Plenty of elevation is gained (and lost) on the numerous rollers.

Season: This trail is ridden year-round.

Services: Most services can be obtained in either Dawsonville or Dahlonega.

Hazards: This is a well-maintained trail. A section of approximately 3 miles incorporates forest service roads, and you may encounter traffic traveling at speeds greater than the law allows. There will also be bike traffic coming from either direction, and some of it will be on the narrower single-track sections. Hunters in search of quarry of all sorts may be marching through the woods.

RIDE 63 · Bull Mountain

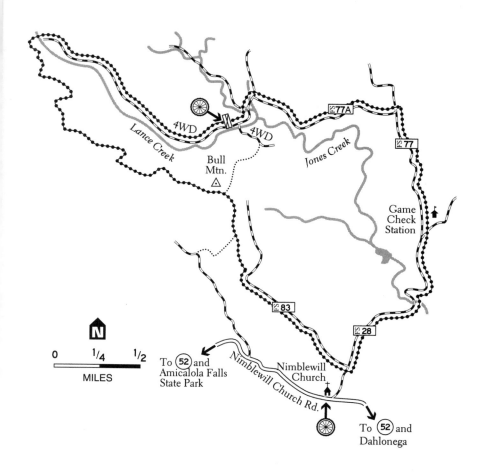

Rescue index: You will be riding on some remote pathways, but because it is heavily used you will no doubt soon be seen should you need help. Getting you out and to someplace where you can get first aid—for either you or your bike— is another story, and a long one at that.

Land status: Located entirely within the Chattahoochee National Forest.

Maps: You can obtain a map of the trail at Bull Mountain from the forest service office in Dahlonega, or you can pick one up at Mountain Adventures Cyclery on Highway 400. A topo map of the Nimblewill quad (7.5 minute series) will show the trail in its basic shape; there are some recently made sections of single-track that will not show up on the topo. Another good map to invest in is the Chattahoochee National Forest map, also available at the national forest service office in Dahlonega.

Finding the trail: Pick your favorite way to go to Amicalola Falls State Park and continue north on Highway 52 if you have a southerly approach. After passing where Highway 136 is accessed on the right, you'll cross the county line. Take the left toward Nimblewill Baptist Church and park at the church. If leaving from Dahlonega, take Highway 52/9 west. Bear right on GA 52 toward Ellijay. Look for the white building on the right and the sign for the church about 7 miles after making the turn onto Highway 52. Park at the church and take FS 28.

Source of additional information:

Chestatee District Ranger's Office
U.S. Forest Service Business Center
102 Memorial Drive
Dahlonega, GA 30533
(706) 864-6173

Notes on the trail: Leave the parking lot near the church and ride down FS 28. Take the left on FS 77. At the bottom of the hill, turn left onto FS 77A to Jones Creek. Take the right turn onto the gated road. The climb along the right bank of Lance Creek is pleasantly strenuous, but nothing compared to the steep grade awaiting you on the other side of Lance Creek. Turn left up the hill until you reach the ridge where the trail dead-ends. Turn left here and watch for the steep descent going off to the left that dead-ends into FS 83. Take a right onto this road and right again after it joins FS 28. The church will be on your right after the blacktop.

RIDE 64 · Amicalola Falls State Park Trail

AT A GLANCE

Length/configuration: 14-mile loop on service roads

Aerobic difficulty: For the big-time pedal pusher looking for a strenuous workout, this is it

Technical difficulty: A beginner will be challenged on this ride

Scenery: Amicalola Falls, Nimblewill Gap, Springer Mountain

Special comments: This trail has probably been responsible for more lost bikers, myself included, than any other I've ever heard of; but by following the specific directions I've included (learned the hard way), you won't have that problem

GA

Georgia's most popular state park lies near the unofficial Deep South trailhead for hikers beginning the Appalachian Trail trek up to Maine. For those who have hiked the eight miles to Springer Mountain (the official AT southern terminus) from Amicalola Falls, the rugged and steep terrain of the bike trail (actually a combination of jeep, ATV, and hiking trails) will come as no surprise. Plan on spending the greater portion of the day completing the 14-mile loop.

The information available at the park's visitor center sets the time for completing this loop at 2 to 6 hours, but it will probably take closer to the upper end rather than the lower for most bikers. Scenic overlooks along the way will be as responsible for slowing progress as will the hike-and-bike sections. Also, if you fail to make the turn at Nimblewill Gap and wind up on the other side of the ridge at Nimblewill Baptist Church, the ride back to Amicalola could take an uncomfortably long time.

After riding this trail, you might enjoy pitching a tent or setting up a trailer at one of the park's many camping spots. Several trails within the park—some with campsites along them—explore the land surrounding the largest falls east of the Rockies, the 729-foot drop of Amicalola Falls. A lodge is also available for those who prefer a soft bed and home-cooked meals.

Amicalola, which means "tumbling waters" in Cherokee, was the site of a different tumble back in the days of Prohibition. Bootlegging has always had a checkered reputation among the hill communities of north Georgia. For many farmers, distilling corn was the only way to make a decent, if not respectable, living. One such man, the object of the local sheriff's hot pursuit, failed to negotiate a turn by the falls. The bumper of his car is still rusting on a ledge by the falls viewing platform. Racing is a popular pastime (if not a downright religion) in north Georgia. For a small-town look at a local-racer-made-big, take a pit stop at the Dawsonville Poolroom to check out the collection of Awesome Bill Elliott's NASCAR racing memorabilia. Or for a slower pace, just down the road a short piece west of Amicalola Falls Park, Burt's Pumpkin Farm offers hayrides for the family between September 1 and December 30—pumpkin season.

General location: The trail is found within the Chattahoochee National Forest, near where Lumpkin, Dawson, Fannin, and Gilmer Counties meet.

Elevation change: From the trailhead at the top of the falls (2,220 feet) to Nimblewill Gap on FS 28 (3,049 feet), several significant climbs and drops occur. This is not a trail for those who do not relish steep climbs and descents. It's a steady, 4-mile climb from Tickanetley Creek on FS 28 to Nimblewill Gap—with an average gain of nearly 300 feet each mile.

Season: There are times during the winter months when the trail and park will be closed due to ice and snow. Call ahead for local conditions if in doubt. Hunting is not allowed inside the park; however, the forest service roads may well be traveled in mid-fall to early winter by hunters. A cyclist should be clad in a liberal amount of hunter orange (500 square inches, minimum) during these times.

RIDE 64 · Amicalola Falls State Park Trail

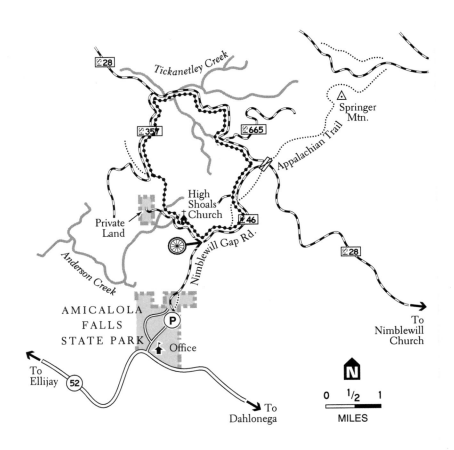

Services: Most services can be found in Dawsonville or Dahlonega. The park, of course, offers all the facilities and conveniences expected at a top-notch park.

Hazards: Vehicular traffic, like jeeps and off-road vehicles, will occasionally be seen, especially on weekends. Rocks, roots, and deep ruts can be expected on the steeper sections of the ATV trail. But perhaps the biggest hazard is straying off the trail and winding up miles from the trailhead, and then having to climb the 25 percent grade 1.5 miles back up to the falls from Highway 52. Ouch! I spoke briefly with Ms. Kincaid at Kincaid's Grocery about riding the bike trail at the park. The first thing she wanted to know was if I had gotten lost. "A lot of people get lost on that trail," she warned. Use the map and directions found in this book, though, and the ride won't be any longer than 14 miles—unless it's by choice.

Rescue index: Depending on the day of the week, you're more likely to encounter a bear than a human on these remote roads. Ride prepared for self-rescue.

Land status: The bulk of the trail is on national forest land and roads, although access to the most convenient trailhead requires entering the state park.

Maps: The topo maps (7.5 minute series) of the Nimblewill, Noontootla, Tickanetley, and Amicalola quads would be a help, but without the map of the Chattahoochee National Forest, lack of recent topo revisions will not show critical junctions correctly. The best bet is to use the map reproduced in this book. Other sources of the trail's directions have been sorely lacking; many misdirected bikers will attest to this fact, as will Ms. Kincaid at the grocery outside the park's entrance.

Finding the trail: Enter Amicalola Falls State Park from Highway 52 and pay the parking fee (unless it's Wednesday, when entrance is free, or unless you tell the gate attendant you'll be going through to the national forest above the park) and take the first left up to the top of the falls. The paved road turns into a gravel road leading up to High Shoals Church. Pull off and park at any of the unimproved national forest camping spots on the right or left before getting to Nimblewill Gap Road (FS 46) coming in from the right. Begin the clockwise loop from the junction of FS 46 and High Shoals Road.

Source of additional information:

Amicalola Falls State Park
Star Route Box 215
Dawsonville, GA 30534
(706) 265-8888

Notes on the trail: The first mile or so leads up to High Shoals Church. Go past the church and down the rocky road, crossing first a small creek, and then the larger Anderson Creek, before making a short climb. Look for the narrow ATV trail appearing shortly on the right, cutting between high banks. The gravel road continues to the left for a quarter of a mile and dead-ends at private property and a gate. The ATV trail intersects with FS 357 at what is a very confusing junction (and where I got lost). The gravel road goes left and right; the ATV trail continues straight across the gravel road. Turn right and ride 2 miles down the hill on the graveled FS 357 until it dead-ends into FS 28. Note the pasture across the road behind a fence at this intersection. Turn right and cross a bridge spanning a small creek before crossing the larger Tickanetley Creek twice more in a valley with some houses. The next hour will be spent pedaling uphill for 4 miles along the rocky ascent to Nimblewill Gap, the most troublesome intersection of the trail (so far as getting lost goes, although I had no trouble here).

Some landmarks to look for before and at this intersection: about a mile from the top, FS 665 (a long dead-end road) goes off to the left, and the frequent switchbacks stop shy of the gap, providing two long, straight stretches just before the gap is reached. At the gap, note several conspicuous landmarks: a set of log steps come down the mountain from the right, the road levels off and widens, a trail goes off to the left toward Springer Mountain, a large tree lies on the ground on the left, a gate (probably open) is in the middle of the right turn of the road you've been climbing, and finally, a rocky road to the right (taking you up another 150 feet or so in the next half mile). It is this rocky road (FS 46) to the right—and up!—that must be taken. After the final climb up FS 46, it levels out before another intersection: a right up to Frosty Mountain. Take the left, however; you've done all the climbing required once you reach this intersection. The rest of the trail drops 450 feet over an extremely rocky roadbed for nearly 2 miles before coming back into High Shoals Road at the bottom. A left leads back to Amicalola State Park. In order to make another 14-mile lap, though, turn right.

RIDE 65 · Chicopee Woods

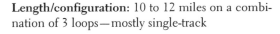

AT A GLANCE

GA

Length/configuration: 10 to 12 miles on a combination of 3 loops—mostly single-track

Aerobic difficulty: Most bikers will receive a thorough workout

Technical difficulty: There is plenty of challenge available

Scenery: Interstate 985 lies to the southeast of the trail, but it doesn't detract too much from the overall pretty ride through rolling hills and along several creeks

Special comments: This is a popular trail, especially on the weekends; its popularity speaks well for the people who built and maintain it; additional mileage has been planned

"Something for everybody," is how my guide for the day, Woody, described the single- and double-track combination of loops outside Gainesville, Georgia. "You can come out here and take the big loop for a three- or four-mile ride. Or you can tack on the red trail, the inner loop, or the lake loop," Woody

RIDE 65 · Chicopee Woods

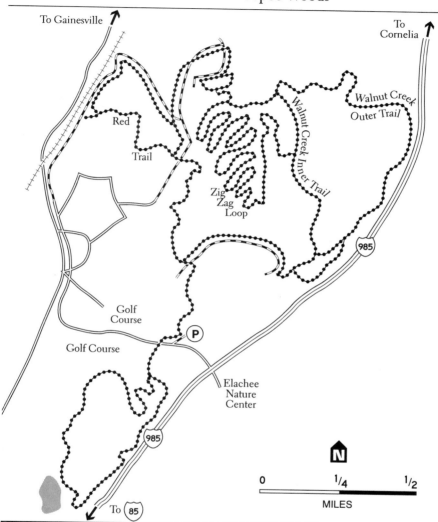

To Gainesville

To Cornelia

Red

Trail

Walnut Creek Outer Trail

Walnut Creek Inner Trail

Zig Zag Loop

985

Golf Course

Golf Course

P

Elachee Nature Center

985

To 85

N

0   1/4   1/2

MILES

told me before we headed out on the quarter-mile approach trail. "If you put it all together," he said, "I think you ride somewhere near 12 miles." With the additional mileage planned for the near future, bikers can expect to ride 15 to 20 miles.

The overall mileage is not nearly as important as the variation. The terrain has the roll of Georgia's foothills, but without the steep climbs found 30 miles to the north. The route crisscrosses the ridge line above the creeks and plunges down to and crosses Walnut Creek. As the clockwise loop is made, a portion of the trail parallels I-985, giving the ride a definite metropolitan flavor. However, it is just as easy to feel deep in the woods. As Woody and I, along with Ned (Woody's dog), made a climb away from Rockaway Creek, I heard a sharp rap. When I looked up, Woody was ahead of me, wordlessly slapping his helmet with his left hand. Two deer were 20 feet off the trail, and he was trying to scare them off before Ned noticed and gave chase. At least, that's what he said. As it turned out, the deer stayed by the trail and watched the three of us pass by. No doubt, they were wanting Woody to hit his helmet again.

General location: South of Gainesville, Georgia, near I-985.

Elevation change: A few climbs may gain a hundred feet, but overall the elevation is not much of a factor.

Season: This is a dry weather trail only, and to enforce it, the gate is closed when it's too wet to ride. Violators should expect—and deserve—rebuke, if not prosecution.

Services: Nearby Gainesville has most if not all you will need, including a reputable bike shop or two. The trailhead, however, is equipped with only a small wooden information station.

Hazards: A couple of creek crossings, not yet bridged, will provide a significant challenge either on or off your bike.

Rescue index: This trail's popularity and relatively compact configuration make it an easy one for effecting a rescue.

Land status: The bike trail lies on part of a 1,200-acre nature preserve.

Maps: The Chicopee Woods Bike Trails map is available at area bike shops.

Finding the trail: Exit I-985 at Oakwood (exit 4) and head north on GA 53. Just past the underpass, Frontage Road turns to the right. Take it until it dead-ends into GA 13. Turn left and travel less than a mile. Look for the prominent sign indicating the right turn to Elachee Nature Center. The golf course will be on the right. A double-track on the left (trailhead for the lake loop) signals the left turn into the parking lot for the other two loops.

Source of additional information:

Elachee Nature Science Center
2125 Elachee Drive
Gainesville, GA 30504
(770) 535-1976

Notes on the trail: The longest loop (the outer one) begins with a quarter-mile approach trail. (Take this section in order to exit the loops and head back to the parking lot.) Although I rode it clockwise, two other bikers were on the trail traveling in a counterclockwise direction. Take your pick. The trail goes down to Rockaway Creek and crosses it before coming into the double-track. The main loop goes to the right, but you can continue straight at this point and take on the more difficult red trail, an out-and-back leading to a double-track, which can be used in combination with some pavement to make a 3- or 4-mile loop. Back on the main loop, the single-track begins again after you cross another creek and reach a right turn. In less than a quarter mile, the inner loop cuts off to the right; the larger loop continues straight. After a bridge crossing, the ride borders the interstate before dropping back down to a creek. After the creek, the double-track climbs back up to where the approach trail comes in on the left.

The lake (or pond) loop begins at the parking lot. Head uphill out of the lot and turn left onto the double-track where a sign has been placed to mark the beginning of the bike trail. After a short approach, the trail forks. The two ends of the loop come together here. Try either a counterclockwise or clockwise direction. A clockwise loop goes above the interstate. The trail turns away from the noise and skirts the edge of a small lake. A bridge crossing begins the last third of the loop, which winds its way back up to regain the elevation lost on the way down to the water. The intersection is easily noted. Take a left back to the parking lot, or a right for another lap.

RIDE 66 · Tumbling Creek

AT A GLANCE

Length/configuration: This is about a 5-mile loop on single- and double-track

Aerobic difficulty: Despite its name, don't expect too much aerobic exertion

Technical difficulty: This is a great trail for beginning bikers

Scenery: It is pretty but not outstanding; however, in a few years after the trees grow larger with lusher canopies, it will be beautiful

Special comments: The bridges spanning the waterways are architectural masterpieces

The five miles of single- and double-track of this Gainesville College loop will not present too great a challenge, even for the beginning biker. But don't let that mislead you to underestimate the fun found here. The trailbuilders—members of Gainesville College Mountain Biking Club, along with help from a wide variety of sources—took extra care to carve a tight track through the mixed woods forest that serves as the boundary around the college and its affiliate, Lanier Tech. Although it carries the name of Tumbling Creek, the primary waterway on this

RIDE 66 · Tumbling Creek

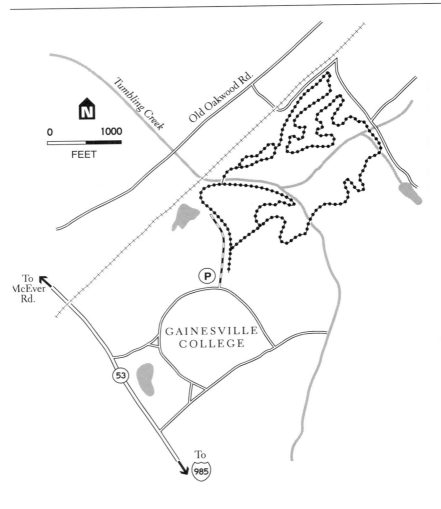

loop is Balus Creek, which empties into nearby Lake Lanier. Two massive bridges carry bikers safely over the fast water at two different spots. I mention this because at least one biker I know was momentarily confused as to whether or not we had already crossed the second bridge. In between the two Balus crossings, you will ride over the surprisingly named Tumbling Creek, a simple trickle.

General location: South of Gainesville, Georgia, just off Interstate 985.

Elevation change: Very little.

Season: This is a dry-weather trail only; please observe the signs requesting that you stay off it until it has dried.

Services: Gainesville, Georgia, has most if not all the goods and services you will likely need, including reputable bike shops.

Hazards: You may encounter hikers and other bikers. A few roots to avoid, and that's about it.

Rescue index: You are unlikely to experience any difficulty in getting rescued here. It's a short walk out, and the interstate is nearby.

Land status: This trail lies on the campus of Gainesville College, a part of the University of Georgia, a state-owned school.

Maps: Ask for the Tumbling Creek map at local bike shops.

Finding the trail: Exit I-985 at Oakwood (exit 4) and head north on GA 53. Approximately a quarter mile on the right, look for Frontage Road and turn right. Education Drive appears on the left, about a half mile farther down, before the intersection with GA 13. Turn left onto Education Drive and take the first right onto Mathis Drive. The next right leads to Gainesville College's plant operations building. Immediately after taking it, turn left into the parking lot. As you stand facing north (downhill), look to the right, on the other side of the pavement. You should be able to make out a track in the grass, which heads into the tree line and the beginning of the trail.

Source of additional information:

Gainesville College Bike Club
Gainesville College
3820 Mundy Mill Road
Oakwood, GA 30566-3414
(770) 718-3674 or 718-3639

Notes on the trail: Begin riding downhill and cross the pavement into the grass, where you'll see tracks where other cyclists have ridden. The tracks should lead to the tree line, where they seem to disappear into a tangle of green. You'll be able to follow the trail easily, though. It winds around on the southern side of Balus Creek for nearly a half mile and then crosses over to the area between Tumbling and Balus Creeks. The trail stays close to the boundary of "Foundation Land." After crossing the second bridge, it returns to the road leading past the plant operations building. You can either go straight and ride an approximate half-mile loop past the pond near the plant operations building, or you can take another lap of the trail you've already covered.

RIDE 67 · Rich Mountain Wildlife Management Area

AT A GLANCE

Length/configuration: A 6-mile loop of mostly single-track, with some lightly graveled double-track

Aerobic difficulty: Some short hills will occasionally make it a slow go and a hard blow; other than that, it's a fairly easy ride

Technical difficulty: Some sections are very technical, but for the most part it's easily handled by a biker with average skills

Scenery: Cartecay River and rolling riparian ridges

Special comments: Also known as the Red and White Trail, for the color of blazes marking the trail

GA

This combination of single-track and rough gravel road leading into the Rich Mountain Wildlife Management Area provides off-road bikers with an opportunity to experience a close encounter with the Cartecay River. Although this trail was ridden for several years by local bikers before it was officially turned into a six-mile loop, the state of Georgia now has a 30-year lease with Georgia Power to manage this land. And lucky for mountain bikers, part of the maintenance includes keeping the off-road trail.

The maniacally steep descent to the Cartecay is where, as Jay Srymanske of Mountain Outdoors Expeditions puts it, "Brakes do no good. You're either on your bike or off." As a result, and as a favor to first-time riders, three orange blazes announce the start of the radically steep section. Once down, the single-track follows the Cartecay for a half mile, passing Clear Creek Falls.

General location: This trail is located off Highway 52 about 5 miles east of Ellijay.

Elevation change: If you had wings, you could fly on some descents. The overall change, however, is not significant.

Season: Hunting occurs in these woods, especially during the fall and spring, deer and turkey seasons. It is an understandable temptation to ride here during these times, but the advice is to hold off until the managed hunt is finished.

Services: Mountain Outdoor Expeditions on Lower Cartecay Road comes highly recommended as a safe zone for vehicles and as a good source of current information on mountain biking opportunities in the area. Known as MOE, it has catered to outdoor needs for many years, even offering a place to stay at its very own MOE-Tel.

RIDE 67 · Rich Mountain WMA

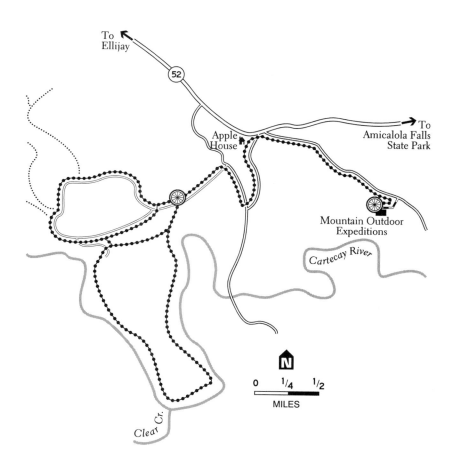

Hazards: The trail has at least one steep spot where most people may be more comfortable walking. Leaving a vehicle unattended for a long time at the gate nearest the single-track "is a day-to-day thing" according to Jay at MOE. "A lot of people just blow the additional [paved] mileage off and park with us." Of course, by parking at MOE, you'll encounter traffic on the paved section.

Rescue index: Some locations on this trail are remote, and rescue may be difficult. Largely, though, gravel service roads and home construction along the Cartecay make this area easily, if not quickly, reached. The weekends draw many bikers here, but weekdays have few bikers showing up.

Land status: This property is leased to the Georgia state government from Georgia Power Company.

Maps: A bike trail map can be picked up at MOE. Ask for Rich Mountain or the Red and White Trail.

Finding the trail: To find MOE, leave Ellijay headed east on GA 52. Turn right on Lower Cartecay Road. About a mile down the road, look for the canoes on the hill to the right. Turn to the right and park by the office. Leave MOE, retracing the route in until you come to Oak Hill Apple House. Turn left here. Go down the road until it dead-ends and turn right. Travel a short distance and turn left at the Rich Mountain Wildlife Management Area sign. The gate there is closed from October 1 through the opening of trout season (usually late March) and you can park to the side of it then. A little farther down, there's another gate on the right. Park here at the wide spot in the road. You can continue until the road dead-ends at the single-track about another mile down, but it's rough and better ridden on a bike. The white-blazed single-track begins at the end of the road, going up the hill over some roots by a large white pine.

Source of additional information:

Mountain Outdoor Expeditions
Lower Cartecay Road
Ellijay, GA 30540
(706) 635-2524
(706) 276-6385, MOE-Tel

Notes on the trail: Beginning with the single-track, watch for the triple orange blazes indicating the steep descent. Scout it first. After hitting the riverside, the trail goes for approximately a half mile before leaving the river. The fork to the right leads back to the gravel road where the trail started. The trail continues left in a wider loop with white on top of red blazes marking the way. Three trails go off to the left: the first one leads to an overlook and dead-ends, and the other two may possibly be overgrown in summer, but they lead down to the river and a beach. The 6-mile loop is completed when you reach the second gate. Returning to MOE (and riding the 2.5-mile approach trail out-and-back from there, 5 miles total) makes the trip almost 11 miles.

RIDE 68 · Ridgeway

AT A GLANCE
—————————

GA

Length/configuration: A 6-mile loop on mostly single-track, with some lightly graveled double-track

Aerobic difficulty: The climbs are not necessarily long, but some are quite steep—more than enough to make you huff and puff

Technical difficulty: It's not a particularly technical ride, but a novice may think otherwise

Scenery: Carters Lake and the Cohutta Mountains

Special comments: This trail was built by mountain bikers, for mountain bikers

This nearly six-mile single-track loop in Ridgeway Park, which stays for the most part high above Carters Lake, got its beginning from local biker and star international trials competitor Doug White. He and a ranger, who also rides mountain bikes, got together and laid out the path for this course, a NORBA-sanctioned race site since 1993. Using old, abandoned double-track in places, the mostly single-track course rolls through forest protected as a part of U.S. Army Corps of Engineers property.

Many trails ridden by mountain bikers follow the old grades left behind by logging operations, which is fine. Loggers and bikers apparently have a lot in common, at least so far as the grades they use are concerned. But what a treat it is to ride a trail cut with the specific character of a mountain bike and its rider in mind. Tight and twisty, the switchbacks are demanding enough so that you can ride them on a good day and not feel bad about walking them the other days.

General location: This trail is located at Ridgeway Park on Carters Lake off Highway 282/76 approximately 8 miles west of Ellijay, Georgia.

Elevation change: According to Doug, "You can't put a baseball anywhere on the trail and not have it roll off." I don't know about that, but I do know that there's more than one section where I had to push my bike up.

Season: It's a good place to ride during hunting season because no hunting is allowed here.

Services: Ridgeway Park has camping pads developed for tents, and you can get water by using the handpumps at several locations in the campground. The rest of the services a mountain biker away from home will need can be found in nearby Ellijay (home to a couple of bike shops), or if the service is specialized enough, a trip to Dalton or Chattanooga may be necessary.

RIDE 68 · Ridgeway

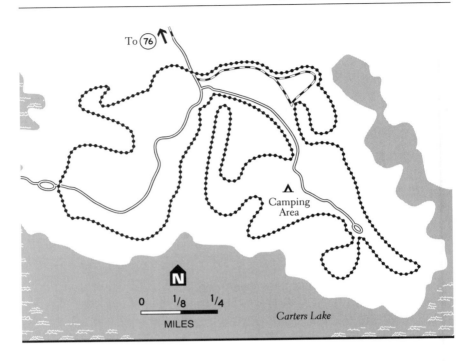

Hazards: Beginners need to be comfortable riding down steep sections of rocky trail before they try to ride all the way on this one. This trail has been designed with one approved riding direction only (counterclockwise), so oncoming bike traffic should not pose a problem . . . but you never know.

Rescue index: The trail does not get much farther away than a mile or so from one of the paved park roads. However, it is fairly remote territory. It takes approximately 10 to 15 minutes to get back to the highway from the camping area. Ride prepared for self-rescue.

Land status: This is land managed by the U.S. Army Corps of Engineers.

Maps: A map of the bike trail is posted on the bulletin board by the boat ramp. Area bike shops may also have copies of the map, Ridgeway Mountain Bike Trail.

Finding the trail: Turn off Highway 282/76, 8 miles or so west of Ellijay at the Ridgeway entrance sign. It's only a little over 3 miles to the camping area, but the gravel road should be driven slowly, so it takes about 10 minutes to reach the pavement of the park. One trailhead occurs just before the turn to the boat ramp. Another trailhead is at the boat ramp, and another one is at the camping area.

Source of additional information:

Carters Lake Resource Office
U.S. Army Corps of Engineers
P.O. Box 96
Oakman, GA 30732-0096
(706) 334-2248

Notes on the trail: After you find the trailhead, the trail is easy to stay on. Orange markers have been placed at all ambiguous intersections. Stay on the trail and follow the recommended, counterclockwise direction. The route occasionally climbs to open areas, looking out across narrow Carters Lake. One section follows the lake bank, but much of the trail can be characterized by frequent climbs and drops along ridges through a secluded, quiet forest.

RIDE 69 · Bear Creek

AT A GLANCE

GA

Length/configuration: A choice of three different rides, done either separately or together: a 2.5-mile (5 miles total) out-and-back single-track, a 3-mile single-track loop, and a 7-mile loop—half single-track and half double-track

Aerobic difficulty: I start breathing heavy just thinking about it, mainly because it's so pretty, but there are some steep, physically demanding sections

Technical difficulty: Except for riding along the creek and crossing the creeks, it's not so technical that a dedicated novice can't easily handle it

Scenery: Bear Creek and the Cohutta Mountains are magnificent!

Special comments: Save some extra time to ride up to Potatopatch Mountain for the wide view of the Cohuttas; Bear Creek is one of the oldest official mountain bike trails in Georgia

Records do not indicate whether or not the Gennett Brothers, Andrew and N. W., owners of this land during the Depression, could have spared enough money to buy a mountain bike. However, their decision to spare a tulip poplar from the teeth of their crosscut saw resulted in another record. The Gennett Poplar, sporting an 18-foot girth at the bottom, is the most remarkable feature

RIDE 69 · Bear Creek

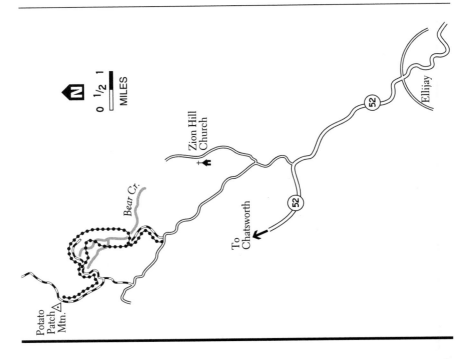

(among many) found on the 2.5-mile out-and-back single-track (5 miles total) and the two loops (a 3-mile single-track, plus a 7-miler, which uses some double-track). The Atlanta REI restored this single-track in a 1992 project, with help from its many friends.

REI knows how to pick them. Hemlocks and wild grapevines hang over portions of the trail so thick you can forget about seeing your shadow. Creek crossings occur near the trailhead before the climb out begins the loop along the ridge. Deer will likely be heard crashing through the undergrowth, and turkeys will probably be seen running out of sight up the slopes to Potatopatch Mountain.

On one ride (I must've been watching wildlife instead of watching the trail), I ran over a stick with my front tire. Normally, this is no problem; mountain bikers often roll over many kinds of trail obstacles. This time, however, the stick (about the diameter of a hot dog) twisted somehow and went through the spokes, which isn't a problem either as long as it's on a climb, which I was. But Murphy must've been in the bushes watching because the stick passed through the spokes, ripping the tube's nipple. The tube went flat in seconds. The spare tube was back at the truck three miles away, so I had no choice but to head back. I did, however, test out the method of stuffing grass inside the tube. It didn't allow me to ride the bike safely, but I was able to run alongside more easily than with an unstuffed tire. Moral of the story: always carry a patch kit, pump, and spare tube. Sure they're heavy, but not as heavy as the disappointment of a long walk back.

Brian takes a break on
part of the double-track
at Bear Creek.

General location: This is one of many trails located in the Cohutta Wilderness Area of the Chattahoochee National Forest in between Chatsworth and Ellijay, Georgia.

Elevation change: Put your "Yee-Haw!" on alert. This is rugged mountain track that provides thigh-burning, lung-bursting climbs in one direction, and a quick descent in the other direction. It took 90 minutes to make the 4.5-mile climb to Potatopatch—and only 30 minutes to come back down.

Season: Periods of high water may make the stream crossings in the Cohuttas ill advised. Hunting season, mid-fall to early winter, is a good time to check out another trail.

Services: This area is about as remotely situated as northwest Georgia can get. Either Chatsworth or Ellijay will be the closest destination for supplies, although basic goods can be picked up at Fort Mountain State Park.

Hazards: Some rocks jut up into the trail. Rocks also lurk under the water on stream crossings. And, yes, sticks can be a problem; try not to ride over them, but if you do, ride over them in the middle. Expect others riding the trail.

Rescue index: It is accessible, but carrying out a rescue could be a difficult chore. Ride prepared for self-rescue.

Land status: Part of the Chattahoochee National Forest, close to the Cohutta Wildlife Management Area.

Maps: Anyone wishing to explore the Chattahoochee National Forest should invest in the map covering the area, which goes nearly all the way across north Georgia. In addition, contact the forest service for its publication, *Mountain Bike Trails–Cohutta Ranger District–Chattahoochee National Forest.* Topo maps are a good idea for a day spent bushwhacking abandoned logging roads. For Bear Creek, acquire the Dyer Gap quad (7.5 minute series).

Finding the trail: Leave Ellijay, Georgia, on GA 52/2 heading west. A little over 5 miles from the square, look for a sign on the right announcing Zion Hill Church and turn. Approximately 5 miles from the turn (just after you cross a small bridge), you should see a forest service sign for Bear Creek Campground to the right; it's a steep cutback to the right, so take it easy and look for oncoming traffic before swinging wide. Signs point the way to the trail. Park at the trailhead or at the campground, seen off to the right just before the trailhead. Parking at the campground adds about another mile one way.

Source of additional information:

> Cohutta Ranger District
> National Forest Service
> 401 Old Ellijay Highway
> Chatsworth, GA 30705
> (706) 695-6737 or 695-6736

Notes on the trail: The trailhead starts both Bear Creek Trail and Bear Creek Loop. A bulletin board has a map of the area and information on the "trail opportunities." Basically, Bear Creek Trail is an out-and-back of slightly more than 5 miles total. Two more loops—a longer 6.7-miler and a shorter 3-miler—are completed by taking right turns at signs along the way. The shorter loop's right-hand turn is just past the Gennett Poplar. This single-track dead-ends into Barnes Creek Road, where another right turn leads back to the parking lot. The longer loop takes a right turn at the junction with Barnes Creek Road. Ride this for about 3.5 miles before turning right onto the trail for the last half mile.

To reach the overlook at Potatopatch Mountain, turn left at the end of Bear Creek Trail onto Barnes Creek Road. After it dead-ends at the normally closed gate, turn right and do a "grind-and-groan" on the gravel road (open to vehicles) up to the overlook.

RIDE 70 · Berry College

AT A GLANCE

GA

Length/configuration: A 7.5-mile loop of mostly double-track, with some single-track off of the basic loop

Aerobic difficulty: A few climbs will give the heart and lungs a workout, but the overall ride only makes moderate aerobic demands

Technical difficulty: Only by riding the single-track will any technical challenges be present on what is a lightly graveled double-track

Scenery: Lavender Mountain, Mirror Lake, Swan Lake, Frost Chapel, the Old Mill, and Berry Wildlife Refuge

Special comments: Make time to cruise the pavement of the former Berry Academy campus

Imagine a school campus where you can turn off a busy highway and view a large pasture on the right where deer graze undisturbed, and on the left in a pine forest strut a flock of turkeys. The backdrop to it all is formed by buildings hewn out of local stone and constructed in a shape reminiscent of castles and the chivalrous days of knights and kings. This, and more, awaits the mountain biker who rides the basic 7.5-mile loop along the gravel service roads and pavement of Berry College. A wide assortment of rides—from the challenge of mountain stream fords to the calm cruise down a country road—can be enjoyed in this section of northwest Georgia. Much of the college campus, with its asphalt roads where the classrooms and dorms are located, seems better suited for 1.25 or 1.5 slicks than knobbies. But a survey of the bikes parked in front of these buildings shows more mountain bikes than road bikes; the temptation to go off-road is just too great.

This biking paradise got its start earlier this century when a remarkable lady named Martha Berry began a school where children who lacked advanced social opportunities could acquire both a practical and an academic education. The magnetic personality of Ms. Berry attracted such notable personalities as Henry Ford, whose partnership resulted in the magnificent buildings seen on the hill upon entering the college. The Keown Mill (at the trailhead for the basic 7.5-mile loop, Mountain Goat Trail) is another symbol of Martha Berry's acquaintances with the rich and influential.

Slightly more than three miles from the college campus on a section called simply the Stretch, the off-road biker can explore the 26,000 acres of the Berry

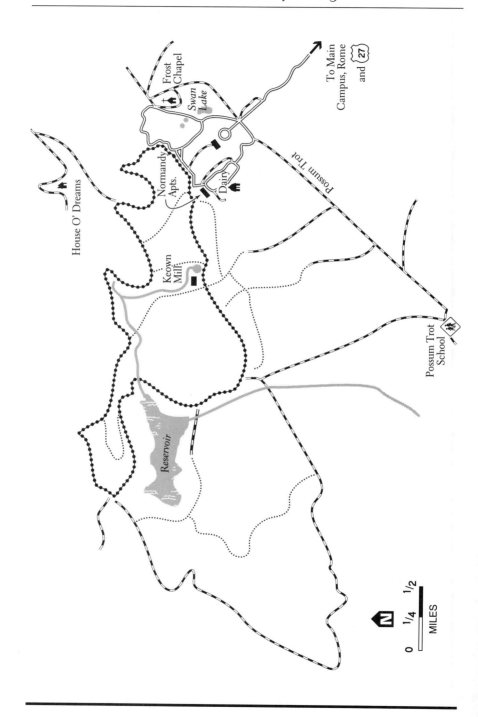

House O' Dreams

Frost Chapel

Swan Lake

Normandy Apts.

Dairy

To Main Campus, Rome and 27

Possum Trot

Keown Mill

Reservoir

Possum Trot School

N

0   ¼   ½

MILES

Wildlife Refuge, making Berry the largest college campus in America. As the pavement ends, turn left and ride down Possum Trot to what is the site of Martha Berry's first school. More of the campus's remarkable architecture is displayed at Frost Chapel, where Berry Academy commencement used to be held and where many weddings now take place. Take time to peek inside Frost Chapel. You can almost hear the shuffle of Academy students on the stone floor as they filed in to Sunday evening chapel services.

The former academy dorms, Friendship Hall and Pilgrim Hall—now housing participants in Camp WinShape—sit on opposite hills facing the chapel. The road between them continues down the hill toward the Old Mill, where the homes of Berry Schools employees are located. The Normandy Apartments lie above an expansive dairy farm, home to hundreds of cows, heifers, and calves.

General location: Berry College is north of Rome, Georgia, on Highway 27. The trails begin back in the foothills, 3 miles down the Stretch.

Elevation change: Moderate climbs and descents make their way along the shoulders of Lavender Mountain.

Season: A remarkable feature of the sandstone base of this trail allows biking during wet days. Except for the noon hour, shade keeps this trail as cool as possible year-round.

Services: Rome, Georgia, has supplies enough, but the basics can be acquired at the college's bookstore.

Hazards: Few hazards exist. As a wildlife refuge, hunting is not normally allowed; however, special hunts are occasionally arranged.

Rescue index: The frequency of use should have someone coming along at regular intervals, especially on weekends. If your car is not removed from the parking space at the Keown Mill by nightfall, regardless of the day, security guards will begin a search. Therefore, a rescue is made somewhat easier than the remote setting would otherwise suggest.

Land status: Berry College owns the land, and the Georgia Department of Natural Resources manages the refuge.

Maps: The map of Berry College showing the trails can be obtained from the school's administrative office or from one of the area's fine bicycle shops, like Bob's Cycle.

Finding the trail: Head north out of Rome on Highway 27. Turn left into Berry campus. Turn right toward the prominent and unmistakable Ford Buildings. Go past them and continue down the Stretch for 3 miles to a speed bump. Bear to the right, continuing past Frost Chapel on the right. Turn left toward Friendship Hall, going past it on the left and down the hill to an intersection with a sign indicating that the old mill is straight ahead. The trail begins behind the gate on the road leading up to the reservoir.

Source of additional information:

Berry College Switchboard
2277 Martha Berry Boulevard
Mount Berry, Georgia 30149
(706) 232-5374

Notes on the trail: Although the basic loop of 7.5 miles stays on seldom-used dirt roads, single-tracks cut off and onto the road above the reservoir in several spots. Plan to explore these possibilities all day, stringing together upwards of 15 miles. But the basic loop is traveled as follows: After beginning the rolling trip up to the reservoir, a couple of signed sections of trail go off to the left, entering the road again above the reservoir. Follow the road along the lake that gravity-feeds the water needs of Berry College 5 miles away. As you cross the small creek, the road bends to the left and up. In the elbow of the turn, notice single-track making its way among boulders on the right. At the top of the climb, in the gap where four roads intersect, take the gated road to the right. This section has obvious single-track coming in and going off to the right, down the mountain. At the **T** intersection with a smooth, gravel road, take a right downhill to Friendship Hall, past the closed gate. Turn right on the pavement and ride down the hill, bearing right at the bottom. At the next intersection, note the sign indicating that the mill is straight ahead. Take a left at this intersection toward the Berry Dairy for a paved scenic route.

RIDE 71 · Pigeon Mountain

AT A GLANCE

GA

Length/configuration: 12.5-mile loop

Aerobic difficulty: Moderate; a couple of short, steep, technical climbs and one long gradual climb back to the trailhead

Technical difficulty: Moderate to difficult; horse use, stream crossings, and washouts

Scenery: Spectacular; the trail follows the perimeter of the flat-topped Pigeon Mountain, allowing for incredible views of the surrounding pastoral valleys and distant Blue Ridge Mountains

Special comments: Pigeon Mountain is a Wildlife Management Area; wear blaze orange or avoid this area during hunting season

*This profile was contributed by Steve Thompson; source material for this profile's map was created by John Derry.

There are a lot of good reasons to visit Pigeon Mountain. Excellent mountain biking is just one of them. This area has many natural features of exceptional value and beauty. More than 13,000 acres are owned by the Georgia Department of Natural Resources and are managed as the Crockford–Pigeon Mountain Wildlife Management Area.

An extensive road and trail system allows visitors to explore Pigeon Mountain's landscape. More than 20 species of rare plants and a few rare salamanders have been found and studied here. There is an extensive cave system that includes Ellison's Cave, a popular destination for cavers from all over the Southeast. No visit to Pigeon Mountain would be complete without the one-mile side hike to Rock Town—a collection of massive boulders popular with climbers. Please be aware that the trail to Rock Town is designated for foot travel only; make sure to stash your bikes well and lock them if you choose to explore this area.

The Pigeon Mountain Trail is a 12.5-mile loop. The majority of the trail (almost nine miles) is single-track, the rest being gravel road. The trail can be quite technical at times, making it hard to enjoy the incredible views. There are several creek crossings and a couple of fairly short but steep technical climbs and descents. For the most part, the trail gently rolls along the edge of this flat-topped mountain on some of the best single-track around.

General location: About 9 miles west of Lafayette, Georgia.

Elevation change: The elevation change is minimal overall. However, there are several steep, technical climbs and descents. The last two miles or so are a gradual climb on gravel road. The rest of the ride is mostly rolling terrain as you follow the contours along the edge of the mountain.

Season: Pigeon Mountain can get hot and dusty (but deserted) during the summer. The ideal time for this area is in the spring, after hunting season.

Services: All services are available in Lafayette. The closest phone is at the check station on Rocky Lane. There is a small convenience store at the intersection of Chamberlain Road and GA 193. While there is no formal campground on Pigeon Mountain, camping is permitted. You'll find campsites scattered beside the road as you drive to the trailhead.

Hazards: Pigeon Mountain is a Wildlife Management Area. Wear blaze orange or avoid the area during hunting season. Make sure to bring plenty of water, as there is no source of potable water once on top of the mountain.

Rescue index: There is a phone at the check station on Rocky Lane. There is also a ranger's residence behind the check station. The area sees a lot of use on the weekends. During the week, it can be fairly deserted.

Land status: This ride is located within the Crockford–Pigeon Mountain Wildlife Management Area, which is administered by the Georgia Department of Natural Resources (DNR).

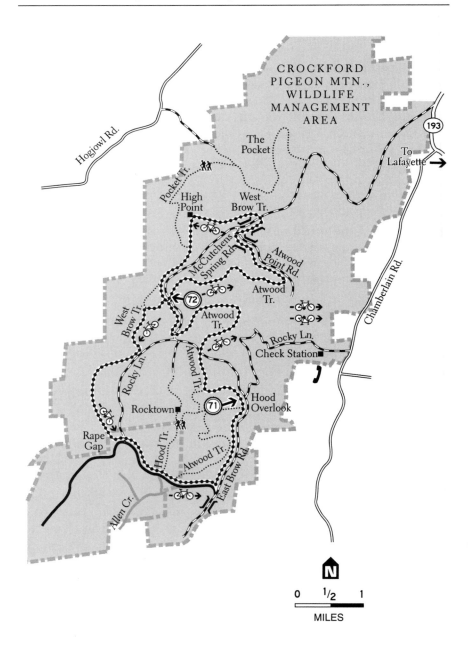

CROCKFORD
PIGEON MTN.,
WILDLIFE
MANAGEMENT
AREA

193

Hogjowl Rd.

The
Pocket

To
Lafayette →

Pocket Tr.

High
Point

West
Brow Tr.

McCutchens
Spring Rd.

Atwood
Point Rd.

West
Brow Tr.

72

Atwood
Tr.

Atwood
Tr.

Chamberlain Rd.

Rocky Ln.

Check Station

Rocky Ln.

Atwood Tr.

Rocktown

Hood
Overlook

71

Rape
Gap

Hood Tr.

Atwood Tr.

Allen Cr.

East Brow Rd.

N

0   1/2   1

MILES

Maps: There are free maps of the trail system available at the DNR check station on Rocky Lane. USGS 7.5 minute quads: Cedar Grove and Lafayette.

Finding the trail: From Lafayette, go north on GA 193 for 2.8 miles. Turn left (south) onto Chamberlain Road. Travel 3.6 miles and turn right (west) onto Rocky Lane. You will pass a big game check station on your left. Continue up Rocky Lane for about 3.5 miles. This section of the road is very rough and can be treacherous when wet. Turn left onto East Brow Road and go about a quarter of a mile to an obvious parking area on the right, next to a large field and across from a rock slab overlook (Hood Overlook). The trail runs west through the field, away from the overlook.

Sources of additional information:

Georgia Department of Natural Resources
2592 Floyd Springs Road NE
Armuchee, GA 30105-2518
(706) 295-6041

The Georgia Conservancy's Guide to the North Georgia Mountains, edited by Fred Brown and Nell Jones, contains a wealth of information about the area. The book is available from Longstreet Press, Inc., 2150 Newmarket Parkway, Suite 102, Marietta, Georgia 30067.

Notes on the trail: Begin at Hood Overlook and head west through the field on a dirt road, which quickly becomes single-track and is marked Atwood Trail (orange blaze). This section of trail is full of short climbs and descents through the woods. At .8 mile, look for Hood Trail (blue blaze) coming in on the left, and continue right on Atwood Trail. Cross Rocky Lane at 1.5 miles and continue on Atwood Trail directly across the road. This portion of trail has a rocky descent and climb that will test your technical skills. Continue on the single-track for about 2 miles, emerge from the forest, and turn right onto McCutchens Spring Road. Climb up McCutchens Spring Road for approximately .2 mile, passing Atwood Road on the left and then turning left on West Brow Trail (white blaze). This is a great 4.5-mile section of single-track that offers great views of Hog Jowl Valley to the west. At 8.5 miles, West Brow Trail intersects with Rocky Lane. Turn left on Rocky Lane, then turn right onto the first gated road you come to (a couple hundred yards). This is Atwood Trail (orange blaze). Continue down Atwood Trail, crossing Allen Creek, which will be a test for all but the most technically skilled riders. After Allen Creek, a side trail to the right heads to a waterfall. After checking out the falls, return to the trail and continue uphill as the trail becomes a dirt road. Proceed along this road until it intersects with East Brow Ridge Road and then turn left. You'll finish the ride with a 1.8-mile climb back to the parking area with outstanding views of the valley below.

RIDE 72 · High Point on Pigeon Mountain

AT A GLANCE

GA

Length/configuration: 8.3-mile loop

Aerobic difficulty: Moderate to difficult; rolling with a few short, steep climbs and a long, steep climb to High Point

Technical difficulty: Moderate to difficult; short, steep technical climbs and descents with plenty of rocks to avoid and logs to bunny-hop

Scenery: Hardwood forest with a spectacular view from High Point

Special comments: Pigeon Mountain is a Wildlife Management Area; wear blaze orange during hunting season and yield to horses

Another great ride on top of Pigeon Mountain is the High Point loop. This 8.3-mile ride on rolling terrain takes you on some great single-track through open forest and offers short, technical pieces that will test your skill. If that isn't enough, the rocky climb to High Point rewards you with a great view of farmland in McLemore Valley and beyond to Lookout Mountain, of which Pigeon Mountain is a protrusion.

Lookout Mountain is the southernmost extension of the Cumberland Plateau and stretches for a hundred miles across Alabama, Georgia, and Tennessee. Lookout Mountain and Chickamauga Valley were the scene of a struggle between Union and Confederate forces in 1863 for control of Chattanooga. This battle site can be visited at the Chickamauga and Chattanooga National Military Park, and you can retrace the conflict of the two great armies at four battlefields: Chickamauga, Point Park, Orchard Park, and Missionary Ridge.

The descent from High Point follows the rim of the mountain and for a short time the Pocket Trail. This trail comes up from McLemore Cove and offers hikers the opportunity to see and climb on unusual geology. This cove is also one of the most remarkable botanical areas in northwest Georgia. After the ride, go ahead and cool off in the pond. It is rejuvenating after sweating in the hot Georgia sun.

General location: About 9 miles from Lafayette, Georgia.

Elevation change: You gain and lose about 1,000 feet of elevation for the entire ride.

*This profile and source material for this profile's map were contributed by John Derry.

Season: It can be hot in the summer, but it's a great place to escape the real heat from the valley below. It's probably best to avoid this trail during hunting season. Otherwise, year-round.

Services: All services are available in Lafayette. The closest phone is at the check station on Rocky Lane. While there is no formal campground on Pigeon Mountain, camping is permitted anywhere there is a pulloff.

Hazards: Because Pigeon Mountain is a Wildlife Management Area, it is important to wear blaze orange during hunting season. Bring plenty of water because there is no source of potable water once on top of the mountain.

Rescue index: There is a phone at the check station on Rocky Lane, with a ranger's residence directly behind it. Many people use the area during the weekend, but during the week the place can be a little deserted.

Land status: Located within the Crockford–Pigeon Mountain Wildlife Management Area, administered by the Georgia Department of Natural Resources.

Maps: There are free maps of the trail system available at the check station on Rocky Lane. USGS 7.5 minute quads: Cedar Grove and Lafayette.

Finding the trail: From Lafayette, go north on GA 193 for 2.8 miles. Turn left (south) onto Chamberlain Road. Travel 3.6 miles and turn right (west) onto Rocky Lane. You will pass a big game check station on your left. Continue up Rocky Lane for about 3.5 miles. This section of the road is very rough and can be treacherous when wet. Continue up this road for 5 miles, then turn right onto McCutchens Spring Road. Start at the campsite.

Source of additional information:

Georgia Department of Natural Resources
2592 Floyd Springs Road NE
Armuchee, GA 30105-2518
(706) 295-6041

Notes on the trail: Start on McCutchens Spring Road and head north past the ponds. At about .7 mile, take the orange-blazed Atwood Trail on the right and head into the woods. This section is great single-track with many short climbs and descents, some being technical.

Turn left onto Atwood Point Road at about 3.2 miles and follow this gravel road until it intersects with McCutchens Spring Road at 4.5 miles. Take a right on McCutchens Spring Road and after .1 mile go around the gate and head downhill.

Around 5 miles, turn left on West Brow Trail. The trailhead is marked with a sign and is blazed blue and white. This is the beginning of the 1-mile climb to High Point.

Finish the climb and take in the view of the valley below and across to Lookout Mountain and great single-track, which is fast and has some bare rock to roll over. Turn right at McCutchens Spring Road and cruise to the start of the ride.

CHEROKEE NATIONAL FOREST

The Cherokee National Forest is Tennessee's only national forest, which sounds bad at first until you consider that it stretches the entire length of the state's eastern edge: all 625,000 acres of it. And if it looks like it's been around for a few years, it has. Since 1911, when the land was bought up from private landholders, most of whom were responsible for clear-cutting and widespread erosion.

You'd hardly know it now. The land has regrown thick stands of forest, looking in some parts like it did when the only humans around were the Native Americans. Deer, squirrels, and even bears and turkeys are nearly as numerous today as they were 200 years ago. Chances are that a ride inside this majestic national forest will bring a mountain biker "tire-to-hide" with one of the forest's full-timers.

Source of additional information:

Ocoee Ranger District
Cherokee National Forest
Route 1, Box 348D
Benton, TN 37307
(423) 338-5201

RIDE 73 · Clear Creek

AT A GLANCE

Length/configuration: An 11-mile out-and-back single-track (5.5 miles each way) that is typically ridden as a downhill connector to an uphill return ride, using either Clemmer or Slickrock.

Aerobic difficulty: None on the downhill, but very tough on the return

Technical difficulty: This is recommended as a ride for intermediate to advanced riders

Scenery: Rock Creek Gorge Scenic Area in between the Hiwassee River (to the north) and the Ocoee River (to the south)

Special comments: This trail has been opened on a trial basis; yield and be courteous to the prime users of this trail—hikers

When I showed up at the Ocoee Ranger District office and talked to Robert Lee, trail coordinator for the district, I was surprised to learn that Clear Creek, a popular hiking-only trail on my last visit, had been recently opened to use by mountain bikers—all of its out-and-back single-track (11 miles total). And not only that, but nearly all of the remaining hiking trails accessed from the Chilhowee Recreation Area had been opened for biking as well. In addition, the Slickrock Trail (a new construction) had been completed. It was clear to see that the Cherokee National Forest had a big hand out to mountain bikers. I asked Robert why the Ocoee District has been so receptive to mountain biking. He told me, "I got a call from someone with the Chattanooga Bike Club who wanted to know why there weren't more trails open at Chilhowee to bikers. I explained how funds were tight, but if the interest was there, some money might be acquired if the club could provide the muscle." Robert was as good as his word, and $7,500 later, volunteers were swinging Pulaskis and tamping tread.

It's good to remember that the answer is always no until you ask. The bike club asked, and the answer was yes. But it doesn't happen by magic. Robert explained, "Whenever there's a work day for the trails, the bikers show, whereas it's been hard to get the hikers and horseback riders here to help." Now doesn't that make you feel good to be a mountain biker? Almost as good as you'll feel when you glide down this classic single-track, from Chilhowee to Parksville Lake.

General location: East of Cleveland, Tennessee, on US 64.

Elevation change: Approximately 1,000 feet.

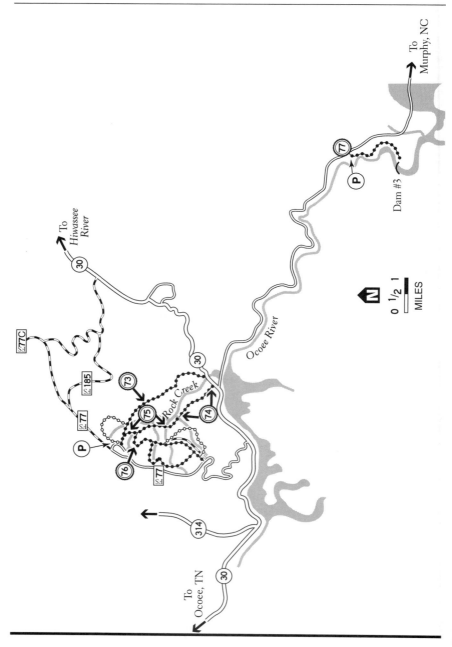

Season: An all-season trail.

Services: The Chilhowee Recreation Area has water and rest rooms (cold showers if you can stand them, or need them) from May 2 until November 13; Parksville Lake Recreation Area is open year-round with warm showers and drinking water.

Hazards: It's a steep descent with plenty of rocks and narrow chutes—not a trail for the timid or technically deficient.

Rescue index: It's not a good place to be rescued from, as it will take moderate to difficult effort.

Land status: Within the Cherokee National Forest.

Maps: A map of the trail system has been placed at the fee station, near the picnic area. The Cherokee National Forest (Ocoee, Hiwassee, and Ranger Districts) map (1984) shows this route. A new, updated map should be released soon and should show all the additions.

Finding the trail: Leave Cleveland, Tennessee, headed east on US 64 to Ocoee. After passing the Ocoee Ranger District office on the left, approximately 7.5 miles east of the intersection with US 411, look immediately to the left. A sign indicating the left turn to Chilhowee Recreation Area should be easy to spot. It's another 5 miles or so to the Recreation Area fee station. After parking in the upper lot by the fee station, look for the Clear Creek trailhead northeast of the lot and adjacent to it.

Source of additional information:

Ocoee Ranger District
Cherokee National Forest
Route 1, Box 348D
Benton, TN 37307
(423) 338-5201

Notes on the trail: Although this trail may be ridden as an out-and-back, it is better as the downhill section of a loop using either Clemmer or Slickrock on the uphill return. Begin the ride up top at Chilhowee Recreation Area. There are two options: Use Azalea Trail as a 2-mile connector to Clear Creek, combined with the three-quarter-mile Arbutus Trail, or stay on Clear Creek from the get-go. It is a fast descent to FS 3111 and TN 30. Turn right at the bottom and go for approximately a mile to pick up Clemmer on the right for the comparatively moderate climb back. Clemmer joins Benton Falls Trail, which leads to the lower parking lot a mile and a half away.

RIDE 74 · Clemmer Trail

AT A GLANCE

Length/configuration: 5.7 miles one way (11.4 miles total) on an out-and-back single-track

Aerobic difficulty: There's approximately 1,000 feet of elevation gained (and lost) in about 6 miles, a pretty good workout on the way back up

Technical difficulty: Some sections will require careful attention to detail, but most of the route is easy to slightly challenging

Scenery: Rock Creek Gorge Scenic Area

Special comments: This route can be made into a 20-mile loop by riding a section of pavement (7 miles) and gravel (8 miles)

The 11.4 total miles (5.7 miles one way) of this Cherokee National Forest out-and-back single-track explores the Rock Creek Scenic Area just north of Lake Ocoee. Rock Creek is formed from four small springs gushing out of the upper slopes of Chilhowee Mountain. The stream drops over Benton Falls on its way to the lake formed by the backed-up waters of the Ocoee River, site of the 1996 Olympic white-water events. An early spring ride down into the gorge most likely will give rise to the smell of the trailing arbutus, an intensely fragrant evergreen creeper. It, and the more common wild grape, are the likely candidates for what the Cherokee Indians were describing when they named this place Ocoee—"land of the apricot vine." In any case, the off-road riding here is as sweet as it gets.

General location: About 18 miles east of Cleveland, Tennessee, just north of US 64.

Elevation change: Approximately 1,000 feet.

Season: This trail can be ridden year-round.

Services: The Chilhowee Recreation Area has water and rest rooms (cold showers if you can stand them, or need them) from May 2 until November 13; Parksville Lake Recreation Area is open year-round with drinking water and warm showers. Cleveland or Chattanooga will be the closest site where more specialized biking services can be obtained.

Hazards: Hikers, deadfalls, rocks, and roots provide the majority of hazards on the single-track; motorized vehicles will be encountered on the paved and graveled sections, should this trail be used for the first section of a 20-mile loop.

An opening in the middle
of a young pine forest.

Rescue index: Both trailheads begin at paved roads, and the trail stays within 3 miles of a paved road. Still, the overall remote nature of the area will make any rescue difficult. Ride prepared for self-rescue.

Land status: Within the boundaries of the Cherokee National Forest.

Maps: A map of the trail system has been placed at the fee station, near the picnic area. The Cherokee National Forest (Ocoee, Hiwassee, and Ranger Districts) map (created in 1984) does not show this route. An updated version of this official map is planned for release soon, and all additions and changes should be shown. The DeLorme *Tennessee Atlas and Gazetteer* shows Clemmer as a jeep trail. See page 258 for our map of this ride.

Finding the trail: Leave Cleveland, Tennessee, headed east on US 64 to Ocoee. After passing the Ocoee Ranger District Office on the left, approximately 7.5 miles east of where US 64 intersects with US 411, immediately look for FS 77 also on the left. A sign indicating the left turn to Chilhowee Recreation Area should be easy to spot. It's another 5 miles or so to the Recreation Area fee station. After parking in the upper lot by the fee station, bike down to the lower lot. A gated road is at the end of the lot. This is the upper trailhead. Follow the trail signs to Benton Falls. In order to park and begin at the lower trailhead on US 64, don't turn left up the mountain on FS 77 and go to Chilhowee Recreation Area; instead, continue straight for a couple of miles past the turn. Just before (west of) where TN 30 intersects with US 64, the trail goes up the mountain. A parking area on the right (lakeside) shoulder is provided and marked for bikers.

Source of additional information:

Ocoee Ranger District
Cherokee National Forest
Route 1, Box 348D
Benton, TN 37307
(423) 338-5201

Notes on the trail: From the upper trailhead at Chilhowee Recreation Area, continue down to Benton Falls. Clemmer continues straight. A fork in the trail occurs at about a mile and a quarter in, with a blue-blazed trail going left and the yellow-blazed Clemmer Trail going right. After about another half mile, just after you cross a creek, the rocky double-track comes in on the right. Clemmer continues straight. (This turn, however, soon enters a wildlife opening, where a double-track is easily seen on the right a few yards into the clearing; it goes up and intersects with FS 5050—unmarked at this point—after a half-mile climb. Left—and up—on FS 5050 for another 1.5 miles leads to paved FS 77. Take a right on it to head back to Chilhowee.) Back on the main Clemmer route, a descent loses about 250 feet over the next 2.5 miles. During the descent, the single-track ends at gravel road FS 33101. Turn left to return to US 64.

An alternate route, the 20-plus-mile loop, uses the Clemmer single-track down to US 64 where a left turn, followed by an immediate left turn onto TN 30, leads up Greasy Creek for approximately 4.5 miles. After the pavement bends away from Greasy Creek, watch for a left turn onto the gravel road, FS 77, 3 miles later. After FS 477 goes to the right, take either FS 77 to Oswald Dome or FS 185 to the left. FS 185 rejoins FS 77 a couple of miles north of Chilhowee Recreation Area, which is reached by turning left. However, FS 105, whose left turn appears a quarter-mile or so after you turn onto FS 185, may also be taken to loop back into TN 30, a mile-and-a-half south of the FS 77 intersection.

RIDE 75 · Benton Falls

<table>
<tr><td>AT A GLANCE

</td><td>Length/configuration: 3-mile loop, almost all single-track

Aerobic difficulty: A few places can cause hard breathing, but just momentarily

Technical difficulty: There are no challenging sections for bikers with experience

Scenery: Some of the best scenery anywhere is found within the Cherokee National Forest, especially in Rock Creek Gorge Scenic Area, where Benton Falls is located

Special comments: This is a national forest fee area; bikers must register at the information station</td></tr>
</table>

This three-mile loop inside the Chilhowee Recreation Area combines single-track and a short piece of pavement for an easy ride through the Cherokee National Forest. The mature mixed hardwood forest of Rock Creek Scenic Gorge is home to a wide assortment of wildlife. It's the unlucky biker who doesn't see at least a deer or two while pedaling these slopes south of Oswald Dome.

Squirrels, mostly the basic gray variety, are frequently seen scampering up the tall trunks of oaks, beeches, and maples. Also, flying squirrels are sometimes seen. It is always a special treat to watch one launch itself from high in the crown—arms and legs akimbo—in what is more a controlled fall than actual flight.

As I took a break near Benton Falls, I happened to catch sight of one of these flying rodents going airborne as it sought refuge from the talons of a hawk. Just as the hawk swooped down on what it must have thought was going to be lunch, the squirrel leapt into the air. It landed on a nearby tree trunk and scurried to a bough where it barked a complaint to the disappearing hawk. But there'll be no complaints for the mountain biker who comes to this part of the Cherokee National Forest looking for classic single-track.

General location: About 18 miles east of Cleveland, Tennessee, just north of US 64.

Elevation change: Total elevation change is less than 200 feet for the entire loop.

Season: This is an all-season trail. The recreation area may be closed from mid-November through the end of April.

Benton Falls drops with a
roar just behind the bike.

Services: The Chilhowee Recreation Area has water and rest rooms (cold showers if you can stand them, or need them) from May 2 until November 13; Parksville Lake Recreation Area is open year-round with warm showers and drinking water. Cleveland or Chattanooga will be the closest site where more specialized biking services can be obtained.

Hazards: Hikers use this popular trail; other than that, no other out-of-the-ordinary hazards exist on this easily ridden route.

Rescue index: You should have no difficulty organizing and carrying out a rescue, although the winding road from Chilhowee Recreation Area to US 64 makes it a slow drive down off of the mountain.

Land status: Benton Falls lies within Cherokee National Forest.

Maps: A map of the trail system has been placed at the fee station, near the picnic area. The Cherokee National Forest (Ocoee, Hiwassee, and Ranger Districts) map (created in 1984) shows most of the available trail. An updated version of the official map, which should show all the additions and changes, is planned for release soon. See page 258 for our map of this ride.

Finding the trail: Leave Cleveland, Tennessee, headed east on US 64 to Ocoee. After passing the Ocoee Ranger District office on the left, approximately 7.5 miles east of the intersection with US 411, look for FS 77 immediately on the left. A sign indicating the left turn to Chilhowee Recreation Area should be easily seen. It's another 5 miles or so to the Recreation Area fee station. After parking in the upper lot by the fee station, bike down to the lower lot. A gated road is at the end of the lot. This is the trailhead. Follow the trail signs to Benton Falls.

Source of additional information:

Ocoee Ranger District
Cherokee National Forest
Route 1, Box 348D
Benton, TN 37307
(423) 338-5201

Notes on the trail: Begin this 3-mile loop by riding around the normally closed gate at the end of the lower picnic area parking lot. Take the left at the first intersection toward Benton Falls. Approximately a third of a mile in on the right, you'll see the entrance to the Slickrock Trail. Continue past it. At about the mile mark, the intersection with Red Leaf Trail occurs; Benton Falls is straight ahead in approximately another half mile. The left turn down to Benton Falls (foot travel only from this point on to the actual falls) is marked by a sign pointing to Clemmer Trail straight ahead. Benton Falls is reached by dismounting the bike and walking the remaining couple hundred yards. To complete the loop, go back to the intersection with Red Leaf Trail and take a right on it. Arbutus Trail intersects approximately a quarter mile farther on. Turn right on Arbutus and then left onto Clear Creek Trail, which leads west back to the campground. Continue up the hill to the picnic area's parking lot and fee station.

RIDE 76 · Slickrock

AT A GLANCE

TN ⊛

Length/configuration: A 5.1-mile single-track loop

Aerobic difficulty: Portions make for a moderate workout, but overall it's not a strenuous ride

Technical difficulty: An occasional challenge, but mostly an easy ride

Scenery: This trail goes through part of the nearly 300,000 acres in the southern section of Cherokee National Forest, adjacent to the Great Smoky Mountains National Park

Special comments: The loop returns along FS 77, a paved road; however, trail construction continues, which may link the single-track to the end of FS 5050

While I was trying to wait out the rain at the Chilhowee Recreation Area parking lot, a ranger drove up. She told me there was a trail partially completed—a mile section of single-track leading to a gated gravel road that joins FS 77 just above the radio towers. "This," she said, "makes an easy four-mile loop inside the Rock Creek Gorge Scenic Area." When I returned six months later, I discovered the trail had been completed, adding up to a total of 5.1 miles.

The Slickrock addition is a recent Cherokee National Forest project designed to provide more separation between different users—i.e., hikers, horseback riders, and mountain bikers. Slickrock represents only one stage of an extensive collaboration between Ocoee Ranger District and local bike clubs. The funds come from the Ocoee Ranger District, with the muscle supplied by local bike clubs. The result, as seen at Slickrock, should inspire us all to volunteer as trail builders.

General location: East of Cleveland, Tennessee, on US 64.

Elevation change: A net gain of approximately 300 feet occurs over the first 2 miles; the return is mostly downhill.

Season: An all-year ride.

Services: Developed camping is found at Chilhowee, and water and showers are available here from May 2 until November 13. Some small stores along US 64 have the basics, but you may be required to go to Cleveland or Chattanooga for more specialized services.

Hazards: Hikers may also be using the single-track.

The alert biker is likely to spot a wide variety of wildlife on the trail. Photo by Pam Jones.

Rescue index: Although a rescue could be easily accomplished here, just getting off the mountain once the on-the-trail rescue is completed may take 15 minutes (or more) by car.

Land status: Part of the Cherokee National Forest.

Maps: A map of the trail system has been placed at the fee station, near the picnic area. The Cherokee National Forest (Ocoee, Hiwassee, and Ranger Districts) map (created in 1984) shows most of the available trail; however, the Slickrock addition does not appear. An updated version of the official map is planned for release soon and will include Slickrock. The tracing made for this guide is based on field notes and a conversation with Robert Lee of the Ocoee Ranger District. See page 258 for our map of this ride.

Finding the trail: Leave Cleveland, Tennessee, headed east on US 64 to Ocoee. After passing TN 314 (Parksville Road) on the left, approximately 7.5 miles east of the intersection with US 411, look for FS 77 and the ranger district office. A sign indicating the left turn to Chilhowee Recreation Area should be easily seen. It's another 5 miles or so to the Recreation Area fee station. After parking in the upper lot by the fee station, bike down to the lower lot. A gated road is at the end of the lot. This is the trailhead. Start riding toward Benton Falls (follow the signs). The Slickrock intersection occurs on the right, a third of a mile in.

Source of additional information:

> Ocoee Ranger District
> Cherokee National Forest
> Route 1, Box 348D
> Benton, TN 37307
> (423) 338-5201

Notes on the trail: The first one-third of a mile shares the single-track route to Benton Falls. A 4-foot-tall carsonite post on the right marks the turn onto Slickrock. After you reach a wildlife opening, a short mile away, take the right onto the gravel double-track, FS 330902. Turn left onto single-track before the paved FS 77. Take an uphill and downhill to the creek, cross it, and turn right at the intersection with FS 5050. At the **T** intersection, turn left and reach the wildlife opening, where a left turn onto Clemmer leads to the Scenic Trail intersection. Turn left again and reach another wildlife opening. Continue straight across the opening, picking up the single-track back to the wildlife opening at the end of FS 330902. Ride straight to reach the trailhead; a left takes you on another lap.

RIDE 77 · Old Copper Road Trail

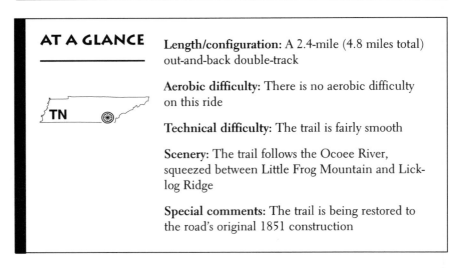

AT A GLANCE	**Length/configuration:** A 2.4-mile (4.8 miles total) out-and-back double-track
	Aerobic difficulty: There is no aerobic difficulty on this ride
TN	**Technical difficulty:** The trail is fairly smooth
	Scenery: The trail follows the Ocoee River, squeezed between Little Frog Mountain and Licklog Ridge
	Special comments: The trail is being restored to the road's original 1851 construction

Few trails in Appalachia can be ridden as easily as this 2.4-mile out-and-back double-track (4.8 miles total), which follows the first road built into the Copper Basin. What it lacks in difficulty and technical challenge, though, is compensated by its scenery and history. Free enterprise is really the mother of invention, and proof lies in the story behind this road's construction. The Dahlonega gold rush, which occurred in the early 1830s, sparked exploration for the twinkling mineral, and prospectors tromping around up north in Tennessee hit a rich vein—of copper, that is. So much copper was found that it sped construction of a road to Ducktown, Tennessee, six miles east of the Ocoee White Water Center trailhead, site of the 1996 Olympics venue for white-water paddling.

Old Copper Road went from the Copper Basin to Cleveland, Tennessee, a distance of 33 miles, where the copper was off-loaded from mule teams and loaded onto trains. All but the remaining 2.4-mile stretch was paved, first in the 1930s and again in 1957, for US 64. The sound of this busy highway will sometimes override the trickle of the diverted Ocoee River, which flows through a large pipe leading to the drop at Dam 3.

General location: East of Cleveland, Tennessee, just north of US 64.

Elevation change: Little to none.

Season: An all-season trail.

Services: The Ocoee White Water Center (OWWC) has water, phones, and rest rooms. For other services and supplies, head either to Cleveland or Chattanooga.

Hazards: Other bikers and hikers are the only significant hazard.

Rescue index: This is an easy trail for carrying out a rescue.

Land status: Within the Cherokee National Forest.

Maps: No maps have been drawn for this trail, other than what appears in this guide (see page 258). A brochure, however, called "Old Copper Road Trail," can be picked up at either the OWWC or the ranger district office.

Finding the trail: From the Copper Basin and the intersection of US 64 and TN 68, head west on US 64 for 6 miles and turn left into the OWWC. From the Cherokee Ranger District office, head east on US 64 for 13 miles, where the OWWC will be on the right. The trail begins at the Legacy Bridge.

Source of additional information:

Ocoee Ranger District
Cherokee National Forest
Route 1, Box 348D
Benton, TN 37307
(423) 338-5201

Notes on the trail: You will cross four different bridges on the way out to Dam 3, the turnaround for this out-and-back.

RIDE 78 · Iron Mountain

AT A GLANCE

TN

Length/configuration: A 12-mile loop, divided nearly equally between single- and double-track

Aerobic difficulty: Two moderately strenuous climbs provide a workout; the final section (4.5 miles) follows an old rail grade

Technical difficulty: Intermediate riders will be challenged

Scenery: The Conasauga River and Cohutta Mountains

Special comments: Two river crossings are required; these are not possible at high water levels or advised during periods of cold weather

This 12-mile loop follows an old railroad grade for about 5 miles on the north bank of the Conasauga River. The southern seven miles, mostly single-track, climb up the side of Iron Mountain, which straddles the Tennessee-Georgia border. The southern section has three distinct climbs, in addition to having two creek crossings before the last ford of the Conasauga River.

The occasionally steep climbs may require a push for short stretches, but the fast, smooth drops make all the work worth it. One especially nice overlook, with Iron Mountain on the left, looks down the Alaculsy Valley. Other views show the peaks of the Cohuttas jutting up on the horizon like biceps.

The last section of the loop, the Tennessee side, uses new trail from the ford to the intersection with Conasauga River Trail. The sound of the large river echoes off the side of Iron Mountain, which rises sharply and looms 700 feet above the trail. Although the track's design encourages a fast pace, the biker willing to slow down is likely to spot a complete assortment of riparian wildlife.

General location: Near Ocoee, Tennessee.

Elevation change: Approximately 1,000 feet of climbing per lap. Some of it is quite steep and will likely require at least one push.

Season: It's best to delay this ride until periods when water levels are lower and not likely to rise. Deer season (mid-fall to early winter) is not a good time to ride here, either, as it's open to hunters.

Services: The trailhead is remote. It's a long ride to the small stores along US 411, which will have the basics. An even longer trip to Cleveland or Chattanooga must be made for special services, like bike shops.

RIDE 78 • Iron Mountain

Hazards: Large rocks and some roots have to be negotiated with care. Loose sections of the new trail may have to be walked down for safety's sake until they become more packed. Distant thunderstorms can create flash floods, making river crossings dangerous.

Rescue index: Ride prepared for self-rescue. The trailhead lies more than 10 miles from US 411, most of it on winding forest road.

Land status: This is land within both the Cherokee National Forest (Tennessee) and the Chattahoochee National Forest (Georgia).

The rocky ribs of the Appalachians fall across each other on the Georgia-Tennessee line.

Maps: I picked up a copy of the Conasauga and Iron Mountain Trail Project from the Cherokee Ranger District Office on US 64, near the Chilhowee Recreation Area.

Finding the trail: Leave the Cherokee Ranger District Office headed toward Cleveland, Tennessee, on US 64. After 7.5 miles, look for the turn onto US 411 South. After driving 6.25 miles, signs for TN 313 will be posted just before the intersection with Ladd Springs Road. Take the left (marked by the sign for Ball Play Baptist Church). There will be a sawmill on the right after 2 miles, and after another 2.25 miles another sign is posted across the bridge and at the beginning of FS 221. Bear right toward Jacks River and Sylco Creek Campground. Almost 5.5 miles farther, Jacks River Trailhead will be straight ahead. Turn right and cross the bridge. Take the right turn into Cottonwood Patch Camping Area. Parking for the Iron Mountain Trail will be three-quarters of a mile farther on the left. Leave the parking area and turn left toward the river to begin the trail.

Source of additional information:

Ocoee Ranger District
Cherokee National Forest
Route 1, Box 348D
Benton, TN 37307
(423) 338-5201

Notes on the trail: Begin the clockwise loop by heading out of the parking lot and turning left toward the river, which will be forded in approximately a quarter mile. Do not continue if the crossing here is too high; the second crossing will be deeper. At the end of the second significant climb, at approximately 4.2 miles, the intersection is reached with FS 1A. This double-track quickly descends downhill to a fork nearly a mile away. Take the right across the creek. At the 6-mile mark, a spectacular view of the Alaculsy Valley, with Iron Mountain on the left, comes into view. A ridge leads to the river, where, at the approximate 7.2 mile mark, the trail begins losing elevation fast. After about 8 miles, at the bottom of the drop, watch for the next (and last) river crossing. Look for the wide ford, which you should cross off-bike, staying upriver of the bike. Nearly 1.5 miles farther along, the Conasauga River Trail is met. Continue riding upriver, crossing two creeks before the parking lot of the Conasauga River Trail. Take a right out of the parking lot and look for the intersection at Jacks River Trail (the same intersection seen on the way in). Turn right and cross the bridge.

RIDE 79 · Indian Boundary

AT A GLANCE

/ TN   ⊛

Length/configuration: 3.5-mile loop

Aerobic difficulty: Minimal; this trail is essentially flat; it's a great place to begin working on your aerobic fitness and/or ride with the whole family

Technical difficulty: Other than a few roots and some twisty sections, there's not much to worry about; the trail has been leveled and graveled, with bridges over all of the creeks

Scenery: Although this ride is adjacent to a recreation area and campground, it feels surprisingly isolated; the Unicoi Mountains provide an impressive setting for this beautiful high mountain lake; the fall leaf season is a great time to do this ride

Special comments: This ride is located within the Indian Boundary Recreation Area ($2 usage fee) near the campground; swimming beach and bathhouse facility at the trailhead

The Indian Boundary trail is a simple 3.5-mile loop that twists and turns along the edge of Indian Boundary Lake. This trail is graveled, essentially level, and offers little in the way of technical difficulty. It does, however, offer

*This profile was contributed by Steve Thompson; source material for this profile's map was created by John Derry.

RIDE 79 · Indian Boundary

much in the way of scenic beauty. The lake is ringed by impressive peaks and ridgelines. In the fall, this area explodes with color as the plentiful sugar maples turn gold and red in contrast to the dark greens of the black balsam and pines. There is a swimming beach and bathhouse facility at the trailhead.

There are many opportunities for other recreational activities nearby. Joyce Kilmer–Slickrock Wilderness, Citico Creek Wilderness, Tellico River, Ocoee River, and Great Smoky Mountain National Park are all within an hour's drive. The full-service campground, swimming beach, and nearby riding, hiking, paddling, and rafting opportunities make this area a great choice for family adventure weekends.

General location: About 14 miles east of Tellico Plains, Tennessee.

Elevation change: None. The trail is essentially flat.

Season: The fall colors are usually outstanding. Indian Boundary Recreation Area is busiest with campers and day users in June and July.

Services: The ride is adjacent to a full-service campground. There is a bathhouse and changing facility at the trailhead. There are several rangers on call in case of emergency.

Hazards: This trail is a popular walking trail for campers in the adjacent campground.

Rescue index: During the camping season (usually Memorial Day through Labor Day) help can be summoned by contacting the "Campground Host." In the off-season, the area can be fairly deserted. Cell phone coverage is weak at best.

Land status: Indian Boundary Recreation Area, Cherokee National Forest.

Maps: USGS 7.5 minute quad: White Oak Flats.

Finding the trail: From Tellico Plains, travel east on TN 165 and follow the signs to Indian Boundary Recreation Area. Once in the recreation area follow the signs to the swimming beach. Park and pay in the parking lot. The trail begins at the base of the steps and heads left toward the campground. This part of the trail is also used by campers heading to and from the beach.

Source of additional information:

Tellico Ranger District
Larry Fleming, District Ranger
250 Ranger Station Road
Tellico Plains, TN 37385
(423) 253-2520
Fax: (423) 253-2804

Notes on the trail: The trail is very easy to follow. From the steps, travel left on the obvious trail. The trail enters the woods and passes the campground on the left. There will be several small foot trails that link the campground with the bike trail. After a couple hundred yards, you will come to the boat ramp parking area. Follow the edge of the parking lot to the right and stay on the gravel bike trail as it passes the ramp. Continue traveling clockwise around the lake. At several points, old logging roads will intersect the trail. Toward the end of the ride you will cross the dam and spillway. Bear right on the trail as it heads up a small hill to the trailhead.

RIDE 80 · Hurricane Gap

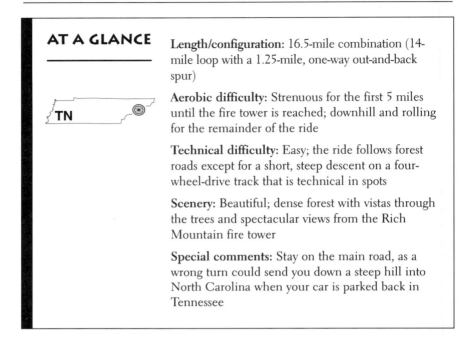

AT A GLANCE

TN

Length/configuration: 16.5-mile combination (14-mile loop with a 1.25-mile, one-way out-and-back spur)

Aerobic difficulty: Strenuous for the first 5 miles until the fire tower is reached; downhill and rolling for the remainder of the ride

Technical difficulty: Easy; the ride follows forest roads except for a short, steep descent on a four-wheel-drive track that is technical in spots

Scenery: Beautiful; dense forest with vistas through the trees and spectacular views from the Rich Mountain fire tower

Special comments: Stay on the main road, as a wrong turn could send you down a steep hill into North Carolina when your car is parked back in Tennessee

An hour after leaving the parking area and riding only five miles, I was beginning to wonder if climbing to the Rich Mountain fire tower was worth the effort. I could just as easily have bypassed this spur and continued the loop along the ridge separating North Carolina and Tennessee. However, climbing the tower and taking in the view was reward enough. Looking southwest, I could see the Great Smokies; and to the east were the Black Mountains, one of which is Mount Mitchell (6,684 feet), the highest peak east of the Mississippi.

This 16.5-mile ride is located in the Paint Creek Recreation Area, which is in the Nolichucky Ranger District of Tennessee's Cherokee National Forest. After making the climb to the fire tower, the remainder of the ride is less demanding aerobically; you will enjoy traveling along the North Carolina–Tennessee state line, riding on dirt roads, and catching views of distant ridges through the dense forest.

Though not a technical ride, and one which could be driven in any four-wheel-drive vehicle, it can be remote in places. Also, a cause for concern is the possibility of taking a left instead of a right and ending up descending quickly into North Carolina rather than Tennessee at the end of the ride. The best piece of advice for not getting lost on this ride: when in doubt, take a right.

Riding is limited to all gravel and dirt roads and horse trails; bicycles are not permitted on hiking trails. There is a $2 parking fee in the Paint Creek Recre-

*This profile and source material for this profile's map were contributed by John Derry.

RIDE 80 · Hurricane Gap

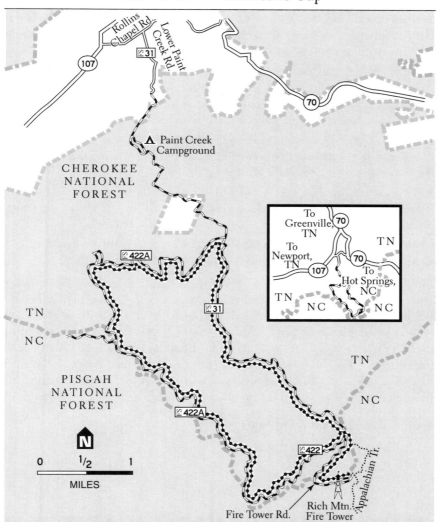

ation Area, and this can be paid at a pay station in the Paint Creek Campground. Most of the ride is open to vehicular traffic, so be careful in turns.

General location: About 14 miles east of Newport, Tennessee, off TN 107 and adjacent to the North Carolina state line.

Elevation change: In the first 5 miles of the ride, about 1,450 feet of elevation is gained, with the steepest section being the last 1.3 miles to the fire tower atop Rich Mountain. The rest of the ride consists of a fast descent down the fire tower road and then a rolling ridge line with short climbs and descents from Hurricane Gap back to the parking area.

Season: Year-round, but it's best when the leaves are off the trees. The air is clear and the views are spectacular from the many vistas. Don't attempt this ride after heavy rains; FS 422 turns into a giant mud puddle.

Services: All services can be found in Newport. Camping is available at the Paint Creek Campground, which is seasonal and runs on a first-come first-served basis ($7 per night). The only amenities provided at the campground are water and pit toilets, but it's laid out nicely with hiking and fishing nearby.

Hazards: All the roads on this ride are also open to vehicles. There is not a lot of traffic, but it is important to remember that others are using the roads. During hunting season, wear blaze orange.

Rescue index: You'll be 8 to 10 miles from a phone during portions of the ride. The Paint Creek Campground does not have a phone. In case of an emergency, phones may be found at houses along Lower Paint Creek Road.

Land status: The entire ride falls within the Cherokee National Forest.

Maps: USGS 7.5 minute quad: Hot Springs, North Carolina.

Finding the trail: From Greeneville, Tennessee, take State Road 70 south for 10.2 miles until you see the Paint Creek Campground sign. Turn right here onto Rollins Chapel Road and go 1.3 miles to Lower Paint Creek Road. Turn left onto Lower Paint Creek Road, which becomes gravel after 1.1 miles and turns into FS 31. The road then winds uphill for 1.8 miles until it enters Paint Creek Campground. Locate the pay station so you can park along the road. Take FS 31 on the right and uphill for approximately 1.9 miles to the intersection of FS 31 and FS 422A. Pull into 422A and find parking along the side of the road.

Source of additional information:

> Cherokee National Forest Office
> 2800 North Ocoee Street NE
> Cleveland, TN 37312
> (423) 476-9700

Notes on the trail: The Forest Service has tried to mark most dirt roads; you should see their road signs for the entire ride. From the parking area, turn right onto FS 31 and proceed up the gravel road for 3.5 miles to Hurricane Gap. This climb is long and steep in sections and will force you to become one with your small chain ring. At Hurricane Gap, bear right and you will see blazes for the Appalachian Trail. Just beyond that is FS 422. Continue past FS 422 and climb 1.3 miles to Rich Mountain fire tower, which offers scenic views of the French Broad River Valley.

Turn the bike around and scream downhill to the intersection, then turn right onto FS 422. This narrow dirt road follows the North Carolina–Tennessee state line for 7.5 miles, climbing and dropping over small knobs and splashing through numerous mud holes. There are many roads and trails that head off to the left, but it's important to stay on FS 422 because some of these roads could drop steeply into North Carolina and would require much effort on your part to get back. At around 11.8 miles, Jack Branch Trail enters on the left; continue on FS 422 and prepare for the bottom to drop out at around 12.7 miles. The road becomes more of a jeep track that is a steep, technical descent, and one heck of a ride. After a mile, the four-wheel-drive track comes to an end in a clearing and intersects with FS 422A. Follow this road for 2.8 miles back to the car.

RIDE 81 · Poplar Cove

AT A GLANCE

TN

Length/configuration: 5.5-mile loop

Aerobic difficulty: Fairly difficult; the first 2 miles are really steep; pushing may be required at times

Technical difficulty: Four-wheel-drives and extensive horse use makes for very rocky conditions, especially on the climb through Poplar Cove; a lot of trees are down across the trail due to a fierce winter storm in 1998; multiple stream crossings will cool you down on hot summer days

Scenery: If you have time to look up from your front wheel, you'll enjoy lush rhododendron thickets next to the creeks, a beautiful stand of fairly mature Poplars, and views of rock outcroppings

Special comments: This ride is located within the Horse Creek Recreation Area; a daily usage fee of $2 per vehicle is required

Make sure you and your bike are in good shape before tackling this 5-mile loop trail. Don't let the distance fool you; this trail is difficult. Poplar Cove throws all kinds of technical challenges at you. The climb through the cove is steep, rocky, and technical. The descent to Jenning's Creek demands your attention as you pick your way down steep, twisty, and tight single-track. Once you get to Jenning's Creek, you'll travel along it (and through it) on rocky and boggy single-track before picking up a gravel, then paved road back to the trailhead.

Poplar Cove will not only challenge your riding skills but also impress you with its scenic beauty. The recreation area is on Green Ridge, which is part

*This profile was contributed by Steve Thompson; source material for this profile's map was created by John Derry.

RIDE 81 · Poplar Cove

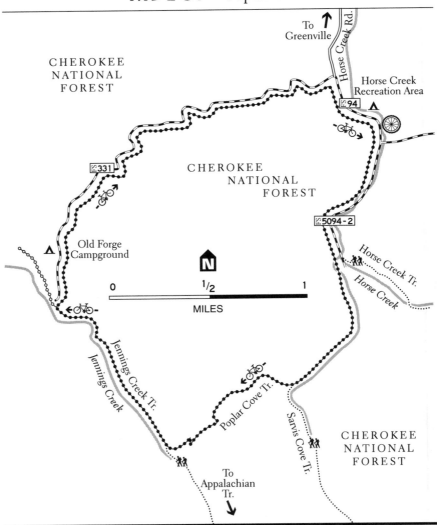

of the Bald Mountains, which in turn are a subset of the Unaka Mountains. The Appalachian Trail is just a couple of miles south, and that section of trail is generally regarded as one of the most rugged and beautiful. You'll occasionally pass hikers coming down to Horse Creek Recreation Area as they head into Greeneville or Erwin.

General location: About 11 miles southwest of Greeneville, Tennessee.

Elevation change: You'll climb for the first 2 miles, the last mile of which is very steep and may require pushing. This is followed by a very steep downhill to Jenning's Creek. From there, it's mostly downhill to the trailhead with a couple of gradual climbs thrown in.

Season: Because of its heavy tree cover and elevation, Poplar Cove stays cool even during the dog days of summer.

Services: You have your choice of two full-service campgrounds: Horse Creek and Old Forge. Both are run by the Forest Service. Greeneville offers all services.

Hazards: You may wish to avoid this area during winter, as there is no way to stay dry on the river crossings. This area is a popular hunting area. If you're going to ride here during the hunting season (usually late fall and early spring), it would be wise to wear some blaze orange or attach a bell to your bike.

Rescue index: There are several rangers on call in the recreation area. You may also find help at one of the two campgrounds on the ride. The Poplar Cove section is fairly deserted during the week.

Land status: Horse Creek Recreation Area is within the Cherokee National Forest.

Maps: USGS 7.5 minute quad: Greystone, TN-NC.

Finding the trail: From the parking lot at the end of the paved road, the trail leads upstream along Horse Creek.

Source of additional information:

Nolichucky-Unaka Ranger Districts
Olin Mason, District Ranger
120 Austin Avenue
Greeneville, TN 37743
(423) 638-4109
Fax: (423) 638-6577

Notes on the trail: From the parking lot, head upstream along Horse Creek. You'll climb for about a mile. Cross the creek at the top of the hill and follow the four-wheel-drive road until it ends. Continue on Poplar Cove Trail (yellow diamond blazes). You'll climb steadily until Sarvis Cove Trail enters on the left. Stay on Poplar Cove Trail and start climbing steeply until you reach the top of the hill. Ride along the ridge for a couple hundred yards until you come to the start of the obvious steep downhill section. There is a small foot trail heading off to the right. Ride downhill until you reach Jenning's Creek Trail. Turn right (downstream) onto Jenning's Creek Trail and follow Jenning's Creek. Little Jenning's Creek enters from the left; bear right and cross Jenning's Creek. Continue to follow Jenning's Creek until you come to a set of old stone steps. This is the entrance to Old Forge Campground. Ride around the perimeter of the campground on a lightly graveled path, then bear right on FS 331. FS 331 will intersect with paved FS 94 (the road you drove into Horse Creek Recreation Area). Turn right on FS 94 and ride back to the trailhead.

RIDE 82 · Buffalo Mountain

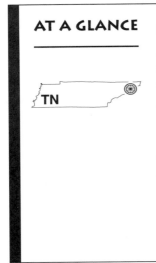

AT A GLANCE

Length/configuration: 6.8-mile loop

Aerobic difficulty: Moderately difficult; the first 4 miles of this ride are uphill

Technical difficulty: Fairly difficult; the last mile of the ride is a steep, technical descent

Scenery: There are great views of the surrounding Unaka Mountains on the climb to Buffalo Mountain ridge; you won't have much time to enjoy the scenery on the downhill

Special comments: Buffalo Mountain's maze of trails are maintained primarily for all-terrain vehicle use, so make sure your bike is in good mechanical shape

If you want to test your aerobic fitness and technical riding skills, this trail is for you. This 6.8-mile loop starts off innocently enough with a quick descent down paved Dry Creek Road. That's followed by a long climb to the top of Buffalo Mountain on a scenic, grassy double-track. You'll enjoy views of nearby Cherokee and Pinnacle Mountains as the trail winds along Buffalo Mountain ridge.

The trail changes character completely once it leaves the ridge and merges with an all-terrain vehicle trail, known locally as the Blue Trail. The Blue Trail will challenge you with a chaotic mix of banked turns, loose rock, sand and mud bogs, roots, and whoop-de-doos. The last mile of this ride is a very technical descent, which can be treacherous in places and even dangerous when wet. Beginners may wish to walk some of the technical downhill.

The Blue Trail is popular with motorcyclists and four-wheelers, many of whom regularly maintain the trail. It is protocol (and safer) for mountain bikes to yield the trail to motorized vehicles. Much of the trail is on private land, but permission to use the area has been granted. There is a $5 per vehicle usage fee required by the Forest Service.

General location: About 7.5 miles north of Erwin, Tennessee.

Elevation change: The first half mile is downhill. You will climb about 1,000 feet before reaching the ridge. From the ridge, the trail is mostly level before plunging back to the trailhead.

Season: Year-round, although the fall colors here are beautiful. This trail can be very hot and dusty during the "dog days" of summer.

*This profile was contributed by Steve Thompson; source material for this profile's map was created by John Derry.

RIDE 82 • Buffalo Mountain
RIDE 83 • Pinnacle Tower

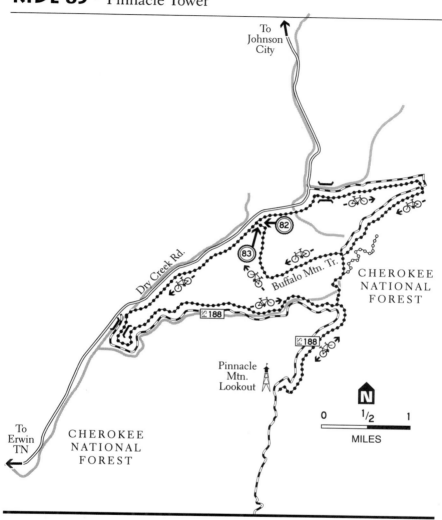

Services: All services are available in Erwin.

Hazards: This is a popular all-terrain vehicle area and can be crowded on the weekends. It's a good idea to pull off the trail and let motorized vehicles pass.

Rescue index: Help can be summoned in either Erwin or Johnson City.

Land status: Much of the trail is on private property; permission to use the area has been granted by the landowner. The rest of the trail is in the Cherokee National Forest.

Maps: USGS 7.5 minute quad: Erwin, TN. *Tennessee Atlas and Gazetteer,* available from Delorme, P.O. Box 298, Yarmouth, ME 04096.

Finding the trail: From Erwin, TN: go 4.1 miles south on TN 81. Turn right onto Arnold Road and travel 1.9 miles to Dry Creek Road. Take a right onto Dry Creek Road and go 5.8 miles to the Buffalo Mountain all-terrain vehicle trailhead parking area. The parking area will be on the right. Park here and pay at the self-pay station near the information board and motorcycle loading ramp. You will begin the ride by heading out of the parking lot and turning right onto Dry Creek Road.

Source of additional information:

Nolichucky-Unaka Ranger Districts
Olin Mason, District Ranger
120 Austin Avenue
Greeneville, TN 37743
(423) 638-4109
Fax: (423) 638-6577

Notes on the trail: From the parking lot, turn right onto Dry Creek Road and go downhill for about one-half mile. There will be a gate on the right just past a gas pipeline crossing. Take a right around the gate and bear left heading up the mountain. You will climb for a long time before hitting the ridgeline at about 4.2 miles. The trail crosses the gas pipeline again. Turn right onto the trail that follows the pipeline. You will come to a trail heading into the woods to the left just before the pipeline heads down a very steep hill. Turn left onto this trail and travel about .1 mile, then turn right onto Buffalo Mountain all-terrain vehicle trail (blue blazes). Follow this trail back to the parking lot.

RIDE 83 · Pinnacle Tower

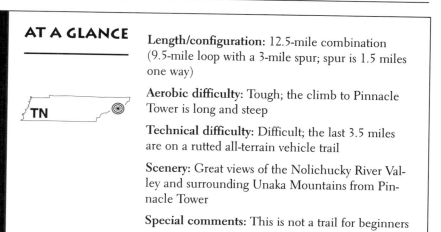

AT A GLANCE
_____

TN

Length/configuration: 12.5-mile combination (9.5-mile loop with a 3-mile spur; spur is 1.5 miles one way)

Aerobic difficulty: Tough; the climb to Pinnacle Tower is long and steep

Technical difficulty: Difficult; the last 3.5 miles are on a rutted all-terrain vehicle trail

Scenery: Great views of the Nolichucky River Valley and surrounding Unaka Mountains from Pinnacle Tower

Special comments: This is not a trail for beginners

This 12.5-mile combination trail (9.5-mile loop with a 3-mile spur; spur is 1.5 miles one way) is very challenging. The five-mile climb on gravel road to the tower is steep in sections and will test your aerobic fitness. The scenery at the tower rewards your effort on the climb with some outstanding views of the surrounding Unaka Mountains and Nolichucky River Valley.

This trail has some pretty tough technical sections. The Blue Trail is sandy, rutted, and rocky during dry periods—muddy, slippery, and fast when wet. There is a very steep, technical descent on this trail. Not only will you have to focus on the trail, you'll also need to be aware of motorized vehicles sharing the trail with you. The Buffalo Mountain all-terrain vehicle trail is popular with four-wheelers and motorcycles; weekends can get crowded.

There is a $5 per vehicle usage fee required by the Forest Service. If you ride here during the summer, bring plenty of water because most of the climb is in direct sun.

General location: About 7.5 miles north of Erwin, Tennessee.

Elevation change: The first 2 miles are screaming downhill on paved Dry Creek Road, followed by a 5.5-mile steep climb on gravel to Pinnacle Tower. The last 2 miles are steep, technical, and mostly downhill.

Season: This trail can be ridden year-round.

Services: All services are available in Erwin.

Hazards: This area is popular with all-terrain vehicle users and can be crowded on weekends. It's a good idea to pull off the trail to let motorized vehicles pass. The steep, technical downhill can get dangerous at times. Beginners may wish to walk the steepest sections.

*This profile was contributed by Steve Thompson; source material for this profile's map was created by John Derry.

Rescue index: Help can be summoned from nearby Erwin. This area is fairly crowded on weekends.

Land status: Cherokee National Forest.

Maps: USGS 7.5 minute quad: Erwin, TN. *Tennessee Atlas and Gazetteer,* available from Delorme, P.O. Box 298, Yarmouth, ME 04096.

Finding the trail: From Erwin, TN: go 4.1 miles south on TN 81. Turn right onto Arnold Road and travel 1.9 miles to Dry Creek Road. Take a right onto Dry Creek Road and go 5.8 miles to the Buffalo Mountain all-terrain vehicle trailhead parking area. The parking area will be on the right. Park here and pay at the self-pay station near the information board and motorcycle loading ramp. You will begin the ride by heading out of the parking lot and turning left onto Dry Creek Road.

Source of additional information:

Nolichucky-Unaka Ranger Districts
Olin Mason, District Ranger
120 Austin Avenue
Greeneville, TN 37743
(423) 638-4109
Fax: (423) 638-6577

Notes on the trail: From the parking lot, take a left onto Dry Creek Road. Ride down Dry Creek Road about 2 miles to FS 188. Turn left onto FS 188 and climb this gravel road. Stay on FS 188 until you reach Pinnacle Tower. From Pinnacle Tower, backtrack down FS 188 about 1.5 miles until you come to the third place that the blue-blazed Buffalo Trail (known locally as the "Blue Trail") crosses the road. Turn right onto Buffalo Mountain Trail. Follow Buffalo Mountain Trail back down the mountain to the parking lot.

RIDE 84 · Panther Creek State Park

AT A GLANCE
_____

TN

Length/configuration: Almost 7 miles (and growing) in a 3-loop combination of single- and double-track

Aerobic difficulty: You won't experience much hard breathing until you reach the advanced loop of 2.5 miles

Technical difficulty: The double- and single-track are fairly easily handled, until reaching the more technical single-track tacked onto the outer loop of the Farm Trails

Scenery: The rolling hills in this region line the southeastern shore of Cherokee Lake and Panther Creek

Special comments: The Appalachian Mountain Bike Club is working with park administrators to expand current mileage

---

These trails are not in the Cherokee National Forest, but I just couldn't pass up the chance to include this nearby scenic area. The three different loops found inside Panther Creek State Recreation Area make up a total of over 6 miles, mostly easy double- and single-track. There is, however, a small single-track section (a 2.5-mile loop west of the boat ramp) that demands expert riding skills. Called simply the Advanced Trail, this route is also the most scenic exploration of land still showing signs of its former days as a farm along Panther Creek.

Panther Creek and Panther Springs are supposedly named from the story of a Virginia gentleman, Colonel Bradley, who returned from a hunting trip claiming he had shot a panther . . . and the beast had fallen in the creek. It was a simpler day back then. Instead of the sound of motorboats whining in the distance, mountain bikers riding the creek banks a hundred years ago would have heard the rhythmic grind of a mill pestle turning corn into meal, and the true breakfast of champions — grits.

The early June morning I was there revealed the largest collection of "blooming" indian ghost pipe I have ever seen. The white of the curled stalks spread across the hill, looking like pockets of drifted snow. I also saw a large herd of deer browsing on mushrooms. Although it was hard to get an exact count, at least 13

RIDE 84 · Panther Creek State Park

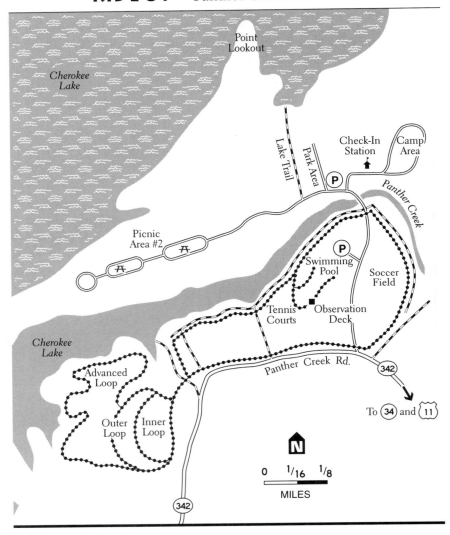

deer interrupted their nibbling long enough to watch me wheel silently through the wonderland of fog. I'm almost sure none of them had a hookah.

General location: Northeast of Jefferson City and southwest of Morristown, in between Cherokee Lake and US 11E, approximately 45 miles northeast of Knoxville.

Elevation change: The Advanced Trail makes use of the radical elevation changes closer to the lake, steep in places but not too long. The rest of the trail has only slight to moderate changes.

Season: This trail network can be ridden year-round, but periods of rain can leave sections muddy and difficult to ride.

Services: The state recreation area has camping, showers, a swimming pool, and hiking trails. Nearby Morristown can provide all but the most specialized services, which can be found in Knoxville, thirty minutes away by car.

Hazards: Hikers and other bikers present the most significant hazards. A couple of park road crossings make it necessary to watch for motorized vehicles.

Rescue index: There is a good chance of being easily rescued inside this park.

Land status: The land is managed by Tennessee's Department of Conservation, Division of State Parks.

Maps: No single map includes all trails, but the 11X17 map entitled "Panther Creek State Recreation Area" includes most of them. A detailed map of the Advanced Trail can be found at its trailhead behind Plexiglas.

Finding the trail: From Knoxville, head north on US 11E. A little over 7 miles north of Jefferson City, look for the sign indicating the left turn to Panther Creek State Park, on Panther Creek Road, State Road 342. Take the right turn into the park approximately 2 miles down SR 342. Continue past the Visitors Center on the left, parking in the swimming pool lot. The trail begins by taking the paved road out of the lot, turning left toward Panther Creek. Turn left onto the double-track just before crossing the creek at the bottom of the hill.

Sources of additional information:

Superintendent's Office
Panther Creek State Recreation Area
2010 Panther Creek Park Road
Morristown, TN 37814
(423) 587-7046

Tennessee Department of Conservation
Department of State Parks
701 Broadway
Nashville, TN 37219-5237
(615) 742-6667

Notes on the trail: After taking the left turn off the paved park road, the easiest loop uses the double-track all the way, past two (single-track) turnoffs on the right, and one turn (also single-track) on the left, which leads to both the swimming pool and observation deck. Cut across an open field before crossing the park entrance road. Follow the fence line up and take the descent to the soccer fields. A single-track loop on the other side of Panther Creek (seen on the right) used to be open to bikes, but was marked "Foot Travel Only" when I was there.

For the more technical route, still use the basic double-track loop. But when you reach the left turn onto single-track up the hill, take it for a short diversion up to the observation deck. A left turn at the fork before reaching the observation deck will lead down to the swimming pool, as will continuing past the observation deck. After enjoying the view from the deck, return to the double-track and turn left. Look for the right turn leading to the boat ramp. It is short but fun. It dead-ends at the gravel road leading to the boat ramp (to the right). Take a left and then a right 20 yards after, which should be posted with a sign indicating the Inner and Outer Loops. They are a mile, and a mile and a half, respectively, marked with either a white dot (inner) or yellow dot (outer).

Before the Inner and Outer Loops split, the trailhead for the Advanced Trail will be visible on the right. This 2.5 miles of looping single-track will test both strength and balance. After completing the Advanced Trail, and back on the Inner/Outer Loops, continue right at the fork to remain on the Outer Loop. The two loops rejoin before ending at the gravel road. Across the road, look for an unmarked single-track (different from the one taken from the double-track) going back into the forest. It will return to the double-track where a right turn completes the basic counterclockwise loop already described.

BIG SOUTH FORK AREA

The Big South Fork National River and Recreation Area was created by an act of Congress in 1974, which set aside funds to purchase over 100,000 acres along the Cumberland Plateau, the western boundary of the Appalachian Mountains. The South Fork Cumberland River—long famous as a paddling destination—cuts north through steep sandstone canyon walls that loom nearly 800 feet above the river's churning surface. With dramatic changes in elevation in such beautiful country, it isn't surprising to discover that mountain bikers can also enjoy many miles of trails here.

This land first rose from the sea over 250 million years ago, squeezing the material underneath to form—among other things—coal. But the sandstone and shale surfaces are those most likely to play a part in any off-road biking adventure at Big South Fork. There will be few worries about having to ride on slick clay here. As the sandstone erodes, the surface provides great traction to a mountain bike's fat tire. However, sandstone's eroded product—sand—collects in long pits, a challenge seldom encountered away from the coast. Other challenges await the brave mountain biker in Great South Fork. Deep stream crossings and radical elevation changes are just two of the conditions that make a ride here extraordinary. But don't expect everything to be extreme. The National Park Service has worked with area bike clubs to build and maintain trails suitable for all experience levels.

For those times when the bike is resting, an extensive network of hiking trails presents a closer look at this unique land. Horseback riding is a popular local activity, and a large number of horse trails—also open to bikers—wind along the plateau. I know, I know. Riding horse trails isn't normally that much fun, but most of the trails shared between bikers and horses inside Big South Fork are tolerable so far as riding conditions go, and they're more than worth the effort. The camping facilities at Bandy Creek and Blue Heron Campground are modern and well built. The swimming pool and laundry facilities make it even more pleasant to stay the week and enjoy the many rides in the area. Or, if a more private and secluded spot is preferred, primitive campgrounds can be found at Alum Ford, or, for that matter, anywhere in the area that hasn't been posted with camping restrictions.

The Big South Fork of the Cumberland River cut the chasm between the 500-foot-tall sandstone walls.

Source of additional information:

Superintendent
Big South Fork National River and Recreation Area
4564 Leatherwood Road
Oneida, TN 37841
(615) 879-3625—Tennessee
(606) 376 3787—Kentucky

RIDE 85 · Collier Ridge

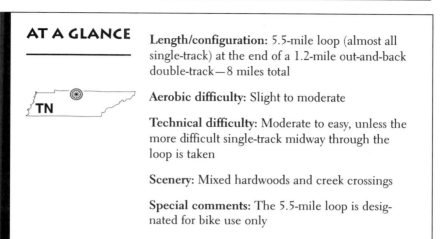

AT A GLANCE

Length/configuration: 5.5-mile loop (almost all single-track) at the end of a 1.2-mile out-and-back double-track—8 miles total

Aerobic difficulty: Slight to moderate

Technical difficulty: Moderate to easy, unless the more difficult single-track midway through the loop is taken

Scenery: Mixed hardwoods and creek crossings

Special comments: The 5.5-mile loop is designated for bike use only

I knew the Big South Fork's popularity as a mountain biking destination was unquestioned when I reached the trailhead of this 5.5-mile loop of single- and double-track. As I rode the 1.2 miles from the Bandy Creek Visitor Center to the trailhead (2.4 miles total, making a near 8-mile ride out of the Collier Ridge Trail), I expected to have the trail to myself on a gray and drizzly morning. However, just as I got to the first stream crossing (North Bandy Creek), I noticed a family returning from their ride. I first met a young boy pushing a bike; he had just crossed the creek. He was closely followed by his two older sisters, both of whom rode through the shallow stream. Across the creek, Dad straddled a mountain bike in the most unusual biking getup I've ever seen. He wore a helmet, to be sure, but he was dressed in a Tennessee Tuxedo. That's overalls to you city folks.

I slowly rode past him and said, "Kind of messy today." His mud-spattered face grinned and he said, "Oh, it gets better." And, boy, was he right!

General location: Big South Fork is located 70 miles northwest of Knoxville and about 10 miles west of Oneida, just south of the Kentucky border.

Elevation change: There are no gut-wrenching climbs, but plenty of elevation changes will keep the pulse perking right along.

Season: This trail holds up exceedingly well in wet conditions. During dry times, it should be even better. Hunting goes on inside Big South Fork—mostly in the fall and spring. Make sure there are no biking restrictions, during hunting season or any other time, by calling ahead.

Services: Modern camping facilities (including a swimming pool) are at Bandy Creek Campground, which makes for a convenient central location for riding all of Big South Fork's trails. Oneida is a good 20-minute ride away and can only

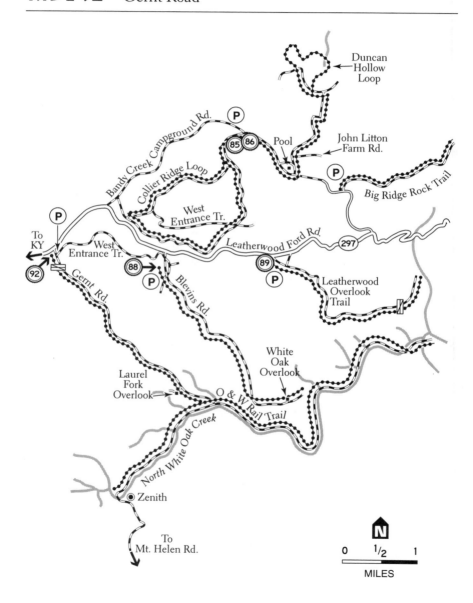

provide the basics. Knoxville is the closest city where a complete and wide range of services can be found.

Hazards: Typical trail hazards: rocks, stream crossings, some downed trees, and limbs. At the beginning of the single-track, hikers may also be using a small section of this trail. An alternate section of trail uses the highway, TN 297, where high-speed traffic will be present. The single-track alternate, though, is a tad more difficult than anything else on this trail. Be prepared to walk certain sections if necessary.

Rescue index: Remote sections of this trail could make a rescue difficult. Ride this trail prepared for self-rescue. TN 297 remains a relatively short walk away, should that be necessary.

Land status: Inside the Big South Fork National River and Recreation Area, a piece of federal property.

Maps: The best map for biking in this region is the National Geographic Trails Illustrated Big South Fork National River and Recreation Area. There is also the free Big South Fork—Mountain Bike Riding map, which can be picked up at the Bandy Creek Visitor Center.

Finding the trail: Leave Oneida on TN 297, headed west. About 10 minutes out of town, TN 297 turns left at Terry and Terry Store where a forest service–brown sign points the way to Big South Fork. Travel several slow, switchbacking miles on the descent into the river canyon, and then climb back out. Once back on top, turn right at the sign pointing toward Bandy Creek Campground on Bandy Creek Campground Road. Approximately 2 miles after the turn, take a left and park in the visitor center parking lot.

Source of additional information:

Superintendent
Big South Fork National River and Recreation Area
4564 Leatherwood Road
Oneida, TN 37841
(615) 879-3625—Tennessee
(606) 376 3787—Kentucky

Notes on the trail: Begin the ride at the Bandy Creek Visitor Center and head west for approximately 1 mile, passing the Katie Blevins Cemetery on the right. A sign for Scott State Forest will be on the left just beyond the cemetery, and it marks the entrance to the bike trail. A nearly half-mile descent to North Bandy Creek follows. Several stream crossings occur at North Bandy Creek, King Branch, and South Bandy Creek before you reach the right turn onto the single-track paralleling TN 297. The sign indicates this section is for advanced riders. Weigh riding the smoother but traffic-infested asphalt highway shoulder (reached by riding straight) against taking the more technical—yet in many ways safer—single-track. My guess is that if you've enjoyed the ride so far, the single-track is the best choice. If it proves too much for your skill, walk the tougher sections.

After about three-quarters of a mile, the single-track rejoins the highway route, coming in on the left. Turn right at the wooden post. (If you elected to take the highway, look for this opening on the right approximately 1.4 miles after the highway). Follow signs marking the next two double-track turns—first a right, then a left—all within the next half mile after you return from the highway. The ride ends with 1.5 miles of single-track section downhill to North Bandy Creek. Of course, if another lap is in order, turn right (instead of crossing the creek, which leads to the trailhead at the Bandy Creek Visitor Center).

RIDE 86 · Duncan Hollow

AT A GLANCE

TN

Length/configuration: 5.3 miles (total) consisting of a loop at the end of an out-and-back; all double-track except for a 1.7-mile section of single-track

Aerobic difficulty: Only one short section demands much aerobic exertion

Technical difficulty: The drop to and the crossing of a small, unnamed creek will be an enjoyable challenge; other than this obstacle, few technical moves are required

Scenery: A mixed hardwood forest, creek crossing

Special comments: The highlight to this short single-track section is the creek crossing

What do you get when you combine nearly 2 miles of double-track gravel road out-and-back (3.6 miles total) with a 1.7 mile section of single-track between two bluffs above the Big South Fork Cumberland River? Duncan Hollow inside Bandy Creek Campground. This short trail offers another good excuse to come to Big South Fork for an extended stay, camp at the modern facilities at night, and ride all the many miles of nearby trails during the day. What better way to top off a breakfast of French toast and French roast than to take the leisurely ride through Duncan Hollow, stretching out the hamstrings and sneaking up on all the wild things?

The double-track part of the ride falls gently through the thick woods of the Cumberland Plateau. Part of the forest, however, is a departure from the mixed hardwoods. Managed jointly by the National Park Service and the University of Tennessee, it is a parcel of hundreds of American chestnuts that have been planted in an effort to develop a blight-resistant strain. American chestnuts are those giants of trees whose hulks can still be seen rotting on the ground, victims of the blight that felled them more than 75 years ago. On the soggy morning I rode here, three deer appeared out of the mist on the shoulder of the road just past the chestnut forest. When they saw me, each whipped up its big white flag of a tail before jumping stiff-legged down the hill. Their noisy flight no doubt alerted the big tom turkey I saw around the next curve; he was already moving at a blur into a tangle of forest. The leisurely pace of this ride is broken on the descent to a small, heretofore unnamed trickle of water. The creek is so small, in fact, that it is left off of the National Geographic Trails illustrated map of Big South Fork, an oversight I have corrected for the map in this book. I have also taken the liberty—in the spirit of Lewis and Clark—to name this body of water: Duncan Loop Branch. After you descend into the cove split by Duncan Loop Branch, the fairly demanding climb out will bring a deep burning to your thighs.

General location: Big South Fork is located 70 miles northwest of Knoxville and about 10 miles west of Oneida, just south of the Kentucky border.

Elevation change: With the exception of the area dropping into and climbing out of the creek bottom, the elevation remains fairly unchanged.

Season: During hunting season (call for details), you may want to find another trail, but other than that, this is a year-round trail.

Services: First-rate camping facilities are located at Bandy Creek, which makes for a convenient central location. Oneida is a good 20-minute ride away and can only provide the basics. Knoxville is the closest city where a complete range of services can be found.

Hazards: Vehicles may be present on the double-track portion, as may horses. Take care to cross Duncan Loop Branch with caution. A loose bank of sand grabbed my front tire, almost sending me over the handlebar for a dunk in the drink.

Rescue index: This is a fairly easy place to get rescued from; the service road stays within a half mile of the single-track.

Land status: Within the Big South Fork National River and Recreation Area, a piece of federal property.

Maps: The best map for biking in this region is the National Geographic Trails Illustrated Big South Fork National River and Recreation Area. There is also the free Big South Fork—Mountain Bike Riding map, which can be picked up at the Bandy Creek Visitor Center. See page 294 for our map of this ride.

Finding the trail: Leave Oneida on TN 297, headed west. About 10 minutes out of town, TN 297 turns left at Terry and Terry Store where a forest service–brown sign points the way to Big South Fork. Travel several slow, switch-backing miles on the descent into the river canyon, and on the climb back out. Once back on top, turn right toward Bandy Creek Campground on Bandy Creek Campground Road. Approximately 2 miles after the turn, look for the road on the left, which leads to the visitor center parking lot.

Source of additional information:

> Superintendent
> Big South Fork National River and Recreation Area
> 4564 Leatherwood Road
> Oneida, TN 37841
> (615) 879-3625 — Tennessee
> (606) 376 3787 — Kentucky

Notes on the trail: Leave the parking lot at the Bandy Creek Visitor Center and cross Bandy Creek Road, heading into the campground itself. Head toward Loop A. Just as the swimming pool appears on the left—and in the middle of a left-hand curve uphill—bear right onto the gravel road. Pass the chestnut forest on the right before the right turn for the John Litton Farm, hiking only. Another trail goes off to the left here, but go straight to the next intersection. The main road veers left here, and the bike trail continues straight ahead (look for the white bicycle painted on a wooden post). Continue riding downhill, making the loop in a clockwise direction. After crossing Duncan Loop Branch, then reaching the top of the hill, turn left to return to the trailhead or right for another lap.

RIDE 87 · Big Ridge Rock Trail

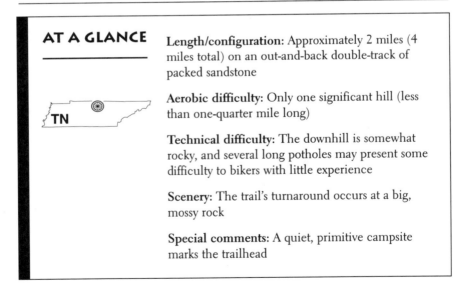

AT A GLANCE

Length/configuration: Approximately 2 miles (4 miles total) on an out-and-back double-track of packed sandstone

Aerobic difficulty: Only one significant hill (less than one-quarter mile long)

Technical difficulty: The downhill is somewhat rocky, and several long potholes may present some difficulty to bikers with little experience

Scenery: The trail's turnaround occurs at a big, mossy rock

Special comments: A quiet, primitive campsite marks the trailhead

I've always heard that it's better to be lucky than good. Well, I was lucky the morning I discovered this approximately two-mile (four miles total) out-and-back, just outside of Bandy Creek Campground. I had seen the double-track road in my headlights the night before, but I decided to go on to the more devel-

The thick, deep moss growing on Big Ridge Rock felt good under bare feet.

oped camping area instead. The next evening, though, after a long day in the saddle exploring some of the area's many trails, I decided to make camp a little way down the gravel road. After setting up and having supper, I took out my newly purchased National Geographic Trails illustrated map for Big South Fork to see where the road in front of the campsite went. The road was not shown on this otherwise detailed and accurate topo map. I could hardly wait to get started exploring.

I set out the next morning after breakfast, expecting the road to dead-end quickly, as so many abandoned logging roads do. Fifty yards from camp I startled a deer and it bolted down the mountain. I had already seen two painted turtles and was just beginning to forget about the odometer when I came to the power lines about a mile from camp. I was happy to see the double-track twisting past the massive stanchions and back into the woods. I surprised a turkey beside a rather large pond on the left. Not long after that, I came to a right turn in the road, marking a long and fairly steep descent. I took it, and at the bottom, I traveled through a ridge-line basin where deep potholes were lined with frogs. When I finally made it to the exposed rock that anchors the northernmost end of Big Ridge, I knew I had found a special spot. The leaves blocked most of the view, but I could tell that in late fall and winter, after the leaves have fallen, I would have a commanding view of the river and plateau. A game trail led down to where I knew the John Muir Trail (hiking only) lay, but I stayed and explored the rock, whose thick carpet of crinkly moss felt good under my bare feet.

General location: Big South Fork is located 70 miles northwest of Knoxville and about 10 miles west of Oneida, just south of the Kentucky border.

Elevation change: Approximately 100 feet, most of it coming on one hill.

Season: Since hunting is allowed on this trail, I would ride one of the other nearby trails when hunters are likely to be about, usually mid-fall to New Year's Day. Call ahead for details.

Services: First-rate camping facilities are located at Bandy Creek, which makes for a convenient central location. Oneida is a good 20-minute ride away and can only provide the basics. Knoxville is the closest city where a complete range of services can be found.

Hazards: Hunters present the only likely hazard.

Rescue index: Unless word has been left with someone, it could be a long time before another trail user happens along. The good news is that it's not too far from a main road. Ride prepared for self-rescue.

Land status: This is part federal and part state land. The ride begins in Scott State Forest, which adjoins Big South Fork.

Maps: The best map for biking in this region is the National Geographic Trails Illustrated Big South Fork National River and Recreation Area. The map found in this guide on page 294, however, was drawn using detailed notes from my ride.

Finding the trail: Leave Oneida on TN 297, headed west. About 10 minutes out of town, TN 297 turns left at Terry and Terry Store where a forest service–brown sign points the way to Big South Fork. Travel several slow, switchbacking miles on the descent into the river canyon and the climb back out. Once back on top, turn right toward Bandy Creek Campground on Bandy Creek Campground Road. Approximately 1 mile after the turn, look for the gravel road on the right. It's in a sharp left-hand curve of the paved road. Park by the road or pull in to the campsite to begin the ride. Or park at the visitor center, on down the road about a mile on the left.

Source of additional information:

Superintendent
Big South Fork National River and Recreation Area
4564 Leatherwood Road
Oneida, TN 37841
(615) 879-3625 — Tennessee
(606) 376 3787 — Kentucky

Notes on the trail: The trail begins where the gravel road intersects Bandy Creek Campground Road. Go across the powerline right-of-way at approximately the 1.2 mile mark. After leaving Scott State Forest (a sign will mark this point), ride downhill and through a low area and climb back up a ways. An old road forks to the right, goes up to the top, and then stops. Take the left fork instead to find the Big Ridge Rock just a quarter mile away. This is a good place to spend some quiet and secluded time.

RIDE 88 · White Oak Overlook

AT A GLANCE
_____

Length/configuration: 6-mile out-and-back double-track of packed sandstone (3 miles each way) with plenty of possible additional mileage

Aerobic difficulty: Only the mile-long section nearest the overlook is demanding

Technical difficulty: Moderate challenges, including a creek crossing, will keep you alert

Scenery: North White Oak Creek and its tributaries

Special comments: The difficulty of this trail increases by taking the part of the North White Oak Loop Trail, which parallels the ridge route

The basic out-and-back (three miles one way, six miles total) on double-track of packed sandstone leads to an overlook above North White Oak Creek. Most experienced riders will take the sand and mud bogs in stride, although a novice biker may feel daunted at times. The ride, however, is worth it to whoever wants a great peek at the Cumberland Plateau. At the overlook, Coyle Branch can be seen and heard dropping into the North White Oak below. The knoll in front of the overlook hides most of Logging Hollow, with its twin branches. On the other side of the North White Oak, Panther Creek (panther included, so they say) drains the north face of Hurricane Ridge, the huge rock mountain to the southeast.

General location: Big South Fork is located 70 miles northwest of Knoxville and about 10 miles west of Oneida, just south of the Kentucky border.

Elevation change: A gradual descent from 1,577 to 1,460 feet.

Season: An all-year trail.

Services: First-rate camping facilities are at Bandy Creek, which makes for a convenient central location. Oneida is a good 20-minute ride away and only provides the basics. Knoxville is the closest city where a complete range of services can be found.

Hazards: Horses and four-wheel-drives may be met on the main road during the weekend and other periods of heavy use.

Rescue index: Even though most of the ride follows along double-track, this is rugged country. Plan for self-rescue.

Land status: Part of Big South Fork National River and Recreation Area.

Maps: The best map for biking in this region is the National Geographic Trails Illustrated Big South Fork National River and Recreation Area. See page 294 for our map of this ride.

In the distance, the Big South flows under the TN 297 bridge.

Finding the trail: Leave Oneida on TN 297, headed west. About 10 minutes out of town, TN 297 turns left at Terry and Terry Store where a forest service–brown sign points the way to Big South Fork. Travel several slow, switchbacking miles on the descent into the river canyon and on the climb back out. Once back on top, continue straight past the right turn to Bandy Creek Campground. Three miles from the turnoff to Bandy Creek, turn left onto Blevins Road; it is probably unsigned. Soon after you turn onto Blevins Road, the West Entrance Trail comes in on the right. Before going down the first steeper section, North White Oak Loop crosses the double-track. Park near where the pavement ends.

Source of additional information:

> Superintendent
> Big South Fork National River and Recreation Area
> 4564 Leatherwood Road
> Oneida, TN 37841
> (615) 879-3625 — Tennessee
> (606) 376 3787 — Kentucky

Notes on the trail: The first 2 miles of this trail are easy. Then, however, a descent into a creek bottom and the following climb combine for a somewhat demanding section. The final descent to the overlook loses 60 feet in its half-mile approach. For those who want to extend this ride and make it a physical workout, take the portion of North White Oak Trail leaving Blevins Road on the right (south), just before Blevins begins a steep descent. Be prepared for at least three additional creek crossings on this 2-mile section. Each crossing comes with its own drop into and climb out of a steep draw. Finally, take a right onto Blevins at the bottom of the hill, just before crossing another creek. Return the way you came.

RIDE 89 · O & W Rail Trail

<table>
<tr><td>AT A GLANCE
</td><td>Length/configuration: More than 11 miles one way (22 miles total) on an out-and-back double-track

Aerobic difficulty: The first 3 miles lose 300 vertical feet; over the next 8 miles, about 80 feet is regained

Technical difficulty: The ride is a piece of cake; the stream crossings, however, especially of North White Oak Creek, require fords across occasionally high and swift waters

Scenery: Even though the ride is at the bottom of the gorge, away from all the overlooks, it is here that the scenery of Big South Fork is at its best

Special comments: Do not ride this trail expecting to stay dry, no matter what time of year it is</td></tr>
</table>

In the fall of 1913, the first track of the Oneida & Western Railroad was laid along the canyon floor northwest of present-day Oneida. Its remnants form a double-track corridor where mountain bikers can pedal the 11 miles (one way) from Toomy to Zenith, a total out-and-back mileage of over 22 miles. With only a slight grade, the O & W Rail Trail is a ride best remembered for its water, mud, and rock. Along the creek, the tops of sheer cliffs loom straight up, allowing little direct sunlight to hit the trail.

The O & W's legacy can be traced back to the tall trees that once grew wherever a root could take hold. After a group of Cincinnati businessmen decided to build the railroad, local land developer and later state senator John Toomy worked with large land owner Bruno Gernt to build a lumber business. It took just 16 years to harvest the trees. With the top side ravaged, companies began filling the O & W's cars with coal dug from local mines. It took 25 years to

RIDE 89 · O & W Rail Trail (East Half)
RIDE 90 · O & W Overlook

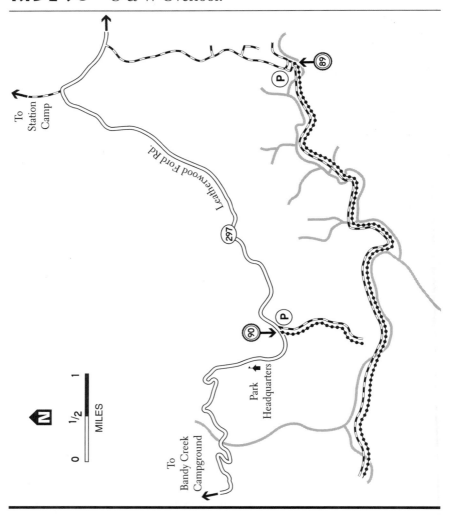

remove enough coal to make business slack, and in 1954, the O & W "pulled the steel" of the four-and-a-half-foot-wide track. It would be another 20 years before Congress passed legislation providing for the formation of the Big South Fork National River and Recreation Area. In 1984, completed construction of nearby facilities at Bandy Creek attracted visitors, some of whom arrived with mountain bikes and rediscovered the tracks of days and ways gone by.

General location: Big South Fork is located 70 miles northwest of Knoxville and about 10 miles west of Oneida, just south of the Kentucky border.

The O&W Rail Trail
crosses the North White
Oak Creek, seen here
near Gernt.

Elevation change: It's basically level.

Season: Periods of high water will make some passages impassable; other than that, when the water's right it's a great run the year round.

Services: First-rate camping facilities are at Bandy Creek, which makes for a convenient central location. Oneida is a good 20-minute ride away and can only provide the basics. Knoxville is the closest city where a complete range of services can be found.

Hazards: The numerous stream crossings—no less then ten, the least of which can be tricky—require extra caution.

Rescue index: Definitely come prepared for self-rescue on this one. Bring extra tubes and food.

Land status: Part of Big South Fork National River and Recreation Area.

Maps: The best map for biking in this region is the National Geographic Trails Illustrated Big South Fork National River and Recreation Area. See page 294 for another map of this ride.

Finding the trail: Leave Oneida on TN 297, headed west. About 8 miles out of town, the small community of New Haven is marked by several farms, one of them a Hereford (polled, I believe) farm on the right, with its sign near the highway. Slow down. Turn left onto the next road on the left (most likely, there's no sign). If you reach the intersection where TN 297 turns left to Bandy Creek, you've gone too far. Turn around and travel just over a half mile. The turn should be obvious this time. Turn right. It's slightly over 2 miles down this road before you reach the trailhead, bearing left at the next intersection with a farm's driveway. A gas well and storage tank will be on the left, near the bottom of an extremely steep descent. For an alternate trailhead, see Ride 91.

Source of additional information:

Superintendent
Big South Fork National River and Recreation Area
4564 Leatherwood Road
Oneida, TN 37841
(615) 879-3625 — Tennessee
(606) 376 3787 — Kentucky

Notes on the trail: The epic adventure begins at Toomy and heads west toward Jamestown for at least 22 out-and-back (total) miles, under occasionally rugged and wet conditions. In those miles to Zenith and back, expect to ford at least ten creeks — twice. It is a navigational no-brainer: just keep on the canyon floor, close to the creek . . . or in it. But for those times when the water's too high to safely cross North White Oak Creek, try starting at Gernt (see Ride 92 for specific directions) and ride the western portion.

RIDE 90 · O & W Overlook

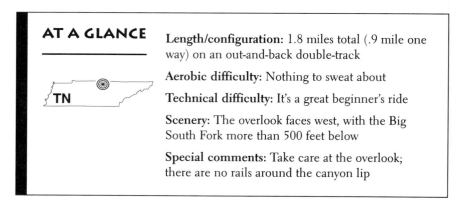

AT A GLANCE

Length/configuration: 1.8 miles total (.9 mile one way) on an out-and-back double-track

Aerobic difficulty: Nothing to sweat about

Technical difficulty: It's a great beginner's ride

Scenery: The overlook faces west, with the Big South Fork more than 500 feet below

Special comments: Take care at the overlook; there are no rails around the canyon lip

TN

The short to-and-fro (1.8 miles total) is a good late afternoon selection, especially after a hard morning's ride. The gentle double-track out to the canyon rim will help work out any kinks, while the beauty of the Big South Fork National River and Recreation Area passes by.

The key feature to this ride, the overlook, gives a wide view of the unique topography of the region. The rolling hills of the plateau have been ground slowly away where two main local bodies of water, the Big South Fork of the Cumberland River and North White Oak Creek, join and rush north through sandstone-capped gorges. Facing north, the canyon coming in on the left was made by the North White Oak. Below, a trestle spans the mighty Big South Fork, remnant of the days when the tracks of the Oneida & Western rattled as boxcars hauled out timber and coal.

General location: Big South Fork is located 70 miles northwest of Knoxville and about 10 miles west of Oneida, just south of the Kentucky border.

Elevation change: It starts out at approximately 1,500 feet above sea level and pretty much stays that way.

Season: An all-season trail.

Services: First-rate camping facilities are at Bandy Creek, which makes for a convenient central location. Oneida is a good 20-minute ride away and can only provide the basics. Knoxville is the closest city where a complete range of services can be found.

Hazards: Rocks are frequently unstable near the cliff's unrailed edge at the overlook; don't be tempted too near the brink.

Rescue index: The ranger's office for the area is located near where the trail begins on TN 297. The highway is no farther away than a mile at any time.

Land status: Part of Big South Fork National River and Recreation Area.

Maps: The best map for biking in this region is the National Geographic Trails Illustrated Big South Fork National River and Recreation Area.

Finding the trail: Leave Oneida on TN 297, headed west. About 10 minutes out of town, TN 297 turns left at Terry and Terry Store where a forest service–brown sign points the way to Big South Fork. After entering Big South Fork, look to the left where a double-track begins. A speed limit sign on the right-hand side of the highway marks the spot. If you reach the ranger's office on the right, you've gone too far. Turn around and go slow, stopping at the beginning of the double-track, which should be the first road on the right . . . this time.

Source of additional information:

Superintendent
Big South Fork National River and Recreation Area
4564 Leatherwood Road
Oneida, TN 37841
(615) 879-3625 — Tennessee
(606) 376 3787 — Kentucky

Notes on the trail: This trail is a good starter for someone interested in beginning off-road biking. Also, the sunset is spectacular from the overlook. Plan it just right and you might catch a glimpse.

RIDE 91 · Leatherwood Overlook

AT A GLANCE
———————————

TN

Length/configuration: Approximately 2.5 miles one way (5 miles total) on an out-and-back double-track of mostly packed sandstone

Aerobic difficulty: No difficult aerobic demands on this ride

Technical difficulty: It's a piece of cake until the last half mile when the chewed-up track from horse traffic makes it a sloppy, slippery, and bumpy affair

Scenery: You go right to the edge of the river canyon wall, and it is magnificent

Special comments: The bridge seen in the distance spans the Big South Fork of the Cumberland River; you can pick out the Overlook on the drive over the TN 297 bridge

For those who can't get enough of Big South Fork, the 2.5-mile out-and-back (5 miles total) leading to Leatherwood Overlook is a relaxing double-track trip. My favorite part, aside from the spectacular view at the end of the ride, is the wildlife opening that begins about halfway to the overlook. It's just under a mile long, and if you ride it at the dusky times of the day, you're sure to spot all kinds of wildlife.

While I was riding through the opening, a half dozen turkeys ran through the hip-high grass away from the pond where they had apparently been drinking. Deer stopped eating near the treeline long enough to look up and switch their white tails over my approach. And, although I couldn't see them, I knew the predators lurked nearby: bobcats, foxes, a panther perhaps. The air above the pasture wheeled with many different birds and insects. Bluebirds picked off grasshoppers, and dragonflies patrolled for gnats and flies. Hawks rode thermals, and vultures flew above them, waiting their turn. There's no telling what you'd see if you really staked the place out. But the place where most of the off-bike time will be spent comes at the end of the trail, at the overlook. The top of the 250-million-year-old canyon walls reach approximately 1,300 feet above sea level. Hopefully, you've packed a lunch or snack because you'll want to stay and enjoy the view. Even better would be to bring along some overnight gear and wake up the next morning to the sight of the Big South Fork 500 feet below.

General location: Big South Fork is located 70 miles northwest of Knoxville and about 10 miles west of Oneida, just south of the Kentucky border.

Sandy double-tracks bend through the wildlife opening on the way to Leatherwood Overlook.

Elevation change: The degree and distance of elevation change is only slight.

Season: An all-year ride.

Services: First-rate camping facilities are at Bandy Creek, which makes for a convenient central location. Oneida is a good 20-minute ride away and can only provide the basics. Knoxville is the closest city where a complete range of services can be found.

Hazards: Both horses and motorized vehicles can be found on the section of double-track that dead-ends at the end of the wildlife opening. Beyond that point vehicles are restricted, but you may still meet horses and hikers on the trail. Some steep, stair-step passages have been created by the abundant horse traffic.

Rescue index: You're no more than a mile from the end of the double-track, which is accessible by four-wheel traffic.

Land status: Inside the Big South Fork National River and Recreation Area.

Maps: The best map for biking in this region is the National Geographic Trails Illustrated Big South Fork National River and Recreation Area. See page 294 for our map of this ride.

Finding the trail: Leave Oneida on TN 297, headed west. About 10 minutes out of town, TN 297 turns left at Terry and Terry Store where a forest service–brown sign points the way to Big South Fork. Travel several slow, switch-backing miles on the descent into the river canyon and on the climb back out. Once back on top, continue past the turnoff on the right to Bandy Creek Campground. About a mile further along on the right, pass White Pine Church; take the second left (about a half mile more) and note the sign on the right side of the gravel road for North White Oak Loop, which comes in immediately on the right after you make the turn. Pull off the road and park.

Source of additional information:

> Superintendent
> Big South Fork National River and Recreation Area
> 4564 Leatherwood Road
> Oneida, TN 37841
> (615) 879-3625 — Tennessee
> (606) 376 3787 — Kentucky

Notes on the trail: This stands by itself as a good short afternoon ride to catch a sunset (the sun will be behind you at the overlook, as the colors dance across the chasm between the canyon walls), but its best attribute is that it ties in to (or is the start for) at least three more trails: North White Oak Loop, Gap Blevins Trail, and Coyle Branch Trail. One of these — Coyle Branch — serves as a link to the classic ride along the old O & W Railbed along North White Oak Creek.

RIDE 92 · Gernt Road

AT A GLANCE

Length/configuration: 3 miles one way (6 miles total) on an out-and-back double-track of packed sandstone

Aerobic difficulty: Most of the trail has a moderate to slight grade, but the sand in some spots makes for strenuous going; if you elect to go down into the canyon, you'll lose approximately 500 feet in a half mile, an extreme challenge on the return climb

Technical difficulty: Be prepared for some sand when you ride on the ridge and some rock hopping down to the canyon floor, both of which require strength and finesse; the ride along the ridge, however, is not difficult

Scenery: Mature hardwood forest and expansive view of 500-foot deep canyon

Special comments: This trail can be taken to Laurel Fork Overlook for a 5-mile total ride, or it can be lengthened as a convenient spur (3 miles one way, 6 miles total) leading to the classic O & W Rail Trail (see Ride 89) along North White Oak Creek

The three miles (one way on an out-and-back double-track—six miles total) to the Laurel Fork Overlook slowly descends a knuckle of 250-million-year-old sandstone, ending abruptly at a high cliff. The overlook faces west, with Darrow Ridge on the horizon looking like an eyebrow. Laurel Fork lies below, and when the water is high, it can be heard dashing down the rocks with a roar. Above, on Gernt Road, water has carved into the sandstone, washing its product—sand—along the ridge to rest in long, fairly level pits that make biking a slippery affair. Fortunately, the sandy stretches last long enough to be fun but not so long that they get tiresome. At the opposite end of the moisture index, small sections of long, watery potholes of unknown depth, which stay that way most of the year, must be passed. The descent into the Laurel Creek Gorge happens quickly. It only takes a scant half mile to lose nearly 500 vertical feet on a section some call the Elevator. Rocks as big as grapefruit are scattered along the double-track. Water from cliffside springs runs down the middle of the road, creating rapids nearly big enough to need names. Once at the bottom, look for signs left over from the old rail community of Gernt.

General location: Big South Fork is located 70 miles northwest of Knoxville and 10 miles west of Oneida, just south of the Kentucky border.

Elevation change: Several sections along the ridge drop 10 to 20 feet over a short distance, but on the whole, it is a gradual grade. That is, until you reach the trail leading into the North White Oak Creek canyon—a loss of nearly 500 feet in almost a half mile. That's about a foot of elevation for every 5 feet in distance.

Season: An all-season trail.

Services: First-rate camping facilities are at Bandy Creek, which makes for a convenient central location. Oneida is a good 20-minute ride away and can only provide the basics. Knoxville is the closest city where a complete range of services can be found.

Hazards: Horses will most likely be encountered on Gernt Road on the weekend; four-wheel-drives may be crawling along the road. And if that's not enough, long sand pits can cause a spill if you don't have a strong, steady grip on the handlebar. The downhill section to North White Oak Creek is extremely steep and has large loose rocks, with and without small streams flowing around them.

Rescue index: At some times of the year, Gernt Road is lightly traveled. Although most of the route is an accessible double-track, the region remains remote and rugged. Be prepared for self-rescue.

Land status: This trail stays inside the Big South Fork National River and Recreation Area.

Maps: The best map for biking in this region is the National Geographic Trails Illustrated Big South Fork National River and Recreation Area. See page 294 for our map of this ride.

Finding the trail: Leave Oneida on TN 297, headed west. About 10 minutes out of town, TN 297 turns left at Terry and Terry Store where a forest service–brown sign points the way to Big South Fork. Travel several slow, switchbacking miles on the descent into the river canyon and on the climb back out. Once back on top, continue straight past the right turn to Bandy Creek Campground. Approximately a mile and a half farther, pass Leatherwood Overlook Road on the left. Three miles from the turnoff to Bandy Creek Campground, Blevins Road is on the left—probably unsigned. The road briefly leaves Big South Fork National River and Recreation Area before you see—and turn at—a sign on the left for Cumberland Valley Trailhead. A small store, the Hitchin' Post, is immediately west of the turn. Follow the gravel road a quarter mile back to the common trailhead for Laurel Fork and West Entrance Trail.

Source of additional information:

Superintendent
Big South Fork National River and Recreation Area
4564 Leatherwood Road
Oneida, TN 37841
(615) 879-3625—Tennessee
(606) 376 3787—Kentucky

Notes on the trail: Begin this out-and-back by heading south on the double-track toward Laurel Fork Overlook, a half hour away at an easy downhill pace, for the most part. The overlook is a good place to stop for several reasons. Besides offering yet another gorgeous look at the canyon, it affords a dramatic look at exactly how steep the descent is. Although tough by any standard, the highlight comes on the ride down a rocky double-track that dead-ends into the O & W Rail Trail (see Ride 89) along North White Oak Creek. Taking a left (east) on the Rail Trail means making a ford across Groom Branch. If you are the least bit hesitant about taking on this crossing, explore the western section for approximately a half mile before you reach Laurel Fork. You won't be any more inclined to ford this creek, however. But if you've come prepared to make a day of it and you don't mind getting a little wet, head approximately 2 more miles to Zenith, where you may find canoes putting in for a run down the North White Oak. Turn around at Zenith and retrace your route back to the Cumberland Valley trailhead.

GLOSSARY

This short list of terms does not contain all the words used by mountain bike enthusiasts when discussing their sport. But it should serve as an introduction to the lingo you'll hear on the trails.

ATB	all-terrain bike; this, like "fat-tire bike," is another name for a mountain bike
ATV	all-terrain vehicle; this usually refers to the loud, fume-spewing three- or four-wheeled motorized vehicles you will not enjoy meeting on the trail—except, of course, if you crash and have to hitch a ride out on one
blaze	a mark on a tree made by chipping away a piece of the bark, usually done to designate a trail; such trails are sometimes described as "blazed"
blind corner	a curve in the road or trail that conceals bikers, hikers, equestrians, and other traffic
blowdown	see "windfall"
BLM	Bureau of Land Management, an agency of the federal government
bollard	a post (or series of posts) set vertically into the ground which allow pedestrians or cyclists to pass but keep vehicles from entering (wooden bollards are also commonly used to sign intersections)
braided	a braided trail condition results when people attempt to travel around a wet area; networks of interlaced trails can result and are a maintenance headache for trail crews
buffed	used to describe a very smooth trail
Carsonite sign	a small, thin, and flexible fiberglass signpost used extensively by the Forest Service and BLM to mark roads and trails (often dark brown in color)

catching air	taking a jump in such a way that both wheels of the bike are off the ground at the same time
cattle guard	a grate of parallel steel bars or pipes set at ground level and suspended over a ditch; cows can't cross them (their little feet slip through the openings between the pipes), but pedestrians and vehicles can pass over cattle guards with little difficulty
clean	while this may describe what you and your bike won't be after following many trails, the term is most often used as a verb to denote the action of pedaling a tough section of trail successfully
combination	this type of route may combine two or more configurations; for example, a point-to-point route may integrate a scenic loop or an out-and-back spur midway through the ride; like-wise, an out-and-back may have a loop at its farthest point (this configuration looks like a cherry with a stem attached; the stem is the out-and-back, the fruit is the terminus loop); or a loop route may have multiple out-and-back spurs and/or loops to the side; mileage for a combination route is for the total distance to complete the ride
cupped	a concave trail; higher on the sides than in the middle; often caused by motorcycles
dab	touching the ground with a foot or hand
deadfall	a tangled mass of fallen trees or branches
decomposed granite	an excellent, fine- to medium-grain, trail and road surface; typically used in native surface road and trail applications (not trucked in); results from the weathering of granite
diversion ditch	a usually narrow, shallow ditch dug across or around a trail; funneling the water in this manner keeps it from destroying the trail
double-track	the dual tracks made by a jeep or other vehicle, with grass, weeds, or rocks between; mountain bikers can ride in either of the tracks, but you will find that whichever one you choose, no matter how many times you change back and forth, the other track will appear to offer smoother travel
dugway	a steep, unpaved, switchbacked descent
endo	flipping end over end
feathering	using a light touch on the brake lever, hitting it lightly many times rather than very hard or locking the brake

four-wheel-drive   this refers to any vehicle with drive-wheel capability on all four wheels (a jeep, for instance, has four-wheel drive as compared with a two-wheel-drive passenger car), or to a rough road or trail that requires four-wheel-drive capability (or a one-wheel-drive mountain bike!) to negotiate it

game trail   the usually narrow trail made by deer, elk, or other game

gated   everyone knows what a gate is, and how many variations exist upon this theme; well, if a trail is described as "gated" it simply has a gate across it; don't forget that the rule is if you find a gate closed, close it behind you; if you find one open, leave it that way

Giardia   shorthand for *Giardia lamblia*, and known as the "backpacker's bane" until we mountain bikers expropriated it; this is a waterborne parasite that begins its life cycle when swallowed, and one to four weeks later has its host (you) bloated, vomiting, shivering with chills, and living in the bathroom; the disease can be avoided by "treating" (purifying) the water you acquire along the trail (see "Hitting the Trail" in the Introduction)

gnarly   a term thankfully used less and less these days, it refers to tough trails

graded   refers to a dirt road that has been smoothed out by the use of a wide blade on earth-moving equipment; "blading" gets rid of the teeth-chattering, much-cursed washboards found on so many dirt roads after heavy vehicle use

hammer   to ride very hard

hammerhead   one who rides hard and fast

hardpack   a trail in which the dirt surface is packed down hard; such trails make for good and fast riding, and very painful landings; bikers most often use "hardpack" as both a noun and adjective, and "hard-packed" as an adjective only (the grammar lesson will help you when diagramming sentences in camp)

hike-a-bike   what you do when the road or trail becomes too steep or rough to remain in the saddle

jeep road,
*   jeep trail*   a rough road or trail passable only with four-wheel-drive capability (or a horse or mountain bike)

kamikaze   while this once referred primarily to those Japanese fliers who quaffed a glass of sake, then flew off as human bombs in suicide missions against U.S. naval vessels, it has more recently been applied to the idiot mountain bikers who, far less honorably, scream down hiking trails, endangering the physical and mental safety of the walking, biking, and equestrian traffic they meet; deck guns were necessary to stop the Japanese kamikaze pilots, but a bike pump or walking staff in the spokes is sufficient for the current-day kamikazes who threaten to get us all kicked off the trails

loop this route configuration is characterized by riding from the designated trailhead to a distant point, then returning to the trailhead via a different route (or simply continuing on the same in a circle route) without doubling back; you always move forward across new terrain but return to the starting point when finished; mileage is for the entire loop from the trailhead back to trailhead

multi-purpose a BLM designation of land which is open to many uses; mountain biking is allowed

off-camber a trail that slopes in the opposite direction than one would prefer for safety's sake; for example, on a side-cut trail the slope is away from the hill—the inside of the trail is higher, so it helps you fall downhill if your balance isn't perfect

ORV/OHV a motorized off-road vehicle (off-highway vehicle)

out-and-back a ride where you will return on the same trail you pedaled out; while this might sound far more boring than a loop route, many trails look very different when pedaled in the opposite direction

pack stock horses, mules, llamas, etc., carrying provisions along trails

point-to-point a vehicle shuttle (or similar assistance) is required for this type of route, which is ridden from the designated trailhead to a distant location, or endpoint, where the route ends; total mileage is for the one-way trip from the trailhead to endpoint

portage to carry your bike on your person

pummy soil with high pumice content produced by volcanic activity in the Pacific Northwest and elsewhere; light in consistency and easily pedaled; trails with such soil often become thick with dust

quads bikers use this term to refer both to the extensor muscle in the front of the thigh (which is separated into four parts)

	and to USGS maps; the expression "Nice quads!" refers always to the former, however, except in those instances when the speaker is an engineer
runoff	rainwater or snowmelt
scree	an accumulation of loose stones or rocky debris lying on a slope or at the base of a hill or cliff
side-cut trail	a trail cut on the side of a hill
signed	a "signed" trail has signs in place of blazes
single-track	a single, narrow path through grass or brush or over rocky terrain, often created by deer, elk, or backpackers; single-track riding is some of the best fun around
skid road	the path created when loggers drag trees through the forest with heavy equipment
slickrock	the rock-hard, compacted sandstone that is great to ride and even prettier to look at; you'll appreciate it even more if you think of it as a petrified sand dune or seabed (which it is), and if the rider before you hasn't left tire marks (from unnecessary skidding) or granola bar wrappers behind
snowmelt	runoff produced by the melting of snow
snowpack	unmelted snow accumulated over weeks or months of winter—or over years—in high-mountain terrain
spur	a road or trail that intersects the main trail you're following
squid	one who skids
stair-step climb	a climb punctuated by a series of level or near-level sections
switchback	a zigzagging road or trail designed to assist in traversing steep terrain; mountain bikers should not skid through switchbacks
talus	the rocky debris at the base of a cliff, or a slope formed by an accumulation of this rocky debris
tank trap	a steep-sided ditch (or series of ditches) used to block access to a road or trail; often used in conjunction with high mounds of excavated material
technical	terrain that is difficult to ride due not to its grade (steepness) but to its obstacles—rocks, roots, logs, ledges, loose soil . . .

topo	short for topographical map, the kind that shows both linear distance and elevation gain and loss; "topo" is pronounced with both vowels long
trashed	a trail that has been destroyed (same term used no matter what has destroyed it . . . cattle, horses, or even mountain bikers riding when the ground was too wet)
two-track	see "double-track"
two-wheel-drive	this refers to any vehicle with drive-wheel capability on only two wheels (a passenger car, for instance, has two-wheel drive); a two-wheel-drive road is a road or trail easily traveled by an ordinary car
waterbar	an earth, rock, or wooden structure that funnels water off trails to reduce erosion
washboarded	a road that is surfaced with many ridges spaced closely together, like the ripples on a washboard; these make for very rough riding, and even worse driving in a car or jeep
whoop-de-doo	closely spaced dips or undulations in a trail; these are often encountered in areas traveled heavily by ORVs
wilderness area	land that is officially set aside by the federal government to remain natural—pure, pristine, and untrammeled by any vehicle, including mountain bikes; though mountain bikes had not been born in 1964 (when the United States Congress passed the Wilderness Act, establishing the National Wilderness Preservation system), they are considered a "form of mechanical transport" and are thereby excluded; in short, stay out
windchill	a reference to the wind's cooling effect upon exposed flesh; for example, if the temperature is 10 degrees Fahrenheit and the wind is blowing at 20 miles per hour, the windchill (that is, the actual temperature to which your skin reacts) is minus 32 degrees; if you are riding in wet conditions things are even worse, for the windchill would then be minus 74 degrees!
windfall	anything (trees, limbs, brush, fellow bikers . . .) blown down by the wind

INDEX

STEVE JONES left his hometown of Marietta, Georgia, shortly after his first shaving accident. Since then, he has milked cows, pumped gas, been shipped across the Pacific on a U.S. Navy tugboat, and flown across the Atlantic in the belly of a 747. He once flirted with respectability by becoming an English teacher, even receiving a college degree from the University of Tennessee. His parents now answer the question, "What's Steve doing these days?" with side-long glances and coughs, but when pressed finally tell the truth: "He's a writer who spends his days riding a bike and his nights tapping out sto-ries." Steve has had articles published in state and national magazines. *Mountain Bike! The Southern App-alachian and Smoky Mountains,* his

fourth book, joins *Mountain Bike! Florida, Mountain Bike! The Deep South,* and *The Nuts and Bolts of Mountain Bike Technique.* When he's not finding, rid-ing, or writing about single-track, you will likely find him home in Dahlonega, Georgia, with his wife and son.